IF IT'S NOT CLOSE,
THEY CAN'T
CHEAT

Other Books by Hugh Hewitt

In, But Not Of

The Embarrassed Believer

Searching For God in America

First Principles

IF IT'S NOT CLOSE, THEY CAN'T CHEAT

CRUSHING THE DEMOCRATS
IN EVERY ELECTION
AND WHY YOUR LIFE DEPENDS ON IT

HUGH HEWITT

NELSON BOOKS
A Division of Thomas Nelson Publishers
Since 1798
www.thomasnelson.com

Published in Nashville, Tennessee, by Thomas Nelson, Inc.

Published in association with Yates & Yates, LLP,
Attorneys and Counselors, Orange, California.

Library of Congress Cataloging-in-Publication Data
Hewitt, Hugh, 1956–
If it's not close, they can't cheat : crushing the Democrats in every
election and why your life depends upon it / Hugh Hewitt.
p. cm.
ISBN 0-7852-6319-5 (hardcover)
1. Democratic Party (U.S.) 2. Presidents—United States—Election—
2004. 3. United States—Politics and government—2001–   I. Title.
JK2316.H49 2004
324.2736—dc22
2004010995

Printed in the United States of America

04 05 06 07 08 QW 5 4 3 2 1

Dedicated, with deep appreciation,
to the men and women of the American
military, without whose service and
sacrifice the freedom within which politics are
conducted would quickly vanish.

*"The secret of happiness is freedom,
and the secret of freedom is courage."*
—Thucydides

CONTENTS

INTRODUCTION

ou don't have to be an alarmist or an extremist of any sort to understand the nature of the times through which we are passing.

There are plenty of very reasonable people who, upon surveying the world conflict that is under way and the sorts of weapons involved, have proclaimed the inevitability of a "clash of civilizations between Islamic extremism and Western liberalism," or at least of an epic struggle between modern, enlightened countries and the remaining authoritarian/totalitarian/theocratic regimes.

You don't even have to be one of these people predicting epic clashes to understand the nature of the times through which we are passing.

You just have to be awake to the fact that the United States is, really and truly, in a war.

From the moment that Winston Churchill entered Great Britain's War Cabinet in 1939 as head of the Admiralty, and especially following his elevation to prime minister in 1940, he worked at a frantic pace—first to assure the survival of his country and then to assure the victory of the Allies. He was sixty-five years old when he reached the highest office, and he attacked his many tasks with a fierce energy that awed his colleagues, his admirers, and even his enemies. He persevered through six years of war, numerous ocean and air voyages that taxed his strength, nights and nights of bombing that destroyed places and people of great import to him and of course cost the lives of tens of thousands of his people. He kept up his focus through all of that and through two heart attacks as well.

He was indomitable, and his example of complete commitment inspired an entire nation to the same level of effort, even as invasion threatened and even through the darkest days of the blitz and the V-2 rockets.

Churchill was impatient only with the patient and the relaxed. No one, no matter his rank, escaped his intensity.

"Why, man, we are at war!" he exclaimed at the United States Secretary of State Cordell Hull when Hull rose from his chair at a midnight meeting, protesting that it was too late to continue the war planning.

How I love that quote. It explains pretty much this entire book and a lot of my radio show these past three years. Since September 11, 2001, I have asked many of my callers and readers whether they are aware that we are in a war—a real, genuine, fight-to-the-death war with an enemy that numbers in the millions, though its armies are in the tens of thousands, and whose weapons, though concealed, may include devices of extraordinary power.

If you don't really believe that the United States is in a war, then this book will make no sense to you, and you are well advised to put it down. The book's premise is quite simple: there are millions of people who would like to see the United States destroyed, or if not destroyed, then deeply wounded and humbled. Among these millions are the tens of thousands of terrorists or would-be terrorists actively engaged in an effort to inflict such injuries upon the United States so as to unhinge it or cower it.

Churchill did not have to stand for election during the course of the war through which he successfully led Great Britain. FDR did. That's the way our country works. Even in the times when politics seems secondary to the greatest issues, politics continues. Even at the height of the Civil War, Lincoln—now seen as the only man who could have saved the Union—was obliged to seek the approval of his fellow citizens.

It is an odd system. But it has worked thus far.

Now we are entering a political season unlike any other in the country's history.

Never before has a presidential election been conducted in the course of a war the very reality of which is denied by a significant portion of the population.

Imagine Thomas Dewey running against FDR in 1944 on a platform that World War II wasn't really the crucial issue of the campaign, or that the European theater was a sideshow and the United States should focus almost exclusively on the Pacific. It can't be imagined because the scenario is absurd. In wartime politics has always taken the fact of war as the central issue.

So should it be in 2004 and beyond. The war in which we find ourselves is likely to continue for many election cycles. It is the single issue on which the campaign of 2004 ought to be conducted, and almost certainly the single issue on which the campaigns of 2006, 2008, and beyond ought to be conducted.

And that's my fair warning to you. Nothing makes sense if you dismiss the idea that we are in a war, if you think the war is a second-tier issue, or even if you think it will be over soon. Fundamental facts are just that: fundamental.

If you are living in a different world from this one, then read science fiction. This book isn't for you.

It is for serious people intent upon the duties of serious citizens.

"Why, man, we are at war!" That pretty much says it all.

PART I

THE
STAKES

*A vote for the Liberals
is a vote for the Boers.*

—Conservative-Liberal Unionist campaign slogan
in Great Britain's Khaki Election of 1900

"I DON'T LIKE YOU BECAUSE YOU'RE GOING TO GET ME KILLED"

W hat you don't know about politics in America could get you killed. In fact, it could get me killed. It could get tens of thousands or hundreds of thousands or even, yes, millions of Americans killed.

The Democratic Party has lost its collective will and collective ability to take the national security of the United States seriously. This is not treasonous or unpatriotic behavior, just selfish and stupid behavior. But the irresponsibility of the Democratic Party extends to every major issue affecting national security, including the size and use of the American military, the deployment of national missile defense, the exploration for new reserves of oil, and the conduct of domestic surveillance against foreigners.

To repeat: the carelessness with which Democrats approach national security issues does not make them unpatriotic any more than a seventh grader cheering for the latest pop star and professing indifference to the conduct of the war on terrorism makes that youngster unpatriotic. The great majority of Democrats are wrong, not rotten, but their errors on these crucial issues are so huge and their indifference to the threats surrounding the U.S. so pronounced that they cannot be trusted with the defense of the U.S. for years and probably decades to come.

Which makes politics so incredibly important for the next four years.

I believe that the return of the presidency to the Democrats or the return of a Democratic majority in either the Senate or the House of Representatives would be ruinous to the national security of the U.S. To paraphrase an old line from P. J. O'Rourke: trusting the national security of the United States to the Democratic Party and its operatives and appointees is like giving whiskey and the car keys to a teenage boy.

It is worse than that because the mayhem that the enemies of the U.S. can inflict upon the U.S. is so much more devastating than even the most terrible accident one young, out-of-control driver can exact.

This book is about winning elections in the new age of post-9/11 politics in America. Beyond a few chapters on why the Democratic Party cannot be trusted to be serious about national security, and a few pages on the internal structures of both parties, this book is about tactics written for the individual who (1) cares about the national security of the United States and (2) wants to effectively work within electoral politics to help elect candidates who will be serious about defending the national security of the United States.

There are, of course, many other issues that matter greatly. I am an evangelical Christian who has watched with alarm as a dominant cultural elite has worked to marginalize the perspective of people of serious Christian faith.

I am a pro-life voter who knows that science is now proving what we have always known to be true: that the unborn are alive and conscious within the womb, they feel intense pain when injured or killed, and they deserve respect and basic human rights.

And I am a professor of constitutional law who is appalled by the conscious, unrelenting assault on the federal judiciary mounted by radical Democratic U.S. senators. Never in the 215-plus years of our Republic had even one nomination of a judge to a federal circuit court of appeal been subject to a filibuster. There are now five such filibusters under way. This relentless attack upon judicial independence, combined with numerous instances of anti-Catholicism, has shocked nonpartisan observers and enraged constitutionalists.

The list of reasons to assist the Democratic Party into an extended stay in the political wildernesses is long, but even if the Democrats stopped assaulting faith, moderated their abortion rights extremism, ended their destructive war on the judiciary, and renounced their anti-Catholic tactics, you still could not vote for a single Democrat if you are serious about defending the country.

Part I of the book summarizes the structure and core beliefs of the two parties, with an emphasis on national defense.

Part II provides a brief overview of why the Democratic Party is addicted to election chicanery and why such trickery can be expected to surface in any close election.

Parts III through VI present the rules of effective political activism and a summary of the issues on which these elections might turn. These rules changed dramatically after 9/11, and the technology of political effectiveness is evolving with lightning-like quickness. These rules are good for 2004 and 2006 and probably 2008. Any attempt to predict politics more than five years out is foolishness. Rule number one is to avoid futurists who clearly see the out years.

Part VII reviews the stakes involved in the elections of the next few years.

Many of my readers will know me from my radio program that is heard from Hawaii to Massachusetts, and from Florida to Washington. Though I am based in Southern California, I have tried to write from a national perspective, and though I am most decidedly a Republican, my listeners know I count many, many hard-core Democrats among my closest friends and I feature partisan Democrats on a weekly basis on the program. I write for the center-right *The Weekly Standard* and the conservative WorldNetDaily.com, but I take pains to read broadly on the Left. I would like nothing more than for our national elections to be fought on issues of economic and regulatory zeal as well as the best methods of assuring the ideals of equal opportunity for all.

Most of politics does not involve issues about which disagreement is ruinous. Tax policy can be wrongheaded and poorly crafted for decades, but it will not destroy the American Republic beyond repair. Mass transit white elephants are expensive exercises in misplaced enthusiasm, but there are no casualty lists associated with such boondoggles.

Lasting damage can be done to the U.S. by its enemies like Al Qaeda, North Korea, and Iran. Whole cities can vanish in a second, and 9/11 demonstrated the wild passion to kill Americans that has come to inflame millions around the globe. North Korea and Iran are ruled by very different sets of tyrants, but both countries possess missile technology and well-advanced nuclear ambitions. The ability to manufacture deadly chemical toxins and biological agents is widespread and their attempted use, inevitable.

Against this backdrop, clear-eyed tactics must be employed in the free elections of America if the party that is serious about combating our enemies is to remain in charge of national security.

Politics can be fun, and the techniques of electoral success are pretty easy to understand. After four years of daily three-hour broadcasts, however, I am convinced that vast numbers of Americans have forgotten or never learned the connection between their actions and the government in D.C. or, having grasped that connection, don't know how to actually do anything to change the government's policies or players.

If It's Not Close, They Can't Cheat seeks to do more than preach to the choir or even the choir plus the undecideds. I aim to change the behavior of the choir, one reader at a time.

Please read the book with a pen, but do more than read it and mark it up. Identify five friends or coworkers who are smart but either apolitical, independents, or Democrats, and buy them copies and schedule a lunch to discuss the book with them.

Try especially to put it into the hands of people who ought to know better but don't, who by accident of birth or geography or race find themselves allied with the Democratic Party. They adore FDR, JFK, or Clinton. They think Joe Lieberman is a thoroughgoing good guy. They are union men or sons and daughters of union men. They care for and serve the poor, and they think the GOP is a wholly owned subsidiary of Halliburton. They love the country, and they reflexively reject the idea that the Democratic Party of

Harry Truman is indifferent to or woefully ignorant of national security.

Most independent and Democratic voters love the U.S. as much as most GOP voters do. Both major parties attract fringe constituencies and wild-eyed absolutists, but the candidacies of Pat Buchanan and Ralph Nader in 2000 revealed that these are relatively small slices of the American electorate.

The cliché popular among Beltway seers is that Americans prefer divided government. This is code for "let the Democrats have some of the power." Most Americans are pretty generous, and most agree that sharing is a good thing, so it's hard to put aside habit and complacency and act on the message that the Democrats have gone off the rails on national security.

Or at least it used to be hard to get that message across. The aftermath of the attack on 9/11, the Democratic second-guessing of the Afghanistan invasion, the back-and-forth on the war in Iraq followed by the second-guessing after its breathtaking and successful execution, the partisan rhetoric over the reconstruction or the false panic over the insurrection, the delay on the creation of the Homeland Security Department over Democratic concerns about union rights for government workers, and the still fierce opposition to higher defense spending generally and national missile defense specifically unmasked the Democrats' recklessness completely.

Democratic recklessness on national defense has never been clearer and never has acting in response to that recklessness been so urgent. The silly response is getting angry. The smart response is winning elections.

This book is about winning elections.

CHAPTER 2

THE SIX-PARTY SYSTEM

In 1998 I wrote an article for *The Weekly Standard* on the three large blocs within both the Democratic and the Republican parties. Each major political party is really three smaller parties stacked in a pyramid. The following chart is a handy reference guide. The critical challenge for each party's elite is to motivate while attracting independents and refugees from the other party.

The Republicans' base is what I call the Party of Faith, the legions of Americans who believe in "the laws of Nature and of Nature's God." The fact that they practice religion defines them. Overwhelmingly Christian, they go to church, read Scripture, and organize their social lives around interactions with other believers. Faith in God and the attempt to obey His will are at the center of their lives.

The Party of Faith has its own subculture. Its most prominent political leader is Dr. James Dobson of Focus on the Family, but there are numerous others, including Pat Robertson, Chuck Colson, and increasingly the dozen or so pastors of the new megachurches, such as Southern California's Chuck Smith, Greg Laurie, and Rick Warren and Chicago's Bill Hybels. When and if these leaders serve notice on the GOP's elite that the Republican Party no longer represents them, the threat will be real. If the base's support for the GOP collapses, the Republicans' ability to contend with the Democratic Party will be gone overnight.

The main reason is that the Democrats' base—the Party of Race—

is solid. This group is fairly united and committed to political action. The two race-related initiatives that dominated California's election cycle in 1994 and 1996—Proposition 187, aimed at controlling illegal immigration, and Proposition 209, aimed at eliminating race- and gender-based preferences—mobilized the Party of Race as nothing has since the civil rights movement of the early 1960s. Indeed, the ill-conceived Prop. 187 guaranteed a new generation of solidly Democratic Latino activists. Strains are emerging between African American and Latino agendas—these strains were on display in California's historic 2003 recall of Governor Gray Davis—but the national dynamics remain favorable for Democrats.

There's another reason the Democrats would easily prevail if the GOP were separated from its base: in the middle tier of the party pyramids, the Democrats again have the advantage.

The Party of Wealth has traditionally made its home in the GOP. From mutual fund managers and some big-business types to small-business entrepreneurs and antitax activists, these folks believe in the bottom line. "If GDP increases, all is well" is their credo. They write checks to campaign coffers, and they vacation out of state. Net worth is the key to their hearts and minds.

There have been substantial defections from this group to the Democrats in recent years, especially from the higher income brackets, where laissez-faire lifestyle politics holds sway over economic concerns. Unfamiliar with the redistributionist zealotry of the old Left (or so rich they don't much care what slice the government takes), these newly wealthy technocrats tend to discount the importance of politics. Their discomfort with the Party of Faith sometimes propels them into the arms of their natural enemies.

The irony, of course, is that the Democratic Party's middle tier, the Party of Government, would love nothing more than to empty the pockets of its counterparts in the GOP. The Party of Government comprises the labor unions, especially the newly dominant public employee unions like teachers; the environmentalists, both nonprofit and bureaucratic; the consumer advocates; and all others who need government to keep them employed and powerful. This is the most rapidly growing sector of

American politics today as the administrative state continues to expand, especially at the local level. This sector demands new tax revenues, without which it cannot grow.

Just below the national leadership of both parties are two further groupings—the Party of National Security and the Party of License. Both are elite, and both carry influence disproportionate to their numbers. These blocs contribute overwhelmingly to the leadership of both parties.

The national security elites are American exceptionalists who believe America is uniquely powerful and organized for the purpose of promoting freedom; the group includes professional foreign policy wonks, the remnants of the anti-Communists, nearly every member of the officer corps of the armed forces, and a solid majority of the enlisted men and women as well. They are secular defenders of the American ideal, and Reagan was their embodiment. As *The Washington Post* military affairs reporter Thomas Ricks pointed out in his brilliant *Making the Corps*, the military is increasingly Republican in its politics, even though its unique culture breeds contempt for the wealthy and it remains at arm's length from the Party of Faith.

Across the divide is the Party of License—the academic Left, the feminist cadre, and the activist gay community. They are everything the national security party is not. Members of these two groups are not for turning, as Margaret Thatcher once remarked about her own convictions. They know the stakes, and they fight each election cycle with vehemence.

The elected elites of both parties thus see below them groupings whose defining qualities will not shift over the next few election cycles, but whose interest in politics will wax and wane.

From 1980 to 2000, GOP leadership held captive the Party of Faith with a threat: "Imagine if the Democrats won everything." For a long while, this worked. But a sea of change has occurred. George W. Bush is an evangelical. Condi Rice is an evangelical. Senator Bill Frist is an evangelical. Speaker of the House Dennis Hastert is an evangelical. House Majority Leader Tom DeLay is an evangelical. The evangelicals have won, but they have done so without explicit demands that an evangelical agenda be implemented. This rise of "good men and women" into positions of leadership has cemented the GOP base to the party as never before.

REPUBLICANS

THE PARTY OF NATIONAL SECURITY

Issues	Military readiness, national greatness
Leadership	Assorted Reaganites
Media	The Weekly Standard, Commentary, talk radio, Fox News Channel
Heroes	Ronald Reagan, John McCain, James Webb

THE PARTY OF WEALTH

Issues	Low taxes, free trade
Leadership	Chamber of Commerce, deficit hawks
Media	The Wall Street Journal, Forbes, Fortune, CNBC
Hero	Warren Buffett

THE PARTY OF FAITH

Issues	Abortion, gay marriage, religious freedom, cultural chaos, drugs, education, violence, corrupt entertainment
Leadership	Family Research Council, Christian Coalition, Fuller and Louisville Seminaries
Media	World, Christianity Today, First Things, talk radio
Heroes	Billy Graham, James Dobson, John Paul II

DEMOCRATS

THE PARTY OF LICENSE

Issues	Abortion, gay marriage, "multiculturalism"
Leadership	NOW, NARAL, ACLU, MoveOn.org
Media	Hollywood, Los Angeles Times, NPR
Heroes	Betty Friedan, Tom Hayden, Ralph Nader, John Kerry, Howard Dean, Teddy Kennedy

THE PARTY OF GOVERNMENT

Issues	Federal spending, union rights and growth
Leadership	NEA, AFL-CIO, Sierra Club
Media	The New York Times, The Washington Post, ABC, CBS, NBC, CNN
Heroes	Bill Clinton, Al Gore

THE PARTY OF RACE

Issues	Affirmative action, identity politics
Leadership	Congressional Black Caucus, NAACP, Mexican American Legal Defense and Education Fund
Media	Narrow-focus radio, newspapers, and magazines
Heroes	Jesse Jackson, Maxine Waters, Al Sharpton, Bill Clinton

The Party of Wealth—shocked by the bursting of the market bubble that was heralded by the Clinton administration's attack on Microsoft and that gathered acceleration as Election 2000 paralyzed Clinton and Gore, making off-limits the tax relief that might have halted the stock skid and recession that followed—is more firmly in the GOP camp than ever before.

And the national security caucus has grown in numbers and influence since the attack on America in September 2001. The idea of permanent security in the aftermath of the collapse of the Soviet Union took hold in the '90s, and there was much talk of peace dividends and unilateral cutbacks in American military might. All of that is gone now, and those who warned against such follies throughout the '90s find their stature unchallenged in a country awake to the threat of international terror.

So the three blocs of the GOP have been strengthened and enlarged since 1998. On the other hand, the three blocs of the Democratic Party have been shattered by repeated blows from the headlines.

The Party of Race has now reached a point where its agenda cannot be satisfied without massive injury to the party's overall appeal. African American leaders demand that reparations at least be discussed, if not implemented, but leadership elites know how disastrous such a debate would be in the eyes of middle-class whites with no tolerance for demands that their taxes be spent paying for the sins of slavery and Jim Crow, no matter how real those sins. Latinos, if they are truly represented by the Latino Caucus in Congress or various California and southwestern elites, may want amnesty for illegals and increased acceptance of cross-border flows of people, but the country, while welcoming, is not in the mood for such policies. President Bush's moves toward expanding work opportunities for illegals undercut further the tenuous hold of the Left on Latino voting blocs.

The Party of Government is not unhappy with the Democratic Party; neither can it grow much larger. There are real limits to the growth of government, and they have everywhere been reached. Demands by teachers' unions, once looked on favorably by middle-class voters, have become too regular and too indifferent to classroom performance to resonate.

Organized labor is not a spent force, but neither is it vibrant. As a percentage of the vote, it continues to drop in significance. The political muscle of organized labor was supposed to deliver the Iowa caucuses of January 2004 to either Richard Gephardt or Howard Dean since both men carried key labor endorsements into the campaign, but both were handily beaten. Labor can no longer deliver the votes it once could.

The Party of License is deeply alienated from the American mainstream. The aftermath of 9/11 stripped away much of the camouflage on the academic branch of this group, and widespread disgust with academic hatreds of America was evident. Noisy abortion absolutists have been crying wolf for decades, even as American opinion solidified around majority positions against partial birth abortion and in favor of parental involvement in the abortion decisions of their minor children. Demands for gay marriage as opposed to lifestyle tolerance also pulled American opinion away from this group, even as the echoes of Columbine continue to gnaw at parents. The president's endorsement of an amendment to the Constitution protecting marriage outraged the Party of License even as it energized much of the GOP and a large bloc of traditionalist Democrats.

The Party of License is weighed down with Michael Moore and Nan Aaron, with People for the American Way, and with Alec Baldwin, Barbra Streisand, Martin Sheen, and Janeane Garofalo. The list of foulmouthed and very dense celebrities is so long and their repeated insults so offensive that Hollywood and the university elites are now an anchor and not an engine for the party.

As the first presidential vote of post-9/11 America draws near, then, all three blocs within the Republican Party are united and energized. All three blocs within the Democratic Party are riven, dispirited, and alienated from the middle class and the independent voters as well as the famed "Reagan Democrats" and the emerging "9/11 Democrats."

The table is set for a referendum on the next generation of politics.

If you take your life, the lives of your family and friends, and the national interest seriously, you will be pleased by the direction of the currents in American politics.

And if you are really serious, you'll help deliver the hammer blows
that shatter Democratic Party resistance to the national security agenda.

CHAPTER 3

THE NATIONAL SECURITY COLLAPSE OF THE DEMOCRATIC PARTY

J ames Traub is a foreign policy maven and essayist and a friend to the Democrats. He wishes the Democratic Party had not lost the confidence of the public on issues of war and peace and on homeland defense, but he's a realist. Traub wrote an extended essay on the foreign policy collapse of the Democrats for the first issue of the new year of *The New York Times Magazine* on January 4, 2004. In the very lengthy piece, titled "The Things They Carry," Traub included this brief, trying-to-be-friendly-to-the-Dems history of the party's retreat from its legacy of national strength and robust, aggressive American interventionism:

> When the Democratic candidates mention John Kennedy—and they do so as often as possible—they are not trying to evoke an image of youth and vigor, or even of commitment to social justice, as Bill Clinton was. No, they are trying to remind listeners of the last time the Democrats were considered the party of national security. In a major foreign-policy address, John Kerry summoned up the ghosts not only of Kennedy but of Truman and FDR as leaders who "understood that to make the world safe for democracy

and individual liberty, we needed to build international institutions dedicated to establishing the rule of law over the rule of the jungle." True enough, but the party's line of descent from those mid-20th century heroes was shattered 35 years ago, and the question of patrimony remains bitterly contested.

The brief history of the intersection of American politics and American foreign policy that followed was hardly comprehensive and not even remotely accurate. While Traub detailed the long slide from John F. Kennedy's robust defense policies, he did not detail the rise of Republican internationalism from President Reagan's determined and successful efforts to keep Nicaragua from becoming a Cuban-style dictatorship under the Sandinistas, or Reagan's far more important deployment of the Pershing II and cruise missiles to Europe in the face of huge opposition from the international and domestic Left. Traub also omitted any mention of the "nuclear winter" crowd or of the Democratic Party's deeply entrenched pacifist caucus among its congressional delegation.

Traub didn't even bother to note Clinton's devastating decision to cut and run from Somalia after his administration's refusal to allow armor to deploy there led to the Blackhawk Down disaster; Clinton's terrible appeasement of North Korea in the 1994 agreement that North Korea had already begun to cheat on before the ink dried; or the theatrical but never serious effort to capture or kill bin Laden or to shatter the Taliban regime that provided bin Laden a base from which to launch the attacks on our African embassies, the USS *Cole*, and New York and Washington on 9/11. Traub's conclusion later in his essay that "the war in Afghanistan had enjoyed near-universal support" was just one more attempt to paint Democratic foreign policy failure with bright colors. There was huge criticism from the Left of the war in Afghanistan, and even the Democrats who seemed to support it did so in a hypercritical fashion. Delaware Senator Joe Biden, for instance, appeared before the Council on Foreign Relations and demanded more "boots on the ground" so that the world would see the U.S. going "mano a mano" rather than cruelly bombing villagers from the sky. Reliable Democratic allies immediately began spinning out worries about the quagmire of Afghanistan, the dangers of the Afghan winter, and the troubling example of the Russian intervention a decade earlier.

In short, Traub's account is as favorable to the Democratic Party as one could expect, which is not surprising since a cover story in *The New York Times Magazine* is pretty much the equivalent of a papal bull when it comes to authority within the Democratic Party.

I refer readers to Traub's analysis not because it is fair or accurate, but because it reveals the Democrats' complete collapse on issues of national security and foreign policy. A friendly writer, willing to airbrush out the worst features of the portrait and ready to overlook compelling data on the side of the GOP, was nevertheless obliged to conclude,

> The attacks of 9/11 ended the brief post-cold-war interval and recreated elements of both the psychological and the strategic environment of the cold-war 1960s. Once again, it was we who were targeted; once again we would be engaged on many fronts against an ideologically committed foe. And Americans probably feel more vulnerable today than they have at any time since the depths of the Cold War. President Clinton once observed that at such moments, Americans prefer a message that is "strong and wrong" to one that is "weak and right." But Clinton, who inoculated the Democrats against attacks on so many domestic issues, never had the opportunity, or perhaps never saw the need, to do so in terms of national security. The terrorist attacks made the moral quandaries of the '90s look like luxuries and restored the old party stereotypes with a vengeance. By the time of the 2002 midterm elections, the Republicans enjoyed an astounding 40-point advantage on the question of which party was best at "keeping America strong"; the election was understood as a referendum on national security policy, and the GOP swept the board.

Traub is right about the elections of 2002, and that same referendum will be held in November 2004 and for many even-year Novembers to come. Democrats hate this. They don't want to fight elections on national security and defense issues. They don't want to talk about the war on terror and its battlefields in Afghanistan, Iraq, and other troublesome places around the globe. They want the center-right to take their word on it: they would be just as vigilant as the Republicans.

But the public knows that isn't true. The people know about the party's pacifist wing. They know that the Vietnam generation bred an entire cohort of Democratic Party leaders who remain, as Robert Gordon Kaufman put it, convinced that "the prime danger to U.S. national security [is] the arrogance of American power," not the threats from Islamist extremism married to weapons of mass destruction or Chinese expansion or any of a number of more distant threats.

The Democratic Party is home to, and accords enormous power and influence to, Barbara Boxer and Barbra Streisand, Jesse Jackson and Patty Murray, Charles Rangel and Ed Markey—all of whom remain fixed on the Far Left fringes of the national security/national defense debates. Presidents must listen to and appoint from the activist wing of their parties. Every president has done so in modern times.

And the activist wing of the Democratic Party cannot be trusted with the national security of the United States any more than a group of hard Left faculty could be trusted with any major university or labor radicals, the AFL-CIO.

Democratic Party apologists want to persuade the public that their pacifist caucus can be contained and kept from the levers of power, but that never happens. The government is too vast; the demands for patronage for the activists, too strong. This dynamic is most strikingly illustrated by Bill Clinton's appointment of Sara E. Lister as assistant army secretary for manpower and reserve affairs. Lister brought an agenda of "feminism first" to the army, and when her candid views on aggressive war fighting surfaced in an October 26, 1997, speech at Harvard University's John T. Olin Institute for Strategic Studies in Baltimore, outrage and her resignation followed.

Lister's statement was targeted specifically at the United States Marine Corps: "I think the Army is much more connected to society than the Marines are. The Marines are extremists. Wherever you have extremists, you've got the risk of total disconnection from society, and that's a little dangerous." This remark betrayed an otherworldly understanding of the military. The U.S. Army and the Marine Corps may have different doctrines and very different styles of war fighting, but whatever their differences, they are much closer to each other than either of them is to the wing of the Democratic Party represented by Sara Lister. The U.S. Army patrols Najaf and the Marine Corps battles in Fallujah, both full of warriors who Sara Lister never understood.

The central trouble with the Democratic Party is that its elites are shot through with a latent hostility to the use of American power and especially American military force born from the long-ago opposition to the Vietnam War and nurtured by three decades of blaming America first, no matter what the issue was.

So deep has this strain of reflexive opposition to serious action against our enemies embedded itself that even a Democrat like Georgia's United States Senator Zell Miller, a self-proclaimed "lifelong Democrat who first voted for Adlai Stevenson in 1952 and has voted for every Democratic presidential candidate the 12 cycles since," was obliged to declare a full year before the November 2004 election that "I will vote for George W. Bush for president." He explained why:

> This is a president who understands the price of freedom. He understands that leaders throughout history often have had to choose between good and evil, tyranny and freedom. And the choice they make can reverberate for generations to come. This is a president who has some Churchill in him and who does not flinch when the going gets tough. This is a president who can make a decision and does not suffer from "paralysis analysis." This is a president who can look America in the eye and say on Iraq, "We're not leaving." And you know he means it.

About all nine of the Democrats who set out to win the party's nomination to challenge Bush, Miller wrote, "They also, to varying degrees, want us to quit and get out of Iraq. They don't want us to stay the course in this fight between tyranny and freedom. This is the best chance to change the course of history in the Middle East. So I cannot vote for a candidate who wants us to cut and run with our shirttails at half-mast."

Democrats objected when Senator Miller issued his declaration in 2003, and they continue to object to this day. These politicians will seek to marginalize this longtime Democratic governor of Georgia and now Georgia's Democratic United States senator as he campaigns for George W. Bush in the summer and fall, and heads Democrats for Bush nationwide.

But they ought not to blame Miller; rather, they ought to ask themselves why a great percentage of their party—probably a majority—is isolationist on matters of national security and in agreement with the views of nations like France and Germany on the irresponsibility of American power. The "blame America first" impulse is alive and dominant in the Democratic Party, and unless and until it is rooted out, the party cannot be trusted with the country's national security.

Democrats would surely object if I were to quote from their party's fringe or from its nuttiest members. Congressman Jim McDermott of Washington State, Congressman Dennis Kucinich of Ohio, and Congressman Jim Moran of Virginia are members in good standing of the Democrats, with many more like them, who exert considerable influence on Democratic Party policy.

But if these people are quoted, the Democrats object that they are not representatives of the party, just like black sheep uncles should not be taken as representatives of a large family.

Yet these and others—including the simple lightweights like California's giggly Sanchez sisters, Loretta and Linda, and the race-card players like Maxine Waters—dominate the Democratic Party in the House, and thus the party's approach to foreign policy. They are not black sheep in a family, but the core of the family—its value-seeding, policy-predicting majority.

Still, when the Democrats veer to the center this fall and every fall in which an election looms, it is useful to keep handy the remarks of their leaders. Perhaps the best statement of Democratic Party sensibilities on matters of foreign affairs from other than a presidential candidate came from House Minority Leader Nancy Pelosi when she delivered the response to the president's State of the Union speech on January 20, 2004.

Pelosi cannot be discounted as an aberration—she is the leader of the House Democrats and will remain there for years to come. She's a full-frontal San Francisco liberal, and because the House is elected every two years, the caucus she leads is representative of the most recent trends in the party throughout the country. That the party as a whole turned to a hard Left West Coast liberal to be its voice in the "people's chamber" is evidence enough of where the party's heart lies, but if there is any doubt, Pelosi made it very clear in her nationally televised address. Here is her address in its entirety. Read it carefully, keeping in mind it was delivered in wartime, even as American military personnel were fighting for freedom around the globe. Pelosi's speech is simply a demand for retreat on all fronts on the war on terror. It is an argument for withdrawing inside America and hoping that the Islamists leave us alone.

The state of our union is indeed strong, due to the spirit of the American people—the creativity, optimism, hard work and faith of everyday Americans.

The State of the Union address should offer a vision that unites us as a people—and priorities that move us toward the best America. For inspiration, we look to our brave young men and women in uniform, especially those in Iraq and Afghanistan. Their noble service reminds us of our mission as a nation—to build a future worthy of their sacrifice.

Tonight, from the perspective of 10 years of experience on the Intelligence Committee working on national security issues, I express the Democrats' unbending determination to make the world safer for America—for our people, our interests and our ideals.

Democrats have an unwavering commitment to ensure that America's armed forces remain the best-trained, best-led, best-equipped force for peace the world has ever known. Never before have we been more powerful militarily. But even the most powerful nation in the history of the world must bring other nations to our side to meet common dangers.

The president's policies do not reflect that. He has pursued a go-it-alone foreign policy that leaves us isolated abroad and that steals resources we need for education and health care here at home.

The president led us into the Iraq war on the basis of unproven assertions without evidence; he embraced a radical doctrine of preemptive war unprecedented in our history and he failed to build a true international coalition.

Therefore, American taxpayers are bearing almost all the cost—a colossal $120 billion and rising. More importantly, American troops are enduring almost all the casualties—tragically, 500 killed and thousands more wounded.

As a nation, we must show our greatness, not just our strength. America must be a light to the world, not just a missile.

Forty-three years ago today, as a college student standing in the freezing cold outside this Capitol Building, I heard President Kennedy issue this challenge in his Inaugural Address: "My fellow citizens of the world," he said, "ask not what America will do for you, but what, working together, we can do for the freedom of man."

There is great wisdom in that, but in it there is also greater strength for our country and the cause of a safer world.

Instead of alienating our allies, let us work with them and international institutions so that together we can prevent the proliferation of weapons of mass destruction and keep them out of the hands of terrorists.

Instead of billions of dollars in no-bid contracts for politically connected firms like Halliburton, and an insistence on American dominance in Iraq, let us share the burden and responsibility with others, so that together we can end the sense of American occupation and bring troops home safely when their mission is completed.

Instead of the diplomatic disengagement that almost destroyed the Middle East peace process and aggravated the danger posed by North Korea, let us seek to forge agreements and coalitions—so that, together with others, we can address challenges before they threaten the security of the world.

We must remain focused on the greatest threat to the security of the United States—the clear and present danger of terrorism. We know what we must do to protect America, but this administration is failing to meet the challenge. Democrats have a better way to ensure our homeland security.

One hundred percent of containers coming into our ports or airports must be inspected. Today, only 3 percent are inspected.

One hundred percent of chemical and nuclear plants in the United States must have high levels of security. Today, the Bush administration has tolerated a much lower standard.

One hundred percent communication in real time is needed for our police officers, firefighters and all our first responders to prevent or respond to a terrorist attack. Today, the technology is there, but the resources are not.

One hundred percent of the enriched uranium and other material for weapons of mass destruction must be secured. Today, the administration has refused to commit the resources necessary to prevent it from falling into the hands of terrorists.

America will be far safer if we reduce the chance of terrorist attack in one of our cities than if we diminish the civil liberties of our people.

As a nation, we must do better to keep faith with our armed forces, their families and our veterans. Our men and women in uniform show their valor every day. On the battlefield, our troops pledge to leave no soldier behind. Here at home, we must leave no veteran behind. We must ensure their health care, their pensions and their survivor benefits.

The year ahead offers great opportunity for progress and perhaps new perils still hidden in the shadows of an uncertain world. But you, the American people, have shown again and again that you are equal to any test. Now your example summons all of us in government, Republicans and Democrats, to a higher standard.

This is personal for all of us, in every community across this land.

As a mother of five, and now as a grandmother of five, I

came into government to help make the future brighter for all of America's children. As much as at any time in my memory, the future of our country and our children is at stake.

Democrats are committed to strengthening the state of our union—to reach for a safer, more prosperous America.

Together, let us make America work for all Americans—let us restore our rightful role of leadership in the world, working with others for "the freedom of man."

I have included the complete text because there is no need to edit for effect. Ms. Pelosi, speaking on behalf of her entire party, refused to confront the threat that faces the country. In a fundamental way she has no answer to the question: What should the president do if he believes an enemy looms and is likely to strike us sometime in the future, but is unable to convince the United Nations to act because the United Nations is full of countries that would not mind seeing the United States struck?

She refused to see the vast coalition assembled by President Bush in Afghanistan and Iraq, even though minutes earlier in the evening, the president had again recited the names of the coalition members at work by our side in both countries. Without France and Germany, the coalition doesn't count for Pelosi.

Her assertions that the "president led us into the Iraq war on the basis of unproven assertions without evidence" and that he has "embraced a radical doctrine of preemptive war unprecedented in our history and he failed to build a true international coalition" were genuine expressions of the soul of the Democratic Party.

If you can read Pelosi and agree with her, vote Democratic. But if you think, as I do, that her analysis reflects a fundamental and enduring inability to be serious about threats to the country and a fundamental and enduring inability to set aside partisan sniping to agree on a serious defense and national security policy, then do not pull a single lever or punch a single card or touch a single screen for a single Democrat from the president to your city's mayor to your local school board commissioner.

Nancy Pelosi, Dennis Kucinich, Jim McDermott, and their Hollywood foreign policy advisors are not aberrations—they are the Democratic Party. Vote accordingly.

There was a genuine, unguarded expression of the soul of the Democratic Party in the hunt for the presidential nomination this year. Until he self-destructed on stage following the Iowa caucus vote, Howard Dean had effectively given a voice to the "blame America first" Democrats, and he had garnered the endorsements of Al Gore, Bill Bradley, Iowa's Tom Harkin, and scores of other leading Democrats and Democrat-dominated employee unions. Howard Dean melted before our eyes, but before his personal demons consumed him, he had truly and obviously identified and given definition to the real Democratic Party base. Which is why when you want to know what the real Democratic Party thinks about the national security and the national defense, you have to remember Howard Dean before the collapse of his presidential ambitions rooted in his personal inability to control himself.

Which is why, before we deal with John Kerry, we have to remember Howard Dean. And we have to understand the supporters who flocked to his banner.

CHAPTER 4

REMEMBERING HOWARD DEAN

A Prince is despised when he is seen to be fickle, frivolous, effeminate, pusillanimous, or irresolute, against which defects he ought therefore most carefully to guard, striving so as to bear himself that greatness, courage, wisdom, and strength may appear in all his actions.

—Machiavelli, *The Prince,* Chapter XIX

B y the end of 2003, Howard Dean seemed to have secured victory in the quest to become the Democratic Party's nominee for the presidency in November 2004. But then, in the blink of an eye, his campaign collapsed.

His temperament brought him down. Angry. Unstable. Truth challenged.

I began to refer to Howard Dean as angry, unstable, and truth challenged in November 2003, and his supporters phoned in angry denunciations. On each occasion that a *Dean Dong* called—a term coined by an e-mailer to my program and first used there—I responded by playing tape of Dean or of other Democrats talking about Dean. Until the night of the Iowa caucuses, lots of people disagreed with my assessment. They stopped arguing after Dean's famous "I Have a Scream" speech.

My favorite Dean snippets aired in December 2003, truly a "December to Remember" for Dean and the electorate. The scream just cemented all of the bricks in place, but Dean had been making bricks for six weeks prior to the caucus.

Why Dean went off the rails even after he had achieved sufficient momentum to secure the nomination will puzzle cynical operatives for years to come, but it will never puzzle me. Dean is the sort of fellow who is quite capable of convincing himself of his infallibility. Having once uttered a statement, he will work the world around him until that world agrees with the statement he has already made. In December 2003, Dean revealed himself as an egomaniac and as a tremendously poor student of the world. But a huge portion of the Democratic Party loved him and continued to love him, even after his collapse.

The first killer declaration came out of the doctor's mouth in an interview with NPR's Diane Rehm on December 1, 2003. Rehm asked Dean about the work of the official commission charged with investigating September 11 and about what Rehm had concluded was obstructionism by Bush:

> DIANE REHM: Why do you think he [Bush] is suppressing that report?
> HOWARD DEAN: I don't know. There are many theories about it. The most interesting theory that I've heard so far—which is nothing more than a theory, it can't be proved—is that he was warned ahead of time by the Saudis. Now who knows what the real situation is?

Historians may well date the collapse of the Dean campaign to this utterance, even though it preceded by many weeks Dean's withdrawal from the race for the Democratic nomination.

It was nutty stuff, this "interesting theory" speculation—sort of like wondering aloud if LBJ had JFK knocked off on orders from Texas money men, or if FDR knew of Pearl Harbor's approach but kept it quiet in order to get us fully into the war.

This sort of walk-on-the-wild-side theorizing makes for great History Channel viewing, but it is very unsettling in a presidential candidate. And Dean was only getting started.

The very same day Dean sat down with Diane Rehm he also sat down with *Hardball's* Chris Matthews before a Harvard audience. Asked by

Matthews whether Osama and Saddam should be tried in the United States or tried before an international tribunal, Dean emphatically declared himself indifferent on the subject, and in so declaring, he exposed himself ignorant of ordinary public opinion and of some pretty basic international law.

International tribunals don't come equipped with death penalty authority anymore. Dean didn't know that or didn't care. Most Americans want Osama hanging by the neck until dead. Strike two.

Strike three came a day after Saddam's capture by American forces on December 14. Dean bluntly declared that "the capture of Saddam has not made America safer." And just to assure you that he had indeed struck out, he followed up this howler with a declaration that America was no safer in December of 2003 than it had been on September 11, 2001.

More would follow in that fateful month. Dean completed his "Dr. Emperor has no clothes" tour with an interview with New Hampshire's *Concord Monitor* newspaper, published on December 26, 2003. The paper asked Dean if Osama should be put to death, and Dean replied,

I've resisted pronouncing a sentence before guilt is found. I still have this old-fashioned notion that even with people like Osama, who is very likely to be found guilty, we should do our best not to, in positions of executive power, not to prejudge jury trials. So I'm sure that is the correct sentiment of most Americans, but I do think if you're running for president, or if you are president, it's best to say that the full range of penalties should be available. But it's not great to prejudge the judicial system.

The "full range of penalties" qualifier is not what a country in the middle of a war is looking for, and on that day I would have written off his candidacy as a serious campaign but for the tidal wave of money being squirreled away in the rabbit holes of the 527 committees about which I will explain more later.

Dean's opponents in the Democratic primaries knew the peril of nominating Dean. Between Christmas and New Year's Day of 2003, Senator

John Kerry and Congressman Dick Gephardt warned their party what would follow a Dean candidacy. Then Al Sharpton hit Dean in a nationally televised debate on Dean's failure to appoint any African Americans to his Vermont cabinets, and Dean looked terrible in response. Then the Dean Dongs arrived in Iowa and put people off. Then Dean lost the caucuses. And then, of course, Dean went gutty or nutty, depending on one's point of view, and his "red-faced rant" (as Dean jokingly made reference to it days later on David Letterman's show) sank the campaign. Dean fought on, but no one climbs out of such a hole. Even his followers were shocked. His campaign ended after an embarrassing finish in liberal Wisconsin.

The key thing to remember about Howard Dean was that his temperament, not his issues, disqualified him with Democratic primary voters. His full-throated opposition to the war, his bizarre speculations about secret information and warnings, his refusal to concede that capturing Saddam made America safer—all these positions are majority positions within the Democratic Party. Dean's 2003 strength revealed that a pacifist, isolationist caucus dominated the soul and spirit of the Democratic Party. Dean brought himself to announce that he supported the war in Afghanistan, but that sentiment was not much in evidence on his blog. He won the MoveOn.org primary and the affections of the Hollywood Left. Martin Sheen and Rob Reiner campaigned with Dean across Iowa. Dean's true believers believed nothing so much as the idea that George W. Bush was a neo-imperialist dominated by sinister neocons.

Howard Dean destroyed his own candidacy, but the fireworks he set off, which ultimately consumed his campaign, illuminated the nature of the core of the modern Democratic Party. And the country saw clearly that the core cannot be trusted with the defense of the United States.

CHAPTER 5

UNDERSTANDING JOHN KERRY

T here can be no doubting the physical courage and patriotism of Senator John Kerry. As a 1996 *New Yorker* article recounted, Kerry was an officer on a "swift boat" in the Mekong Delta during the Vietnam War, and on February 28, 1969, that boat came under rocket attack. The article excerpted the military report about the incident:

Kerry's craft received a B-40 rocket close aboard. Lieutenant (j.g.) Kerry ordered his units to charge the enemy positions . . . (his craft) then beached in the center of the enemy positions and an enemy soldier sprang up from his position not ten feet from (Kerry's craft) and fled. Without hesitation Lieutenant (j.g.) Kerry leaped ashore, pursued the man behind a hootch and killed him, capturing a B-40 rocket launcher with a round in the chamber.

The *New Yorker* piece quoted Kerry as recalling, "It was either going to be him or me. It was that simple." Kerry received the Silver Star for his valor.

Just as there is no questioning his courage or patriotism, there is no defending John Kerry's judgment.

Kerry's antiwar activism upon his discharge from the military is well known. Kerry became a spokesman for Vietnam Veterans Against the War and participated in the "throw somebody else's medals away" gambit. Days after the medals toss, Kerry testified to the U.S. Senate Foreign Relations Committee about "war crimes committed in Southeast Asia, not isolated incidents but crimes committed on a day-to-day basis with the full awareness of officers at all levels of command."

Professor Mackubin Thomas Owens, a professor of strategy and force planning at the Naval War College in Newport, Rhode Island, is also a Vietnam veteran, one who led a U.S. Marine infantry platoon in the war in 1968–69. He has written about the crucial question concerning Kerry's antiwar activism and rhetoric, and the judgment and character issues they raise about Kerry:

> If [Kerry] believes his 1971 indictment of his country and his fellow veterans was true, then he couldn't possibly be proud of his Vietnam service. Who can be proud of committing war crimes of the sort that Kerry recounted in his 1971 testimony? But if he is proud of his service today, perhaps it is because he always knew that his indictment in 1971 was a piece of political theater that he, an aspiring politician, exploited merely as a "good issue." If the latter is true, he should apologize to every veteran of that war for slandering them to advance his political fortunes. (*National Review Online*)

Professor Owens will not get his apology, of course, but the fact that it is owed helps us understand John Kerry. He is a calculating, synthetic man of the Left, and his devotion to the Left, as was his devotion to the antiwar movement and before that his devotion to duty, is complete.

That's the crucial thing: John Kerry is fully formed. He's not from the center. He's not from the center Left. He's from the hard Left side of the Democratic Party, and all the campaign camouflage in the world isn't going to change that.

Nor is it going to change the hard Left's opposition to the use of force in a preemptive fashion to prevent the threats of attacks on America from becoming realities of attacks on America.

John Kerry was born on December 11, 1943, and was educated at Yale (Skull & Bones to boot, like President Bush) and Boston College Law School. After a stint as Massachusetts' lieutenant governor, he won a seat in the U.S. Senate in 1984 and won reelection in 1990, 1996, and 2002.

John Kerry is to the left of Teddy Kennedy. Don't believe me. Believe the gold standard of judging liberals: the Americans for Democratic Action (ADA). The ADA maintains lifetime ratings when it comes to senators' devotion to liberal ideas. Each year the ADA looks at the twenty most important votes from the hard Left's point of view. If a senator voted the liberal line on all twenty, he gets a 100 percent rating. A senator's life-time rating accumulates all of his votes from his entire career.

Ted Kennedy's lifetime rating as of the end of January 2004 was 88. John Kerry's was 93.

As I was saying, John Kerry is to the left of Teddy Kennedy. The non-partisan, highly respective *National Journal* agrees, naming Kerry the most liberal member of the United States Senate in 2003.

One analyst of Kerry's record, Peter Huessy, the president of GeoStrategic Analysis and senior defense associate at the National Defense University Foundation, summarized Kerry's national security record this way:

[Kerry] cares about as much for national security as a giraffe. From his first days in Congress, the Massachusetts liberal has been to the very far left of the political spectrum in his national security views.

During the height of the Cold War, Mr. Kerry opposed the entire strategic modernization effort proposed by President Reagan—the Peacekeeper, B-1 and B-2 bombers, the Trident sub-marine and D-5 missile—even though his Democratic colleagues Sam Nunn, Al Gore, Norman Dicks, Sonny Montgomery and Les Aspin, for example, sided with Mr. Reagan. He supported the nuclear freeze, which would have placed U.S. nuclear forces in permanent obsolescence just as Soviet strategic nuclear forces were becoming most formidable.

Mr. Kerry opposed the deployment of the INF Missiles in

Europe that Mr. Reagan successfully achieved. The ground-launched cruise missiles and Pershings in England, Germany, Holland and Italy turned out to be one of the turning points of the Cold War, and hastened the end of the Soviet empire. Mr. Kerry was not only wrong on this crucial issue, but opposed the non-strategic modernization of the defense budget as well. The purchase of additional C-5 airplanes by Mr. Reagan turned out to be critical to rescuing U.S. allies in trouble later in the decade—and Mr. Kerry opposed that as well . . .

Mr. Kerry said he opposed Mr. Reagan in Central America. Indeed, Mr. Kerry supported the Sandinistas in Nicaragua and their war against their own people and against their own neighbors. Not once did Mr. Kerry denounce Nicaraguan leader Daniel Ortega and his communist thug friends, or their sponsors in Cuba and the Soviet Union. Indeed, even after becoming a member of the Senate, Mr. Kerry couldn't shake his firm belief that communism posed no threat to the United States, as he stated in the early 1970s when he testified before the Senate Foreign Relations Committee. (*The Washington Times*)

In short, Kerry's judgment on every major issue of the last phase of the Cold War was wrong.

Kerry's judgment did not improve with the defeat of the Soviet Union and the collapse of that evil empire.

The most important Senate vote of the 1990s was the vote on whether to authorize the first President Bush to go to war to liberate Kuwait from Saddam's clutches.

John Kerry voted no.

If John Kerry had been president in 1991, not only would Saddam still be holding on to Kuwait and its oil, his massive armies intent on perhaps also occupying other victim states, but Saddam would also still possess warehouses full of weapons of mass destruction that not even the crankiest member of the Left denies Saddam had prior to the Gulf War of 1991.

And, chillingly, had John Kerry been in charge in 1991, Saddam today would be a member of the nuclear club. Icon of the Left, Hans Blix testified to the United Nations that post–Gulf War inspections of Iraq in 1991 and 1992 revealed that Saddam's nuclear programs would have produced hydrogen bombs within twelve to eighteen months of Saddam's invasion of Kuwait. Even if Kerry had ever summoned the will to strike at Saddam's Republican Guards, if it had occurred a year later than the fall of 1991, Saddam could have had a nuclear response waiting.

John Kerry had it wrong—again.

Now John Kerry argues that he is tough enough to lead the country in war. Against his lifelong record of failed judgment he can produce only his impressive record of heroism in Vietnam.

George McGovern was also a war hero. Being a war hero doesn't signify national security judgment one way or the other.

Recorded votes on issues affecting national security do.

To repeat: John Kerry is to the left of Ted Kennedy. He is George McGovern returned to try again.

As Kerry maneuvers to escape a record that will cause millions of Americans to conclude he cannot be trusted to protect the United States or to vigorously wage war against our enemies, it will be useful to keep Kerry's record front and center. It will also be useful to keep handy Kerry's responses to six key questions.

These "six critical national security questions" were posed in 2003 by the Council for a Livable World to all candidates for the Democratic Party nomination.

The council is hard Left, like the majority of the Democrats' primary voters. Senator John Kerry submitted his answers. Here are the questions and answers in full:

COUNCIL'S QUESTION: Do you support researching, building and possibly testing a new generation of nuclear weapons, including a high-yield nuclear weapon designed to destroy deeply buried targets and a low-yield nuclear weapon? Please feel free to discuss your Administration's overall nuclear weapons policy.

KERRY'S ANSWER: "Oppose. I oppose the U.S. beginning a new

nuclear arms race by building nuclear bunker buster bombs that are not necessary to achieve our missions."

COUNCIL'S QUESTION: Do you support or oppose the current plan to deploy a ground-based version of a national missile defense in Alaska and California by the fall of 2004? Please feel free to discuss your Administration's plan for missile defense.
KERRY'S ANSWER: "Oppose."

COUNCIL'S QUESTION: Do you support or oppose a multilateral international ban on placing weapons in space? Please feel free to discuss your Administration's space weapons policy.
KERRY'S ANSWER: "Support."

COUNCIL'S QUESTION: Do you support or oppose proposals for a major expansion and acceleration of cooperative threat reduction efforts (including the Nunn-Lugar program), designed to ensure that weapons of mass destruction and their essential ingredients around the world are secured and accounted for as rapidly as possible, reducing the risk that they could fall into the hands of terrorists or hostile states? Please feel free to discuss your Administration's non-proliferation policy toward the former Soviet Union and the rest of the world.
KERRY'S ANSWER: "Support."

COUNCIL'S QUESTION: Do you support or oppose the strategy of aggressive or preventive military action against other states that may pose security threats as a principle policy choice of the United States? Please feel free to discuss your Administration's plans for dealing with potential weapons of mass destruction threats from abroad.
KERRY'S ANSWER: "Oppose. American Presidents have always had a right to preemption to address imminent threats. I support the right of preemption in the force of an imminent threat, but the

Bush doctrine of preemptive war is a dangerous departure from the time tested principles of American foreign policy that have kept us safe."

COUNCIL'S QUESTION: Do you support or oppose negotiations with North Korea that would include providing North Korea with strong incentives to verifiably end its nuclear weapons program? Please feel free to discuss your Administration's plan for dealing with the nuclear weapons program of North Korea.
KERRY'S ANSWER: "Support."

There are a number of remarkable aspects to Kerry's responses to these questions. (I expect, in fact, that he will be obliged to ask the council to "expand and extend" his responses when attention inevitably comes to them as the campaign accelerates. But the first set of responses, reproduced in full and with painstaking accuracy, is quite revealing.)

First, all of the other candidates who responded—General Clark, Howard Dean, Senators Edwards and Lieberman and Congressman Kucinich—provided much lengthier and more nuanced responses. Kerry's four one-word answers, conveying his certainty and his lack of nuance, tell us either that he didn't much care what he answered or that the transparent bias of the council's phrasing made the questions very stilted but still very easy to answer for a candidate whose views are as stilted as the council's questions. One-word answers sufficed because the council and Senator Kerry think alike.

The casual but complete opposition to national missile defense is the most breathtaking of all the declarations. Kerry stands with the loopy Kucinich and against his competitors' varying degrees of support for the concept. The Democratic Party is in reality deeply opposed to deployment of a national missile defense, but the candidates, except Kerry and Kucinich, generally understand the need to disguise that opposition.

For Senator Kerry, a genuine man of the hard Left, "Oppose" will do.

Look long and hard at John Kerry. I'd warn you not to listen to his campaign rhetoric, but his monotone, horrible delivery all but guarantees your anticipating and acting on that advice. Reread his responses. Think on his record. Consider his vote in 1991.

If elected president of the United States, Kerry could be counted on to change radically the course of the war on terrorism. He would cede initiative to the United Nations, and he would almost certainly attempt appeasement with North Korea and Iran, the remaining two threats on the axis of evil.

Do not mistake Kerry's portentousness for seriousness.

He's not serious. And the fecklessness toward the national security of the United States, which has been his consistent theme and practice since his return from Vietnam, will increase the chances of another devastating attack on the United States.

Think on all these things, and then consider them in comparison to the words and record of President Bush.

CHAPTER 6

GEORGE W. BUSH
AND THE WAR

M ost presidential elections are fought and most presidencies evaluated on a wide range of issues.

The election of 2000 between then Vice President Al Gore and then Governor George W. Bush was fought over tax policy in light of record surpluses, the status of Social Security and Gore's promise of a lockbox versus Bush's ideas for partial choice for younger workers while maintaining the existing system for retirees and older workers, and prescription drug benefits.

Most of the campaign's dynamics were actually unrelated to issues, but pivoted on concerns about Gore's penchant to exaggerate or simply conjure up résumé-enhancing accomplishments, and Bush's arrest for driving under the influence of alcohol two decades prior to the election season. Each of three debates between the two candidates featured expectations that Gore would maul the less-experienced Bush, but Bush handily turned back Gore's attacks and won each contest. Gore's problems with makeup, loud sighing, and passivity mixed with stalking worked to cement his image with the public as an odd, strangely disconnected candidate. Only the DUI controversy combined with a blatant appeal to racial fears made the election close, and only the erroneous call of Florida for Gore on election night allowed Gore to douse GOP enthusiasm and turn-out operations, thus allowing him to capture the popular vote while losing the election.

The election of 2000, then, was a peacetime election fought over small stakes and small print as well as personality.

There will be no such elections for a long time to come.

Prior to the collapse of the Soviet Union, no presidential election could take place free of the shadow of the threat posed by Russian militarism. The only Democrats who could win under such circumstances were genuine cold warriors like JFK and LBJ, or flukes like the post-Watergate Jimmy Carter.

The triumph of Reagan and his policies over the USSR ushered in a new era, however, one in which the simple-minded like California's Barbara Boxer could prattle on about peace dividends and a new era in international relations. The collapse of the Democratic Party on national security, begun in the Vietnam War, reached its climax in the absurdities of the Clinton nineties (as detailed in Chapter 3).

In the elections of 1992, 1996, and 2000, there were obligatory questions and answers about foreign policy, but the nation's security was never much in doubt, if at all. We had entered an era where the one superpower—us—might not be able to call every shot, but we certainly weren't losing sleep about threats to our people.

Now presidential politics have changed back to the era when voters had to take seriously the candidates' qualifications on the central issue of keeping the nation safe. Indeed, after 9/11, while the economy and social policy still motivate some voters, the majority of Americans are running a never-ending assessment of their president and the candidates who would replace him: Will they keep the country safe? Are they tough enough for the job? Are they talented enough for the job?

The election of 2004 and all foreseeable future presidential elections will be fought over the question of which candidate will better protect the United States. There are excellent reasons to conclude that the Democratic Party as a whole is structurally incapable of seriousness on national security, no matter how good a game the nominee might talk—be it John Kerry in 2004 or Hillary in 2008.

But even if this fall's or a future Democratic nominee does present a credible claim to respect on issues of war and defense, still the incumbent and his Republican successors in '08 and beyond will have a presumption that he and they are better able to defend the U.S.

Why?

Because when war broke upon us, President Bush responded with war. And when our enemies presumed to threaten us, President Bush began the process of removing them.

It is that simple. Democratic candidates can promise to be tough enough to wage a war on terror. President Bush has actually waged one.

Of longer duration and greater consequence than his actions in Afghanistan and Iraq, however, is the Bush Doctrine that the president has laid down. The attack on America birthed a complete reorientation in American defense policy, one that was developed and articulated in a series of five speeches the president gave beginning on September 14, 2001, and concluding almost exactly a year later with an address to the United Nations on September 12, 2002.

I have included the texts of these five speeches as appendices because they are the crucial documents of our time, laying out as they do a comprehensive statement of what has happened and how the United States has responded and will respond in the future:

1. President Bush's remarks at the National Cathedral on the National Day of Prayer and Remembrance on September 14, 2001 (see Appendix A)

2. President Bush's Address to a Joint Session of Congress on September 20, 2001 (see Appendix B)

3. President Bush's State of the Union Address to Congress on January 29, 2002 (see Appendix C)

4. President Bush's Commencement Address at the United States Military Academy, West Point, New York, on June 1, 2002 (see Appendix D)

5. President Bush's Remarks to the United Nations General Assembly in New York, New York, on September 12, 2002 (see Appendix E)

This quintet of speeches forms a whole, and in retrospect, an amazingly comprehensive whole, one that moves from the raw emotion and grief in the aftermath of the attacks in the address at the National Cathedral, to the initial statement of resolve on September 20, 2001, to the comprehensive statement of the immediate threat in the State of the Union in January of the new year, to a detailed doctrine of American defense strategy in the new era at West Point at the beginning of the summer, to the forceful statement to the world assembly of America's new resolve a year after and within miles of the attack's devastation.

Phrases in each of the speeches will always resonate with Americans who lived through the horror of September 11. That is why I have included the texts in the appendices.

The key paragraphs of the speeches, however, are all a voter needs to know in order to judge the president.

"We are here in the middle hour of our grief," the president began in the National Cathedral in perhaps the most solemn public moment I can recall. It took him only moments to sum up the crisis: "War has been waged against us by stealth and deceit and murder. This nation is peaceful, but fierce when stirred to anger. This conflict was begun on the timing and terms of others. It will end in a way, and at an hour, of our choosing."

And the president chose to invoke God at the moment of national grief, reminding the country that "neither death nor life, nor angels nor principalities nor powers, nor things present nor things to come, nor height nor depth, can separate us from God's love. May He bless the souls of the departed. May He comfort our own. And may He always guide our country."

From the beginning then, President Bush cast the war not as one between interests and nations, but as a conflict between good and evil. The language of moral uncertainty is useless in a war and alien to genuine war leadership. About the president's conviction of America's essential goodness or of its enemies' essential evil there has never been any doubt. His words, because they were true, were effective in shaping the American response in the war that had been launched against it.

Six days later, the president used his address to the joint session of

Congress to lay down a hallmark of war leadership: directness with the enemy. He laid out specific demands for the Taliban in Afghanistan to consider, and he concluded, "These demands are not open to negotiation or discussion. The Taliban must act. They will hand over the terrorists, or they will share in their fate."

On the broader issue of the ideology of our enemies, the president also spoke directly, with a bluntness most welcome in wartime:

> These terrorists kill not merely to end lives, but to disrupt and end a way of life. With every atrocity, they hope that America grows fearful, retreating from the world and forsaking our friends. They stand against us because we stand in their way.
>
> We are not deceived by their pretenses to piety. We have seen their kind before. They are the heirs of all the murderous ideologies of the 20th century. By sacrificing human life to serve their radical visions—by abandoning every value except the will to power—they follow in the path of fascism, and Nazism, and totalitarianism. And they will follow that path all the way, to where it ends: In history's unmarked grave of discarded lies.

And the president closed with the promise of resoluteness and victory necessary in wartime:

> I will not forget this wound to our country or those who inflicted it. I will not yield; I will not rest; I will not relent in waging this struggle for freedom and security for the American people.
>
> The course of this war is not known, yet its outcome is certain. Freedom and fear, justice and cruelty, have always been at war, and we know that God is not neutral between them.

Four months later, President Bush returned to Congress and, in the 2002 State of the Union Address, reported on the lightning success of the first battles in the war:

The American flag flies again over our embassy in Kabul. Terrorists who once occupied Afghanistan now occupy cells at Guantanamo Bay. And terrorist leaders who urged followers to sacrifice their lives are running for their own.

America and Afghanistan are now allies against terror.

Then the president laid down the outlines of the threat that lay immediately beyond Afghanistan—the famous "axis of evil":

Our second goal is to prevent regimes that sponsor terror from threatening America or our friends and allies with weapons of mass destruction. Some of these regimes have been pretty quiet since September the 11th. But we know their true nature. North Korea is a regime arming with missiles and weapons of mass destruction, while starving its citizens.

Iran aggressively pursues these weapons and exports terror, while an unelected few repress the Iranian people's hope for freedom.

Iraq continues to flaunt its hostility toward America and to support terror. The Iraqi regime has plotted to develop anthrax, and nerve gas, and nuclear weapons for over a decade. This is a regime that has already used poison gas to murder thousands of its own citizens—leaving the bodies of mothers huddled over their dead children. This is a regime that agreed to international inspections—then kicked out the inspectors. This is a regime that has something to hide from the civilized world.

States like these, and their terrorist allies, constitute an axis of evil, arming to threaten the peace of the world. By seeking weapons of mass destruction, these regimes pose a grave and growing danger. They could provide these arms to terrorists, giving them the means to match their hatred. They could attack our allies or attempt to blackmail the United States. In any of these cases, the price of indifference would be catastrophic.

The president then went on to promise cooperation with our allies and the deployment of a national missile defense. But he was candid concerning the dangers:

> We'll be deliberate, yet time is not on our side. I will not wait on events, while dangers gather. I will not stand by, as peril draws closer and closer. The United States of America will not permit the world's most dangerous regimes to threaten us with the world's most destructive weapons.
>
> Our war on terror is well begun, but it is only begun. This campaign may not finish on our watch—yet it must be and it will be waged on our watch.
>
> We can't stop short. If we stop now—leaving terror camps intact and terror states unchecked—our sense of security would be false and temporary. History has called America and our allies to action, and it is both our responsibility and our privilege to fight freedom's fight.

A State of the Union speech must by necessity deal with domestic as well as national security concerns, but at its conclusion, President Bush returned to the central focus:

> Steadfast in our purpose, we now press on. We have known freedom's price. We have shown freedom's power. And in this great conflict, my fellow Americans, we will see freedom's victory.

The immediate necessity of destroying the Taliban regime and the Al Qaeda headquarters had been accomplished, and now the near term centers of threat were coldly outlined. Many on the Left reacted negatively to such blunt talk, and certainly the trio of regimes named as the world's greatest rogue regimes complained.

Wars require focus. Americans seemed quite content for plain speech and bald warnings. Even as the president's poll numbers slipped as a result of the slow pace of job creation, the solid majority of Americans never wavered in supporting the direction of the war on terror. Even as the count of dead soldiers, sailors, airmen, and Marines tragically rose in Iraq through 2003 and 2004, the center of the country's majority did not waver from the resolve expressed in the president's speech.

Four months after his State of the Union address, on June 1, 2002, at the commencement exercises at West Point, President Bush expanded on the theme of American resolve by outlining a change in defense strategy that was as radical to American elites as it was obviously necessary to ordinary Americans. President Bush laid out and defended the idea of preemptive action in a half-dozen paragraphs that serve as the core doctrine of his presidency:

In defending the peace, we face a threat with no precedent. Enemies in the past needed great armies and great industrial capabilities to endanger the American people and our nation. The attacks of September the 11th required a few hundred thousand dollars in the hands of a few dozen evil and deluded men. All of the chaos and suffering they caused came at much less than the cost of a single tank. The dangers have not passed. This government and the American people are on watch, we are ready, because we know the terrorists have more money and more men and more plans.

The gravest danger to freedom lies at the perilous crossroads of radicalism and technology. When the spread of chemical and biological and nuclear weapons, along with ballistic missile technology—when that occurs, even weak states and small groups could attain a catastrophic power to strike great nations. Our enemies have declared this very intention, and have been caught seeking these terrible weapons. They want the capability to blackmail us, or to harm us, or to harm our friends—and we will oppose them with all our power.

For much of the last century, America's defense relied on the Cold War doctrines of deterrence and containment. In some cases, those strategies still apply. But new threats also require new thinking. Deterrence—the promise of massive retaliation against nations—means nothing against shadowy terrorist networks with no nation or citizens to defend. Containment is not possible when unbalanced dictators with weapons of mass destruction can deliver those weapons on missiles or secretly provide them to terrorist allies.

We cannot defend America and our friends by hoping for the best. We cannot put our faith in the word of tyrants, who solemnly sign non-proliferation treaties, and then systematically break them. If we wait for threats to fully materialize, we will have waited too long.

Homeland defense and missile defense are part of stronger security, and they're essential priorities for America. Yet the war on terror will not be won on the defensive. We must take the battle to the enemy, disrupt his plans, and confront the worst threats before they emerge. In the world we have entered, the only path to safety is the path of action. And this nation will act.

Our security will require the best intelligence, to reveal threats hidden in caves and growing in laboratories. Our security will require modernizing domestic agencies such as the FBI, so they're prepared to act, and act quickly, against danger. Our security will require transforming the military you will lead—a military that must be ready to strike at a moment's notice in any dark corner of the world. And our security will require all Americans to be forward-looking and resolute, to be ready for preemptive action when necessary to defend our liberty and to defend our lives.

In a few hundred words, George W. Bush redefined American national security policy in a far-reaching and necessary way. Because of the threats posed by weapons that can kill tens or hundreds of thousands in an instant, the United States no longer enjoys the luxury of complacency. We cannot conduct our foreign policy on the assumption that the country can absorb a blow or two from all but the strongest nations, and that the strongest nations would be deterred by mutual assured destruction.

It was not enough for President Bush to address only his fellow citizens on this change in doctrine. It was necessary as well to announce formally the new resolve and the new doctrine to the world. President Bush did so a year and a day after the attacks on America, in an address to the United Nations General Assembly on September 12, 2002.

The speech is a double indictment—of the criminal regime of Saddam Hussein, and of the United Nation's complacency in the face of Hussein's refusal to submit to international demands. The case for force against Iraq was detailed and irrefutable, and it depended not on the presence of weapons of mass destruction being found in Iraq, but on the necessity of obliging rogue states to conform to international authority.

The president concluded with blunt words:

My nation will work with the U.N. Security Council to meet our common challenge. If Iraq's regime defies us again, the world must move deliberately, decisively to hold Iraq to account. We will work with the U.N. Security Council for the necessary resolutions. But the purposes of the United States should not be doubted. The Security Council resolutions will be enforced—the just demands of peace and security will be met—or action will be unavoidable. And a regime that has lost its legitimacy will also lose its power.

Events can turn in one of two ways: If we fail to act in the face of danger, the people of Iraq will continue to live in brutal submission. The regime will have new power to bully and dominate and conquer its neighbors, condemning the Middle East to more years of bloodshed and fear. The regime will remain unstable—the region will remain unstable, with little hope of freedom, and isolated from the progress of our times. With every step the Iraqi regime takes toward gaining and deploying the most terrible weapons, our own options to confront that regime will narrow. And if an emboldened regime were to supply these weapons to terrorist allies, then the attacks of September the 11th would be a prelude to far greater horrors.

If we meet our responsibilities, if we overcome this danger, we can arrive at a very different future. The people of Iraq can shake off their captivity. They can one day join a democratic Afghanistan and a democratic Palestine, inspiring reforms throughout the Muslim world. These nations can show by their example that honest government, and respect for women, and the great Islamic tradition of learning can triumph in the Middle East and beyond. And we will show that the promise of the United Nations can be fulfilled in our time.

Neither of these outcomes is certain. Both have been set before us. We must choose between a world of fear and a world of progress. We cannot stand by and do nothing while dangers gather. We must stand up for our security, and for the permanent rights and the hopes of mankind. By heritage and by choice, the United States of America will make that stand. And, delegates to the United Nations, you have the power to make that stand, as well.

With this address, the UN had been put on notice that a new American resolve would mark our country's deliberations in the Security Council and General Assembly. A different era had begun. In the aftermath of Operation Iraqi Freedom, critics of the American policy have proclaimed that the failure to find weapons of mass destruction makes the war illegitimate. These are the arguments of fools or knaves because no one can deny what has been found: secret and illegal missile programs and weapons laboratories that inspectors never would have found and that Saddam had concealed even from the inspectors he had allowed to return to the country when the threat of war loomed.

Saddam would never have complied with the UN demands. Eventually he or his sons would have waited out the UN and resumed his malignant expansionist dreams. The killing inside Iraq never paused, and Iraq's attacks on its neighbors would have returned when the United Nation's resolve eroded. In a country that openly hosted terrorist Abu Nidal, and whose ties to Al Qaeda were at least as mature as any other nation in the world save Afghanistan, the danger of the pairing of technology and terrorism was real and unavoidable. The president insisted that the United Nations not turn its head from the unpleasant and difficult work of international security.

In the aftermath of the war, even as evidence piled up of Saddam's hideous barbarism and of widespread Saddam-orchestrated corruption within the United Nation's oil-for-food program, Democrats attacked the president for launching the war. He replied to these voices in his State of the Union Address of January 20, 2004:

> Our greatest responsibility is the active defense of the American people. Twenty-eight months have passed since September 11th, 2001—over two years without an attack on American soil. And it is tempting to believe that the danger is behind us. That hope is understandable, comforting—and false. The killing has continued in Bali, Jakarta, Casablanca, Riyadh, Mombasa, Jerusalem, Istanbul and Baghdad. The terrorists continue to plot against America and the civilized world. And by our will and courage, this danger will be defeated.

The emphasis was on "active" defense, and in case his critics missed the point, the president underscored it a few moments later:

> From the beginning, America has sought international support for our operations in Afghanistan and Iraq, and we have gained much support. There is a difference, however, between leading a coalition of many nations, and submitting to the objections of a few. America will never seek a permission slip to defend the security of our country.

No line more starkly conveys the essential difference between the president and the Democrats than the "permission slip" line. It is fair, in fact, to refer to all of the Democrats who sought the nomination of their party to stand against the president in November, except for Joe Lieberman, as "permission slip Democrats" because each criticized the president for initiating the war without the support of France, Germany, and Russia.

John Kerry has never wavered in his criticism of Bush's approach to the world and the threats it contains. Indeed, John Kerry has been a reflexive critic of the use of American force and the expansion of American military capabilities since his return from service in Vietnam. His testimony against the Vietnam War, delivered in 1971 to the U.S. Senate's Foreign Relations Committee, began a thirty-three-year record of hostility to the use of American force in any unilateral fashion and to the proposition that America's military didn't require strengthening via various weapons systems, including the MX missile, the M1 Abrams tank, B-1 and B-2 bombers, the Patriot Missile System, the Aegis cruiser, or any land-based missile defense system. Kerry's worldview could not be more different from the president's.

The choice between what columnist James Lileks calls the "AWOL" Democrats—angry, white, out-of-touch liberals like Howard Dean, Teddy Kennedy, Al Gore, and of course, John Kerry—and George W. Bush could not be clearer. Neither could the choice between the GOP's approach to national security and the isolationist retreat advocated by leading Democrats. The only tactics that Democrats have been able to employ against the standing of the president on the issue of war-time leadership is to attempt to buttress the carpings of the fired Paul O'Neil or the passed-over Clinton holdover Richard Clarke, or to suggest archly that "Bush knew." All of these allegations run up against the record Americans have seen of decisive action in Afghanistan and Iraq, and the resulting liberation of more than 50 million people as well as the dismantling of Libya's nuclear program and the destruction of that state's WMD. The effects of Bush's purposeful conduct of the war against terrorists and the rogue states that support them is increased national security.

The elections of 2004 and beyond may involve scores of issues, but only the choices on the conduct of the war carry with them the immediate risk of disaster. Vote accordingly.

CHAPTER 7

ALLIES, OPPONENTS, AND ENEMIES

T ime now to turn to politics and to the most basic political rule: there are no real neutrals.

Everyone with experience in politics knows that there are only allies and opponents—there are no disinterested third parties.

Sure, there are tens of millions of Americans who won't vote in November. They have never voted in any November in the past and will never vote in any November in the future. But they don't count, and they have no influence on the political process. They are as relevant as Canadians to winning elections. They are as connected to American politics as you are to Australian professional soccer.

Inside the vast game, however, it's all shirts and skins, blues and reds. Someone is either on your side or against you.

An individual's status can change in a moment, of course, and you may have insufficient knowledge about how to categorize an individual perfectly. In that case treat him as an opponent.

But do not confuse this blunt understanding of how politics works with a declaration of love and hate for allies and enemies, respectively. Far from it.

James Carville and Mary Matlin are political opponents who are married and, by all accounts, happily so. They are deep political opponents. It is their job to be opponents. But they are not enemies.

As I have explained many, many times over the years in print and over the air, my closest friend since 1977 has been Mark Gearan. Mark is currently the president of a fine old college in upstate New York, Hobart and William Smith College. It is a place where Hillary and Bill have vacationed. They do so because Mark is an able and loyal member of the Clinton tribe, having served Bill as a senior campaign aide in 1992, as a deputy chief of staff and communications director in the White House, and as director of the Peace Corps. Mark has never spoken a negative word about the Clintons to me in the more than a dozen years he has been associated with them.

I don't think I have ever spoken a positive word about them to him. Rather, I think that they are the worst things to have happened to American politics in the twentieth century, and that Bill Clinton makes Richard Nixon look like a saint. I don't despise the Clintons as people, but their politics are of a low, vicious sort, and their ambitions have always been about themselves, never about the country.

Mark and I are political opponents and very close, indeed, inseparable, friends.

He's just wrong about nearly everything, and I hold out very little hope of his ever changing. He's a John Kerry man, of course, because Mark is a Massachusetts liberal and John Kerry is a Massachusetts liberal.

Despite our friendship, I wish Mark endless bad luck in his political life and a lifetime's exile from real power. There is a no ill will here, just reality. Mark's party, if it returns to power, could get me killed before my time.

Once you can understand the dichotomy between politics and the rest of life, then politics gets easier. Keep an eye on your political opponents, and never seek their advice or take any advice they offer. It's a political death match, and your opponents are playing to win. Treat Democrats like the NFL team on the opposite side of the line of scrimmage.

Politics is a zero-sum game. For every win there is a loss, and every loss inflicted on any member of the opposite side is a win for your side.

Don't do favors for your enemies. Disraeli was the great British prime minister who remarked that nothing was more injurious to political parties than for the victorious party to make gestures of conciliation to the losing side. Small tokens like a few jobs of prestige or the continuation of contracts favorable to the supporters of the other side are crazy concessions to losers. Worse, these are foolish weaknesses, and the other side understands them as weaknesses.

Occasionally, for purely public relations' sake, a GOP president might appoint a Democratic Party member to some job. That's fine, providing it is done to advance the party's interests by advancing a reputation for broad-mindedness.

But genuine bipartisanship is a silly and absurd concept, favored by Lefties tricked out as above-the-fray objective analysts.

Democrats seem to understand the rule of opponent or ally much more genuinely and practice it much more thoroughly than Republicans do. It was learned behavior in the big political machines of New York, Chicago, and St. Louis. Favors didn't go to out-of-machine men and women. There was endless demand for favors inside the machine.

Help political allies. Never help political opponents.

But be very slow to declare any American an enemy of America. There is a very small percentage of Americans who would like to see the country disabled. There always has been. Alger Hiss, a close advisor to FDR, was the real deal: a genuine Communist spy working undercover to destroy the United States. There have always been Benedict Arnolds, and there still are. But they are rare, and it is wrong to name opponents as enemies of the United States. In waging political war, don't charge over that cliff.

In this regard, keep in mind the essential similarities between Democrats and adolescents. They are, almost all of them, patriots. And they are, almost all of them, poorly equipped to understand and fashion the national security policy of the United States. Whether talking with a Republican, an independent, a Green, or a Democrat, never forget: he or she is always an ally or an opponent.

PART TWO

A BRIEF HISTORY OF DEMOCRATIC CHEATING

The ruler of [New York] during the greater part of the forty years of my acquaintance with the state government has not been any man authorized by the Constitution or by the law.

—Elihu Root, U.S. secretary of state and Nobel laureate,
1915 speech to the New York State Constitutional Convention

Until we get rid of these political machines who now control the [Democratic] Party, we might as well not go to the polls.

—FDR, 1912 interview

The one pervading evil of democracy is the tyranny of the majority, or rather of that party, not always the majority, that succeeds by force or fraud, in carrying elections.

—Lord Acton

CHAPTER 8

THE REPUTATION

The Democratic Party has a reputation for cheating when it comes to elections.

It richly deserves this reputation.

The reputation is grounded in the history of the party, and as recently as the fall of 2003, in the California recall campaign, the party did nothing to alter the aroma that surrounds its day-to-day operations.

The face of the modern Democratic Party is Bob Mulholland, the political director of the California Democratic Party, a post he has held in some fashion since the early '70s.

Mulholland is a repulsive character, a bizarre and twitchy thug who threatened Arnold Schwarzenegger with "real bullets" when the then actor decided to run for the statehouse he now occupies. Mulholland was obliged to apologize, just as he was obliged to step aside briefly in 1992 when he slimed Republican senatorial candidate Bruce Herschensohn with the charge that Herschensohn frequented strip clubs.

But the Dems always bring Bob back because it's a brass-knuckled party and Bob's a brass-knuckled guy.

Recall the Clinton scandals—they weren't all about having sex in the Oval Office and lying under oath. They included renting the Lincoln bedroom, accepting foreign money, and having "no controlling legal authority."

Recall as well Al Gore's loose allegiance to the truth, whether it pertained to inventing the Internet, traveling with a FEMA director to fires in Texas, or citing the cost of drugs for his dog, Shiloh.

The Democrats play to win, and if winning requires cheating and lying, so be it.

"I'm not like George Bush," Al Gore said during Campaign 2000. "If he wins or loses, life goes on. I'll do anything to win."

This general attitude among Democrats, articulated so perfectly by Gore, is the reason that it is important for Republicans not merely to win elections. Republicans must win by comfortable margins. If it is close, you can count on the Democrats cheating. You can count on dirty tricks. Putting a close election in front of the Democratic Party is like putting a beautiful woman in a bikini on a kickboard in the *Jaws* movies. Cue the music.

You can count on Florida 2000.

Elite media like to skip over the legacy of the Dems when it comes to cheating, but it is the job of Republicans to keep the Democrats' record front and center.

Here are the key words and phrases: *Tammany, Pendergast, and Daley; Kennedy in Texas and Illinois in 1960; Clinton and the Chinese in 1996; Gore and the military absentee ballots in Florida in 2000; Torricelli in New Jersey in 2002; the Ninth Circuit and the California recall.*

Each of these phrases is shorthand for stories of Democratic Party corruption and cheating in the electoral setting. These accounts cannot be repeated too often. Voters are disgusted by such tactics practiced by Democrats, but others tend to forget the headlines of the past and the Left's friends in elite media are in no hurry to assign resources to the effort to catalogue Democratic scandals.

A case in point. In the same California recall campaign in which Bob Mulholland threatened the spouse of a Kennedy with "real bullets," the *Los Angeles Times* dispatched a huge team to dig for dirt on Schwarzenegger on the Thursday before the election, but it backfired as the public rejected the transparent partisanship of the paper. The number of canceled subscribers soared into the thousands, and the paper's reputation—already in tatters after a decade of agenda journalism—plummeted even farther.

The paper was criticized not just for its relentless attacks on Schwarzenegger—all four of its regular columnists, for example, were vehemently anti-Schwarzenegger—but also for sins of omission. The paper hemorrhaged resources on the campaign to get Arnold, but left Davis alone, imitating its coverage from the 2002 campaign cycle in which the Davis "pay-to-play" governorship was allowed to escape serious scrutiny while GOP nominee Bill Simon was ripped for owning a company that lost a lawsuit—the result of a runaway jury's laughable verdict that was later reversed.

The imbalance in the *Los Angeles Times* political coverage is a common feature of most major American newspapers and of all the television network news operations except at the Fox News Channel. As a result, the Democrats' addiction to shady tactics is allowed to slip down the memory hole.

Which is why the GOP needs to work hard to keep reminding the electorate of the key words and plans outlined above: Tammany, Pendergast, and Daley; Kennedy in Chicago and Texas in 1960; Clinton and the Chinese in 1996; Al Gore and the military vote in Florida in 2000; the big Bob Torricelli switch in New Jersey in 2002; and the attempted judicial coup in California in the fall of 2003.

You don't need to give a dissertation on each of these subjects, just a little reminder. It isn't news that the Democrats cheat. It's just an unpleasant reality that most folks would prefer to forget.

But Democrats worked hard to earn their reputation for shady tactics and knock-down, brass-knuckled vote stealing. Make sure they keep what they earned.

CHAPTER 9

THE LEGACY
OF THE MACHINES

T he Democratic Party grew up cheating. Tammany Hall was born in the same year the Constitution was ratified, so it is accurate to remark that Democratic dirty tricks are as old as the Republic.

Tammany is the name given to the corrupt New York City political machine that began in 1789 and endured well into the twentieth century when Democratic Party cheating was decentralized and thus made much more difficult to identify and prosecute.

But Aaron Burr really started it. Burr is the rogue who schemed to divide the infant Republic when his ambition to become president was frustrated, and who shot and killed Alexander Hamilton in a duel. Burr is a compelling symbol for modern Democrats. The Tammany machine he led can be said to have invented many techniques of electoral fraud that remain regular features of the American political landscape on the Democratic side.

Tammany figured out how to spring cons from jail so they would vote in elections.

Tammany figured out how to register the newly arrived in the country, despite their ineligibility, in order to swell turnout.

Tammany practically patented widespread and blatant cheating. The first Tammany mayor of New York, Fernando Wood, won reelection amid epic ballot laundering, with Republicans counting more than ten thousand fake ballots. Wood relied on the criminal gangs that were featured in Martin Scorsese's *The Gangs of New York*, and even his defeat when he ran for a third term did not finish him off—he moved on to the House of Representatives.

Even more legendary bosses followed, such as William Marcy Tweed, John Kelly, Richard Croker, and Charles Francis Murphy. Each in turn looted the public treasury but kept the men organized and voting. Only the rise of La Guardia and other reformers in the Depression era would largely kill off Tammany, yet even then its power lasted into the 1960s.

The Pendergast brothers of Kansas City, Missouri, picked up and improved upon all of the techniques of Tammany.

James Pendergast, a saloon keeper and city alderman, got the machine started in the late 1800s, and he passed its control to his younger brother, who came to be known as Boss Tom.

Boss Tom began his rise as "superintendent of streets," and his career as king maker lasted until his convictions for fraud in the late 1930s. He even spent fifteen months in federal prison. Pendergast appointees looted Kansas City for nearly forty years. According to historian Lyle Dorsett, "Nearly three thousand people were on the city payrolls who did nothing but pick up their checks."

The Pendergast operation was a national force in politics. It provided crucial help to Franklin Roosevelt in the 1932 Democratic Party convention, and FDR repaid the favor with many key appointments to Pendergast men during the New Deal.

Boss Tom also famously launched Harry Truman's career, installing him as a county judge in 1922, and using the machine to secure Truman's election as senator from Missouri in 1934.

Thus, both FDR and Truman owed debts to corrupt political machines. JFK would be no different, but he would owe Richard Daley, mayor of Chicago and the third name associated with Democratic Party corruption.

The tactics of Tammany and Pendergast were taken to new levels by Richard Daley, the six-term mayor of Chicago. Just look at the titles of the books about him: *Boss, American Pharaoh, Don't Make No Waves, Don't Back No Losers.*

Daley perfected modern machine politics. As the *Chicago Tribune* had occasion to editorialize: "Once an election has been stolen in Cook County, it stays stolen."

"Organization, not machine," Daley would growl. "Got it? Organization, not machine." Why did the word matter? Because Daley knew that crooked tactics didn't sit well outside the ward. Today's Democratic Party knows the same thing, but try as it might, the legacy of Tammany-Pendergast-Daley still animates the party.

Daley's rules were pretty simple: pay back those who help you support the entire ticket, not just the Democrat you like. Don't ask questions. Don't get caught.

Pretty simple stuff, and the stuff of awesome political power. At its height, Daley's machine controlled ten congressional seats, the Democratic caucus in both houses of the state legislature, the governorship of Illinois, and every aspect of political life inside Cook County and Chicago.

The techniques ranged from handing out free turkeys or booze to making sure that the government jobs pipeline—estimated at thirty thousand—was open only to loyal Democrats. Power begot power, and Daley made it run seamlessly.

"I'm not the last of the old bosses," Daley declared. "I'm the first of the new leaders."

He was right. The modern Democratic Party remains true to Daley's focus on winning, regardless of the rules.

CHAPTER 10

DEMOCRATS AND CLOSE ELECTIONS: WHATEVER IT TAKES

A party with a tradition of cheating as rich as the Democrats' finds it easy to bend the rules or to celebrate those who do. An Al Davis/Oakland Raiders "Just Win Baby" attitude permeates modern Democratic Party tactics. Even if winning means suppressing the absentee votes of military serving overseas—well, that's just a price that has to be paid.

The tone for the modern Democratic Party approach to winning was set in the 1960 presidential election. On November 8, 1960, John F. Kennedy won the presidency with 303 electoral votes. Richard Nixon gathered 219 electoral votes. At least that's what the records show.

Illinois had 24 electoral votes, and Texas had 27. Switch those votes from the Kennedy column to the Nixon column, and Nixon wins the presidency, 270 electoral votes to JFK's 252.

There is no certainty that Nixon won both Texas and Illinois. What is certain, however, is that massive voter fraud on Kennedy's behalf occurred in both states. In Texas, Kennedy's margin of victory was 46,000 votes, but Lyndon Johnson's Lone Star state political machine could easily have provided that number. In Illinois, Kennedy won by a bare 9,000 votes, and Mayor Daley, who held back Chicago's vote until late in the evening, provided an extraordinary Cook County margin of victory of 450,000 votes. No thorough investigation of the massive irregularities was ever conducted, and partisans of both Kennedy and Nixon still debate the bottom line. No fair observer then or now denies that the Democratic Party—caught in a tight spot—reverted to form and began cheating at every turn.

The tradition of stopping at nothing to win surfaced in the 1996 Clinton fund-raising scandals. Clinton's obsessive hunt for money with which to wage political war led to huge irregularities and illegalities, including both the famous "renting" of the Lincoln bedroom and Al Gore's defense of his dialing for dollars from his vice presidential office—that "no controlling legal authority" prevented the practice. John Huang became infamous for his incredible fund-raising proficiency—of the illegal variety—and the stink of the Clinton fund-raising excesses lingers.

The lowest point of Democratic underhandedness when it comes to winning took place in the aftermath of the presidential election of 2000. Al Gore's decision to contest the Florida vote wasn't cheating, of course, though it broke a two-centuries-old tradition in American politics of keeping presidential politics out of the courts. Nor was it illegal for Gore to resort to piecemeal litigation in Florida counties where he thought he might gain an advantage from a recount while skipping demands for a recount in the counties where a close look at the votes might add votes to the Bush tally.

There is a difference between ruthless and rotten. Gore's rampage through Florida after the Bush victory was announced and then verified was ruthless, but it wasn't corrupt.

What was corrupt was the Gore team's decision to use whatever means necessary to suppress absentee votes from military personnel serving overseas. More than 3,700 ballots arrived from military voters serving overseas, and the Gore campaign convinced election officials spread across Florida to have many of these votes excluded based on technicalities relating to postmarks and signatures, a move that when exposed led to intense criticism of the Democratic tactics.

The Democratic effort to exclude the votes of the military serving overseas stunned Americans of all political persuasions. Across the political spectrum, disgust with this move erupted. That disgust lingers, and it is crucial to remind voters again that not a single Democrat stepped forward to condemn the Gore campaign's decision to win, even if the cost of winning included the illegal disenfranchisement of thousands of soldiers, sailors, airmen, and Marines. "No one who aspires to be Commander-in-Chief," said Bush advisor Karen Hughes at the time, "should seek to unfairly deny the votes of the men and women he would seek to command."

Hughes's point was a good one, but it is crucial to keep in front of the public the complicity of all Democrats in this exercise in power at all costs. John Kerry likes to talk about his desire to champion the causes of veterans. Most veterans would count among their causes the protection of the voting rights of those currently serving in the military. Kerry did nothing to protect that "value" in December 2000.

The Gore decision to litigate the results in Florida was not cheating, though it was a shocking abandonment of past practice. It wasn't long before the new tactic—sue, even when your cause is palpably absurd, since a lot of nutty judges are out there—swept the Democratic Party.

Two episodes from the recent past illustrate the quick addiction of the Democrats to winning via courtroom antics.

The first involved, in the eyes of many, the most obviously corrupt United States senator of recent times: New Jersey's Robert Torricelli, or as I called him on the radio show, Bobby "Rolexes" Torricelli, or as his friends called him, The Torch.

When The Torch arrived in the Senate in 1996, his Democratic colleagues enthusiastically embraced him. The Torch returned the favor(s), raising more than $100 million to help elect Democrats in 2000. But even as his colleagues lavished praise on him for his fund-raising prowess, the law was catching up with Torricelli.

Torricelli had expensive tastes, and at least one friend, David Chang, catered to those tastes, whether in wrist wear, televisions, jewelry, oriental rugs, or assorted haberdashery. The investigations started and gathered momentum. The Senate censured Torricelli, but the Democrats hung tough with him as his reelection campaign got under way.

But when polls revealed Torricelli would certainly lose to Republican nominee Douglas Forrester, the Democratic Party muscled Torricelli aside, telling him that the interests of the party trumped his own interests.

Such a judgment isn't illegitimate, of course, but the tactics employed by the Democrats to enforce their decision were.

Torricelli had easily won his renomination primary. The laws of New Jersey also appeared to be clear: the New Jersey legislature had to provide for procedures to govern "in the event of a vacancy, howsoever caused, among candidates nominated at primaries." But the New Jersey legislature had dictated that those procedures would govern only if the "vacancy shall occur not later than the 51st day before the election." Had Torricelli abandoned his race before September 16, 2002, the Democrats could have used these procedures to substitute a candidate.

He hung on past that deadline, however. Torricelli and his supporters wanted to see if any conceivable combination of tactics and events could persuade New Jersey voters to keep their ethically impaired incumbent in office. When it became obvious that the voters would not forgive him, Torricelli announced he was dropping out of the race—in early October, well after the September deadline. Democrats sued to replace Torricelli's name on the ballot with that of former United States Senator Frank Lautenberg.

Even though Torricelli was not impaired in any way other than ethically and politically, even though the election campaign had been waged for months and absentee votes had already been cast, the Democrats demanded the right to switch candidates a month before the election—a transparent dodge never before accomplished in the history of American elections.

And it worked because the New Jersey Supreme Court, like the Florida Supreme Court in 2000, cared more about Democratic wins than about the rule of law. Torricelli's name was erased from the rolls, new ballots printed, and a campaign of twenty-eight days conducted that put Lautenberg back in the Senate.

Whatever it takes. Whatever it takes.

The last act in the recent abandonment by Democrats of all pretense to electoral ethics occurred in the Golden State. Gray Davis was the worst governor in California history, an inept, dull, and paralyzed apparatchik who rose to power with a combination of prolific fund-raising and even more prolific favor-granting. When California's economy sank under the weight of Davis's sweetheart deals to public employee unions and trial lawyers, it brought down the state budget, and when the borrowing and green-eye-shade tricks ran out, the state found itself facing economic ruin as well as massive deficits that, standing alone, equaled the deficits of most of the other states combined.

The voters revolted and began collecting the signatures to recall Davis from office.

Davis and his allies tried lawsuit after lawsuit to halt the clearly delin-eated procedures governing recalls. The state judges refused to stay his political execution, realizing perhaps the state's voters would scalp an elected official who stood in the way of removing Governor Clouseau.

Finally a desperate attempt by the ACLU caught a lucky break with a three-judge panel of the United States Court of Appeals for the Ninth Circuit composed of the court's most reliably left-wing, hyperpartisan judges: two Carter and one Clinton appointees. Those three judges issued an order canceling the recall election.

The reaction across the state and, indeed, the country was outrage at the naked alliance between out-of-control judicial imperialism and Democratic Party politics. So outraged was the public and so embarrassed were the bar and bench by the transparent meddling in democratic forms by aging dinosaurs of the Left dressed in robes that the Ninth Circuit's other judges demanded a quick rehearing, which was held before eleven judges.

All eleven judges voted to reverse their out-of-control colleagues. The election went forward, and Arnold is now busy repairing the enor-mous damage done by Davis.

You must not forget that Democrats had a small legion of lawyers standing by on recall night to try to litigate the results if Davis was within spitting distance of hanging on to power. The lawyers were prepared to argue that the voting machines used in some places in the state discriminated against minorities.

Only the large margin by which Davis was thrown out and by which Arnold was installed stopped the lawyers from opening their briefcases. It wasn't a sudden conversion to the rule of law and then recommitment of the party's elites to the will of the majority. Just the futility of battling a landslide.

That was the lesson of the California recall: if it's not close, the Democrats can't cheat.

They'll want to cheat, but you can't sneak away with an election that's been won handily.

Democrats will want to cheat in 2004, 2006, and beyond. It's in their blood. It's in their genes. And now they have learned new tricks, and Democratic judges have seen what's expected of them in close elections like those in Florida, New Jersey, and California.

John Kerry's early exposure as a terrible candidate in March and April of 2004 raised concern about another new gambit, which I started calling "The Torricelli Option" over the airwaves and in print. Kerry's cursing at a secret service agent, his stonewalling of the release of his complete military file, the refusal to release his wife's tax returns, his thin-skinned responses to criticism of his senate voting record, and his now-legendary addiction to flip-flopping—all of these episodes and more woke Democrats to the reality that their "presumptive" nominee is a stiff. This recognition in turn raised Republican fears of another episode in Democratic ruthlessness: a dump-Kerry manuever late in the political season. Even if such an unprecedented and startling development would not alter the fundamentals of the 2004 campaign, which would remain a choice between vigorous prosecution of the war and appeasement, don't underestimate the flexibility of the Democrats.

So it is the responsibility of the Republican Party not merely to win, but to win big.

PART THREE

PARTIES

Conscience indeed.
Throw conscience to the devil
and stand by your party.
—Congressman Thaddeus Stevens

Damn your principles! Stick to your party.
—Benjamin Disraeli

CHAPTER 11

PARTIES
MATTER A LOT

For much of the recent past, academics and pundits were predicting the demise of the two major parties. They were dinosaurs, we were told, and the rise of big money in politics and of independent voters doomed them to minor roles outside the presidential nominating process. That was the refrain of my years as an undergrad at Harvard in the middle '70s. Political scientists across the spectrum were busy burying the Republican and the Democratic parties.

Their argument turned on the facts of the revolution in government employment that destroyed widespread patronage.

Patronage was the practice of giving government jobs and government contracts to allies. Civil service reforms pushed by good government types took most federal and state jobs away from the control of elected officials and the party bosses who managed them, and government contracting become highly regulated and closely scrutinized. Parties began to wither. As money came to dominate politics, grassroots organizations also saw their temporary eclipse.

But then ideology sorted political activists back into parties along the lines of Chapter 2. The Dems now have three key subparties, and the Republicans have three key subparties. While there remain a few jobs for parties to distribute, political struggle these days is not about patronage but about how the country will be organized and run; how high taxes will be; how onerous the laws will become on the private sector.

Politics is also about who should be in charge during a war.

The parties have become sharply defined. And even the occasional individual thought to be a mold breaker, like Joe Lieberman or Arnold Schwarzenegger, isn't really that different from most of his party colleagues on most issues.

Parties have surged in importance because the labels "Republican" and "Democrat" now generally mean something.

Democrats are generally for lower defense spending, multilateralism and the UN, higher taxes, and more benefits of an incredible variety for lower-income people. They favor the use of race and gender in the award of benefits, and they support anything that is vaguely believed to be pro-environment.

Republicans are aggressive proponents of the national interest and builders of the national defense. President Bush is pretty much perfect pitch for the GOP, which is why his approval rating within the Republican Party is sky high and will stay that way.

The GOP is very much the party that favors lower taxes, religion in the public square, restrictions on unlimited abortion, and greater freedom for the private sector from regulatory excess. It is largely pro-life and almost inevitably traditionalist. It is widely perceived as more patriotic than the Democratic Party to the extent that patriotism means pride in the country because Democrats are far more likely than Republicans to see faults in American government, and Republicans are far more likely than Democrats to take offense at slights delivered to America from envious internationalists and hostile allies like France and Germany.

Republicans generally don't see much wrong with America at all, other than the problems that Democratic Party excess has brought about. Democrats see deep and enduring flaws.

With the emphasis on fund-raising, voter turnout, and communication networking, parties have experienced a dizzying return to political prominence in the last quarter century, one that is accelerating as we speak. The new laws on campaign finance further strengthen the parties.

I want to stress the next point: independents aren't really all that independent at any given time. They are really "leaners."

Independents typically declare themselves to be outside the party structure for reasons related to their own identity, but their voting patterns, if fully disclosed, would reveal an undeclared party affiliation. It's just that their pattern is not deeply defined and their ties not secure. But they do "lean" in one direction over time. These people are in flux, and their votes typically hold the key to most national elections.

The election of 2004 requires them to make a serious, serious choice. They have to decide which party's nominee is more serious about the war on terrorism. They are forced to choose between very starkly different candidates in President Bush and John Kerry. It is a choice between far more than Texas or Massachusetts. It is a life-and-death choice. They may be independents formally, but they are going to declare for one camp or another, and given the likelihood of the central issue of 2004 remaining the central issue in American politics for a generation to come—do we take the offense against terrorists and their sponsors, or not?—the decisions of the independents in 2004 will have a lasting effect on American politics. The party that captures an independent's vote in 2004 is going to keep it for many elections to come.

So if you are partisan, understand that perhaps more than any election in your lifetime, the election of 2004 deserves your undivided attention and effort.

Greens are useful only as a bleeding device on Democrats, and Libertarians only as a bleeding device on Republicans. Both Greens and Libertarians are good for chuckles, but it is an absurd choice to ally oneself with one or the other and marks the self-declared Green or Libertarian as a naïve and beside-the-point political nonentity.

There's no point being involved in politics unless you are an active Republican or Democrat. If you are an independent or a minor party candidate, you have no say in things. Nor will you in your lifetime.

If you are ready for this book with an intent to understand and influence politics, then commit to the D or the R. The other choices are meaningless.

CHAPTER 12

PARTIES CAN'T GOVERN WITHOUT MAJORITIES OR PLURALITIES OF SEATS

Americans generally want *everything* exactly as they imagine it should be. Think about it. As a culture, we are extremely demanding about the details.

That's why we emphasize consumer choice so much and why the best companies provide dizzying arrays of choices within product lines, why automobile manufacturers provide long lists of options and colors, why even small coffee vendors provide at least three blends every morning to the passersby. Americans generally have very firm opinions on everything and want what they want to be "just so."

Unfortunately this demand for particularity doesn't work at all when applied to politics. In fact, insistence on personal taste is disastrous for political parties. There are only two real choices in America—Republican or Democrat. To demand more is to be disappointed before you begin, and to hand a victory to the set of choices most repellent to you.

Let me emphasize that if you walk away from politics because you can't have everything your way, you are helping the people win who are *least* like you and most opposed to your views.

I have been an active Republican since 1974, when I first volunteered for a campaign. (My candidate, Republican Congressman Paul Cronin, got hammered by newcomer Paul Tsongas in the GOP bloodbath that was 1974. All across the country Republicans were swept out of office in a tidal wave of disgust over Watergate. It was painful at the time, but at age eighteen, I picked up some crucial lessons that I haven't forgotten. Especially the lessons that revolve around why winning is better than losing.)

Since 1974, the hardest thing to communicate in politics is that the victories of individual candidates don't matter, outside the presidency. Unless a party has a majority of seats in a legislative body, it has very little influence on what gets done.

Majorities matter. Majorities matter. Majorities matter.

Sometimes when a purist Republican calls my show and denounces this or that RINO (Republican in name only), I despair of ever teaching anyone the importance of majorities. For some reason, conservatives and especially evangelical Christians are stubborn when it comes to the importance of majorities.

These purists are generally wonderful people, and usually people of good or even great character or conscience. They care passionately about aspects of politics. Many are single-issue voters, concerned about the lives of the unborn.

These purists cannot bring themselves to vote for Republicans who don't share their particular views, even if the election of a Republican majority in Congress hangs in the balance.

The example of the U.S. Senate is the easiest to grasp.

There are one hundred seats in the U.S. Senate, two for each state in the union.

The party that controls fifty-one or more of these seats controls most of what the Senate can accomplish and can absolutely block any legislation or appointments it does not like.

This reality was vividly illustrated in 2001 when Senator Jim Jeffords of Vermont switched his allegiance from the Republican Party to the Democratic Party. Before Jeffords jumped, the Senate was divided 50/50—with 50 Republicans and 50 Democrats. Vice President Cheney could cast his deciding votes, if necessary, so Republicans had the thinnest of theoretical majorities.

With that majority, Republicans moved President Bush's first tax cut through the Senate and confirmed many of his controversial appointees to their jobs. Attorney General John Ashcroft, a favorite of conservatives and especially evangelicals, would likely never have been installed in his job had the Democrats controlled the Senate in January 2001.

When Jeffords switched sides and began voting with the Democrats (he branded himself an independent but voted with Democrats on the key organizational votes), control of the Senate business switched to Tom Daschle, Ted Kennedy, Hillary Clinton, and Patrick Leahy. Suddenly the president's agenda came to a screeching halt. Senator Leahy, especially, used the new power of his Senate Judiciary Committee Democratic majority to dramatically obstruct President Bush's appointments to the federal courts. Democrats also used their majority to delay passage of a bill establishing a Homeland Security Department because Democrats wanted the bill to include more generous protection for public employee unions. Democrats interfered with the president's request for defense spending, meddling, for example, with President Bush's request for missile defense funding. Democrats launched biased investigations into Enron's collapse and assorted other matters, intended more to wound the president than uncover corporate wrongdoing.

In short, the loss of one vote—even though it was the vote of the most liberal Republican senator—caused enormous damage to the Republican agenda, the president's agenda, and the conservative agenda. Confirmations stalled. Bills died. The platform from which the agenda could be spotlighted and sold collapsed.

That's how government operates. In a majority rule system like ours, either the Republican Party or the Democratic Party is in charge. Defections from one party help the other party. It is that stark. It is that simple.

Some conservatives put fingers in their ears and make noises in an attempt to avoid the message, as though shouting ever changed words printed on a page. They don't like the system. They want it their own way. Just as there's no dealing with tantrum-throwing two-year-olds, there's no dealing with some voters. No appeals to reason and no number of repeated demonstrations of basic math matter to them.

These are not real conservatives. These are not even real single-interest voters. These are self-centered and selfish voters, and it is best not to spend too much time worrying about whether they will take their ball and go home. We cannot change the rules and we cannot change their minds, so there isn't much point in trying.

But there is a great point in spending time explaining the basic importance of majorities before particular choices are presented to voters. If the theory of majorities and their importance gets laid out and is really absorbed before particular candidates get out there among voters, it is much easier to remind voters why they want to hold their noses and vote for the party despite misgivings over the individual.

When you explain the importance of majorities, use a familiar example, like a church congregation or a homeowners association. Ask your friends if, faced with a vote of a congregation to keep or dismiss a pastor or of an HOA to allow or reject a home addition or other remodeling project, they want to be on the winning side of the vote. They will answer "yes" if they are anything other than permanently irascible.

Once they say they want to have a majority on their side in any particular situation, then ask them if they care about the various motivations behind the votes of those who agree with them.

Most people might pause, but in practice the answers are almost invariably "no." If your friend wants the pastor to get tossed out, he doesn't care why others are voting for the pastor to get the boot. It doesn't matter why others in the majority are voting no. What matters is the tally that conclusively ousts the minister.

If you want to add an upstairs level to your home, it doesn't matter a bit if the three votes on the five-member homeowners association board denying your plans are cast for different reasons. The result is a unitary one: no building that second story. The majority dictated the result.

In my first job in the executive branch of the federal government, I worked for Attorney General William French Smith as a special assistant. The job got me an invite to the AG's weekly senior staff meeting in the magnificent formal conference room on Justice's fifth floor.

Each Friday morning, the AG, the deputy AG, associate AGs, and a couple of dozen senior lawyers and associated criminal justice officials like the director of the FBI would fill the room for a review of the week just ended and a look ahead to the next week. Once a month during the months in which the Supreme Court heard cases and delivered decisions, the solicitor general would brief the meeting on the happenings at the nation's highest court.

At the time the solicitor general—the individual who represents the Justice Department before the Supreme Court—was Rex Lee, a brilliant and affable academician who had served previously as the dean of Brigham Young University Law School and would return to BYU as its president after his government service.

I think Rex began every briefing I heard him give in this setting with a reminder of "the rule of five." "You have to be able to count to five," he'd patiently explain, "and if you can't, we don't want to bring the case."

There are nine justices. Rex was reminding the crusaders in the room (and there were plenty of crusaders in the Reagan Justice Department) that you needed five justices to agree with your position in order to win a case.

You needed a majority.

To get majorities in the House and Senate, Republicans need 218 and 51 (or 50, if the GOP holds the White House), respectively. Bigger margins allow for greater maneuverability because the party doesn't then need every vote of its members to carry a vote on a particularly difficult bill, but 218 and 51 are the magic numbers.

Go one seat below 218 or 51 and the body in question shifts to the control of the Democrats, and that brings chaos and bad policy.

Which is why you should always vote for the Republican ticket from top to bottom in a general election.

And which is why you should always ask yourself if the candidate you support in a primary is electable in a general election. You have to look ahead to the general election's likely opponent and ask if your candidate has the capabilities to win the contest that matters. It is no victory to support a candidate who wins a primary, only to lose the general election.

It is an individual who governs as president, but it is the party with a majority that legislates. It is simply foolish to condemn as unsuitable any denominated member of a party on grounds of issue divergence.

If I disagree with the two most liberal members of the GOP Senate caucus—probably Lincoln Chafee of Rhode Island and Olympia Snowe of Maine—on 75 percent of all issues, and I cannot applaud their votes on 80 percent of all legislative matters, still I want them to remain Republicans. If tomorrow both of them pulled a Jeffords, we would again see Patrick Leahy as chair of the Judiciary Committee and Joe Biden as chair of the Senate Foreign Relations Committee.

The GOP needs Chafee and Snowe—without a question and without exception. If you don't understand that, you have to start over with this chapter because nothing that follows is even remotely close in importance to this legislative fact.

We are engaged in a vast global war against deadly enemies whose tactical desire is to inflict massive civilian casualties on America so that their strategic goals—first, withdrawal of America from the parts of the globe where Islam is dominant and, then, radical and continuing Islamization of the globe—can be advanced.

Joe Biden fundamentally does not understand this threat. In the fall of 2001, he fundamentally misunderstood the Afghan theater and displayed his ignorance in repeated public pronouncements over what the president should do next. He loudly demanded more "boots on the ground," just prior to the overwhelming victory over the Taliban that the boots already on the ground delivered. Not only is he usually wrong, Biden is also widely regarded as irascible and vindictive, a small-vision, small-stakes, small-potatoes pol in a time when we need great minds struggling with great problems.

We cannot afford Joe Biden as chair of the Senate Foreign Relations Committee.

Similarly most members of the U.S. Supreme Court are quite old, and vacancies are looming. We need serious judges of accomplished ability and conservative instincts. Such nominees will not emerge from a Patrick Leahy–chaired Senate Judiciary Committee.

Leahy is perhaps the Senate's screwiest member, an oddball given to underhanded tactics and low attacks on honorable people. Even the center Left *New Republic* confirmed as much in a 2002 article about Leahy by Michael Crowley.

We cannot afford a Senate Judiciary Committee chaired by Patrick Leahy.

Thus, Republicans need to keep a majority of Senate seats in Republican hands; thus, we need liberal GOP senators as well as very conservative GOP senators and all those in between.

Which brings me to the subject of incumbents, especially those of your own party that you don't like much.

Throughout 2003, a small group of conservative activists attempted to rally support to the insurgent candidacy of Pennsylvania Congressman Pat Toomey, who declared against incumbent Republican Senator Arlen Specter—a liberal Republican.

The Toomey candidacy came very close to unseating Specter, but it failed by a few thousand votes because serious conservatives understood that Specter keeps the Senate in GOP hands. Even had Toomey won in the primary, he would have been left open to withering attacks in the general election—with no money and Specter "moderates" practicing paybacks—as well as leaving disaffected the GOP voters who have stood with the iconoclastic Specter for many years.

Similar efforts have been launched in the recent past, including one against John McCain by Arizona conservatives who believe McCain to be insufficiently pure.

All such efforts against incumbents of all ideological shades are ill conceived and harmful, with one exception: where an incumbent is too weak to win reelection.

This happened in 2002 in New Hampshire where Senator Bob Smith, the Senate's oddest Republican duck and an unreliable Republican—he bolted the party once, only to return later—was trailing the likely Democratic nominee in polls. A congressman, John Sununu, took on Smith in a primary and won, and he went on to hold the seat for the GOP in the fall 2002 elections. It was the sort of challenge to an incumbent that made sense, but it is rare.

Neither Specter nor McCain is a weak incumbent in general elections. Conservative purists should not only leave both men alone; they should enthusiastically support their reelection efforts. All the money and effort that goes into campaigns to push them out would be far better spent on helping folks like John Thune in South Dakota (www.johnthune.com), a more conservative candidate then either McCain or Specter, but also a Republican running against a powerful Democrat—Tom Daschle.

Please absorb this basic fact about American politics: majorities, not individuals, govern. Without an understanding of this, the GOP's return to near permanent minority status—and the powerlessness it includes—is all but guaranteed.

CHAPTER 13

REGULARS, OCCASIONALS, PRINCIPLED PRAGMATISTS, MOVEMENT ACTIVISTS, AND FANATICS

The Five Orders of Political Partisans

n the various reaches of the blogosphere, I have been described by quite smart people like Virginia Postrel (www.dynamist.com) and Kevin Roderick (www.laobserved.com) as a "fierce partisan" and a "partisan shill," respectively I glory in the former title and reject the latter. I am a noun, not an adjective, partisan.

So should you be. In the greatest struggle of our time, one of two major parties is fully and wholly committed to the defense of the national security, and one is reckless and feckless concerning that security.

How proud the title of "Churchill partisan in the '30s." Today, one party is serious, and one is foolish. Thus, serious people have to be partisans. To reject partisanship is to be at best indifferent to the moral epic unfolding around us. Although the GOP has been winning more elections in recent years, the internal political battle over the direction of the country is very, very close indeed. The result of the internal political battle for power will decide our external political battle for survival.

You need to choose sides. You need to be a partisan. But there are different sorts of partisans. In fact, there are far too many types to catalogue in a short book designed to influence political behavior. But five major groupings are easy to delineate and useful in explaining strategies in the internal political battle under way in what, at least prior to 9/11, was a 50/50 country.

1. REGULARS

My maternal grandfather, A.T. Rohl, was a regular Democrat. A fireman who was employed throughout the Great Depression, he loved FDR and voted a straight Democratic ticket his entire life, which was long. As with many senior citizens, he watched a lot of C-SPAN in his later years, but only to confirm his opinions, never to influence them. He was a party man, but not an activist.

My dad was the same, but he was a GOP regular. To my knowledge, he never attended a political event other than a parade for then Vice President Nixon through Warren, Ohio, in 1960, to which he felt obliged to take his oldest son, my brother, who never has cared much for partisan politics. Politics did not much interest my dad even after I got deeply involved with Nixon and then Reagan and the world of political punditry. He had many opinions on politics and always voted GOP, but his activism never left the voting booth—another regular.

2. OCCASIONALS

The fair-weather fans of politics, the occasionals rise and fall with the rise and fall of particular candidates, usually of the presidential variety.

Most recently the arrival of the armies of Howard Dean in the spring, summer, and fall of 2003 brought a new crowd of occasionals into the Democratic Party.

David Tell, a fine observer of politics at *The Weekly Standard*, detailed in an October 2003 article how momentum brings out such occasionals, and the dangers and false hopes they present:

There is the predictable level of bumper-sticker grandiosity every presidential campaign emits like car exhaust. And then there is this: the broken-muffler variety, a vaguely "progressive," cyber-savvy transmogrification of Pat Buchanan, up to and including the "King George" and peasant-rebellion material. Howard Dean is smart enough to know better, of course. But the additional supporters such rhetoric tends to attract may not be. And there are more and more of them every day, sprinkled through his street rallies, always dominating his official blog. It is a type. Each of us knows someone like this, or was one himself while in college: people who imagine themselves righteously "political," but actually have little practical experience or understanding of politics, and consequently little concern for its daily requirements and limitations. These are undependable supporters, in other words, to whom politics is primarily a vehicle for the projection of an idealized sensibility, not a set of plans and convictions. The chosen candidate is their mirror. They will love him—"I want to have your baby!" *The Washington Post* reports hearing one transfixed young woman yell at a recent Dean rally—until they don't anymore.

The occasionals are not serious, long-term participants in the political battle for power, but certainly are useful shock troops in some instances. (They turn up in both parties, by the way, most recently in California's Arnold campaign.)

3. PRINCIPLED PRAGMATISTS

These partisans are partisans for ideological reasons. They may be pro-union or anti-closed shop; pro-life or abortion rights absolutists; religion-in-the-public-square enthusiasts or antiporn activists; or missile defense or unilateral disarmament visionaries. They have passion about a particular set or sets of ideas.

But they also have prudence. They vote for and contribute to and organize on behalf of any candidate in their party, the victory of whom will advance their agendas even in tiny increments and even if that candidate occasionally slams their views. Thus, an ardent pro-lifer could work for Arnold Schwarzenegger's election as governor because of Arnold's ability to assist in the election of GOP Senate candidates and, of course, President Bush's reelection because Bush's reelection advances the core pro-life agendas.

These are the principled pragmatists. They believe in coalitions within the party.

4. MOVEMENT ACTIVISTS

These purists will not compromise their core, motivating ideas by assisting any candidate who does not embrace their ideas.

Often movement activists believe you have to take a few steps backward before moving forward. Purification in order to establish priorities and to clearly communicate agendas seems more effective to these partisans than coalitions. They'd rather see a nonpure Republican candidate lose than adulterate the GOP.

Even before the war of terrorists on Americans became obvious to most Americans, these partisans were simply wrong. Their theory of purification doesn't work in the Democratic Party for environmentalist zealots or in the Republican Party for strict pro-lifers. Majoritarian opinion in the U.S. stands opposed to crucial portions of the agendas of all movement activists. Without the coalitions that pragmatists embrace, their ideas will never advance, their agendas never materialize.

After the onset of the war, however, the insistence on ideological purity by GOP-leaning purists on any issue other than national security is quite evidently suicidal. Leaving the Democrats in power is likely to make the agenda of these activists beside the point.

5. FANATICS

Each party has them. Combine ideological zeal with antisocial behavior, and the fanatics are identified.

Each party, in a 50/50 country, *needs* its fanatics.

The math dictates that the 5 percent at the edge of each party are absolutely crucial to winning elections. Antisocial behaviors such as screaming at fellow party members for insufficient zeal is not sociopathic behavior, and extreme commitment is not illegitimate, though, of course, violence of either Far Left or Far Right is illegitimate. (The Unabomber, ELF arsonists, doctor assassins, and militia bombers are *not* partisans. They are criminals, condemned by all citizens committed to rule of law.)

I am a "triple P"—a principled but pragmatic partisan. You should be as well. One aim of this book is to persuade regulars and movement activists alike that they need to embrace their style of partisanship because the stakes of the war are so high and the consequences of Democratic victories so dire.

It is also in part a manual on the management of occasionals and fanatics.

CHAPTER 14

MAJORITIES REQUIRE THE VOTES OF SOME NOT-VERY-BRIGHT PEOPLE

I n the fall of 2003, *The Weekly Standard* managing editor and Fox News contributor Fred Barnes assembled and published the evidence for the argument that Republicans were becoming the country's dominant political party. He summarized the evidence in a table.

These numbers are impressive, and the case that Fred laid out was persuasive. Throughout the decade following the election of Bill Clinton to the presidency, the Republicans made steady gains at every level of government.

The elections of 2002 provided even more evidence of the trend when Republicans regained control of the U.S. Senate that the defection of Jim Jeffords had handed the Democrats, and the House shifted even more decidedly into Republican hands.

Thousands of contests are summed up in that table. Again and again, a Republican matched up against a Democrat and won more often than lost.

But the margins of the wins and the losses were not great. George W. Bush won Florida by around 537 votes. Senator Harry Reid, a Democrat from Nevada, won his 1996 campaign by 428 votes. Senator Tim Johnson, a Democrat from South Dakota, beat Congressman John Thune in 2002 by about 524 votes.

The Republican gains may have been steady, but the margins in many victories have been small, just as the margins in many losses have been narrow.

In a crucial congressional race in Colorado in 2002, Republican nominee Bob Beauprez beat Democratic nominee Mike Feeley by 121 votes out of 172,879 cast.

You should now be convinced that small numbers of votes matter a great deal. Now start thinking about who these voters are.

You are reading a nonfiction book about politics.

Huge numbers of people who simply cannot read a sentence vote in elections.

Close elections inevitably turn on the votes of illiterate people.

That's an uncomfortable thought, but true.

Just like the uncomfortable fact that all elections depend upon the votes of grade school and high school dropouts. Except for criminals, everyone gets to vote if they want to. Even though most illiterates don't vote, vast numbers do as do vast numbers of dropouts.

Elections are decided by people you wouldn't want to change your oil or make change at the local supermarket.

Which explains why politics requires simple messages.

A lack of education does not mean a lack of character or a lack of patriotism. It can often mean, however, that the individual without much education is not in a position to respond to intricate arguments and big words.

Politics often comes down to slogans and pictures and music because candidates need to communicate with broad ranges of people, some of whom don't have the mental equipment to deal with policy papers.

The mandatory simplicity of a lot of politics puts off some people.

They want to talk big ideas and they scorn simple speech.

A lot of intellectuals and pseudo-intellectuals fall into the trap of ignoring the need to communicate with every possible voter.

Recall that in the months after 9/11, some of President Bush's critics mocked him for his repeated condemnations of "the evildoers" and "the evil ones."

But what Bush was doing then, and has successfully continued to do, was to assure that every segment of the American population could understand what the war was about. The shocking pictures of the collapse of the World Trade Center are certainly burned in the brains of most Americans, but Bush had to go far beyond these pictures. He had to explain the breadth and depth of the enemy, and he had to completely delegitimize and ostracize Al Qaeda and its supporters.

The brilliant repetition of the word *evildoers* might have amused Bush's critics, but it cemented into place the American public's understanding not only of the terrorists, but also of President Bush's understanding of the terrorists.

Bush communicated through stark language and repetition that he was not going to indulge any softheartedness about the attackers, that there could be no excuse for them, and that no quarter would be given.

The message was sent and the message was received, loud and clear.

That is effective communication.

In the fall of 2002, the president and Republicans in Congress wanted to pass a bill establishing the new Homeland Security Department. Time was of the essence because terrorists remained at large then (and, of course, terrorists are still plotting to kill as many American citizens as possible by any means possible).

Democrats led by Senator Tom Daschle wanted to modify the plans for the new department that had been drawn up by the president and his allies in Congress.

Democrats wanted the new department to be friendlier to public employee unions.

The president would not compromise on this point, so no bill was passed, and the issue of the shape of the Homeland Security Department was among those debated in the fall elections of 2002.

Democrats got whomped in those elections in part because they had held up the creation of an agency that most voters thought was urgently needed in order to try to win concessions for a Democratic Party constituency that is not highly regarded.

Try explaining to average Americans why their personal security from a terrorist threat should be delayed so that unionized federal workers would receive additional benefits.

To begin with, these workers aren't seen as union men and women in the way, say, steel or automobile workers are. Rather, government workers are seen as bureaucrats.

Try as they might to persuade the electorate that their opposition to the new bill was correct and principled, the Dems could not shift the argument away from the simple fact of the urgent need for the reorganization and the simple fact that Daschle and his colleagues were delaying the much needed reorganization in order to help bureaucrats.

Across the country President Bush and GOP candidates pounded away on Democratic obstructionism. It was a simple message and easily grasped: Democrats in Congress preferred the interests of the union members over the safety of Americans promised by the arrival of the new department.

The decision of Democrats to put union priorities ahead of national security priorities a year after a devastating attack on America hurt them badly. As it ought to have hurt them. A stark choice was put before the electorate, and the electorate rejected the Democrats.

It doesn't take an advanced degree, a college degree, or a high school diploma to understand what the Democrats' position meant.

It meant that even in a time of war, Democrats would not abandon their special interest posturing.

Everyone understood. And voted accordingly.

Since that time, Democrats and their allies in the commentariat have complained that the campaign of 2002 falsely accused them of being unpatriotic. They especially love to cite the defeat of Senator Max Cleland at the hands of Saxby Chambliss in Georgia. They complain that Chambliss ran ads attacking Cleland's patriotism and linking him to Osama bin Laden. Senator Kerry often travels the country with Cleland at his side, a sort of shield against anyone attacking Democrats for lacking courage. And Kerry has repeated the absolutely false charge that the GOP attacked Cleland's patriotism in '02, even as he argues, again falsely, that the GOP is attacking his own patriotism.

Kerry specifically and Democrats generally repeat their refrain, in the hope that they can delegitimize future appeals to the electorate based on national security. It won't work because the initial charge is false.

No one who saw the ads attacking Cleland, which featured pictures of Osama bin Laden, concluded that the triple amputee war hero Cleland had thrown in with Osama.

But they did conclude—rightly so—that Cleland was not voting the right way on the Homeland Security Department.

Because of his personal sacrifice, Democrats thought Cleland ought to have been immune to attacks on his national security judgment.

But he wasn't because the fact of his siding with the unions and against the president's bill in a time of war was so stark that even his manifest honor could not excuse his fecklessness on the issue.

Kerry seems to think his three Purple Hearts and his Silver Star ought to shield his three decades of radicalism and antidefense votes from scrutiny.

The Georgia Senate campaign of 2002 is the most important exhibit in the Hall of Fame of Simplicity. Long-winded dissertations on the need to retain hard-won protections for civil servants vulnerable to the whims of political appointees just didn't stand a chance against the demand for action.

The higher-educated end of the voting spectrum understood the choice, and so did the lower-educated end of the spectrum. That's why Cleland was evicted from office. That's why Kerry's transparent attempt to silence his critics by denouncing their criticisms by labeling them attacks on his "patriotism" will fail as well. As U.S. Senator Zell Miller, a close friend of Cleland's who campaigned for Cleland all across Georgia in 2002 has firmly stated on my program, the questions raised about both Cleland and Kerry are questions about their voting records, not their patriotism—legitimate questions. Kerry and other "soft on security" Democrats can expect these attacks to continue.

Political campaigns cannot aim their message at voters with college degrees. They have to aim their message at everyone.

No matter whether the battle is for the presidency or for the school board, the issues to put at the center of any contest have to be able to be understood by all voters and have to be communicated in terms that all voters get.

The theme of 2004 is simple: the Democrats aren't serious about terrorism. They talk a good game, but they don't fight a good war. Their hearts aren't in it, and they'd rather have the UN manage such stuff. They don't like the idea of killing people. Period. And they have been suspicious of the military since Vietnam.

There is a scene in *Die Hard 3* where Samuel L. Jackson shouts at Bruce Willis: "I don't like you because you're going to get me killed!"

John Kerry and his allies in the Democratic Party are going to get us killed.

I often play that line from *Die Hard 3* on the radio, almost always in connection with some incredibly shortsighted posturing by the Democrats on a national security issue.

Everyone gets it. All we need now is the repetition.

CHAPTER 15

PEOPLE CHANGE THEIR PARTY AFFILIATIONS SLOWLY AND ARE EMBARRASSED TO DO SO

In the article I mentioned in the last chapter, Fred Barnes included some key facts about party registration.

In 1982, the Harris Poll found the electorate divided with 40 percent declaring themselves Democrats, and 26 percent declaring themselves Republicans. (The rest were independents or members of other small parties.)

In 1992, the Democrats grabbed 36 percent, and the Republicans, 30 percent.

In 2002, another couple of ticks: Dems were at 34 percent, and Republicans at 31 percent.

Steady progress, for sure, but very slow: over twenty years the GOP increased its slice of the pie only by 5 percent! Democrats lost only 6 percent. Combined, the two trends meant great news for the GOP, but it was not a sudden or dramatic shift.

The reason that people are slow to change their party identification has to do more with psychology than anything else. Party identification is part of self-image, and we change our self-image very, very slowly and often with great reluctance.

California Assemblyman John Campbell is a regular guest on my radio show. John is among the most successful elected officials I have ever met. Part of a talented elected official's bundle of gifts is charisma, part is discipline, part is a willingness to ask for dollars, and part is pure brainpower.

John has each of the talents, and on the brainpower front, he has few peers.

Before John went into politics, he'd made a small fortune in the car business, putting his UCLA business degree and his master's in accounting from USC to work in the fierce, cutthroat world of automotive retail in Southern California, where he owned numerous dealerships. He was so successful that GM offered him senior leadership positions, which he declined because he'd already decided he'd enter politics.

But he's still a car enthusiast, and in one of many conversations on the subject, John confirmed what I'd long suspected: 90 percent of the buyer's decision of which car to buy is made on the basis of the purchaser's self-image. I will leave it for another day to detail the various statements that various cars make, but John explained that this fundamental fact of car buying is no secret within the industry. Everyone knows it, and the business of selling cars depends upon understanding this central fact of automobile life.

As with cars, so with party identification for many people. It begins with an emotional decision that quite often either confirms a set of parents' choices or rebels from them. A second group of voters make their choice of party in response to their perceived understanding of what a party stands for and their acceptance or rejection of that set of priorities and values. Sometimes it is as simple as attachment to a particular figure. As I already noted, my gramps loved FDR—and I mean loved him. He could no more have become a Republican than an astronaut.

For me, the initial choice was more fluid. As a twelve-year-old, I had a poster of Bobby Kennedy in my bedroom, a Peter Max-Lite psychedelic version, and that was perhaps a function of my Roman Catholic roots and parochial school education, mixed with RFK's undeniable and electric charisma. My parents were GOP regulars, but not party partisans, and they didn't bother to try to raise their sons in either party. RFK's murder was an extremely shocking and saddening day for all of us, and I imagine had he lived, much of my political life would have been delayed.

My initial serious attachment to politics came via reading Solzhenitsyn's *One Day in the Life of Ivan Denisovich*, which made me an anti-Communist. Being anti-Communist in the turbulent years of Vietnam meant being a Republican. Nixon's fall did not shake that conviction, and four years at Harvard under the teaching influence of Harvey Mansfield, Alan Keyes, and Bill Kristol cemented my politics.

It would take an enormous shock to change my party ID.

My closest friend since college days, as noted earlier, is Mark Gearan, a Democrat's Democrat. A friend and longtime aide to the Clintons, Mark grew up Irish-Catholic in Massachusetts and could no more become a Republican than I could become a Democrat.

Many people's political IDs are not as fixed as mine or Gearan's, but neither are they very flexible on the issue. It is like changing from Buick to Toyota, or from Ford to Chevy. It's not impossible, but it's not easy either.

When Democrats stop being Democrats, they typically have to cross over the stigma that the Republican brand carries: indifference to the poor.

That brand was affixed by Hoover, who presided over the sudden and sharp beginning of the Great Depression, as well as by a lot of stupid Republicans since Hoover, and indeed there remain some Republicans who are completely callous to the privations of the underclass.

Voters who have great amounts of compassion and who are Democrats have a hard time pulling the Republican lever. At a psychological level, they see it as voting against the poor.

This is not objectively true. But buying a car isn't an objective process, and neither is affiliating oneself with a party.

Why bother to write this down? Only because it may increase your patience in changing a friend's mind.

There is tremendous turmoil in the Democratic Party today, a result of the Democratic leaders' failure to respond to 9/11 as a majority of Americans expected them to respond.

The sniping at the president began even on the days immediately following the attack, with Maureen Dowd in *The New York Times* and Howard Rosenberg in the *Los Angeles Times* giving voice and bicoastal bookends to the thoughts and feelings of many Democratic ideologues.

Dowd, in a column that appeared on September 12, 2001, donned her national security advisor suit and blasted the president:

> For much of the day we weren't sure where the president was. There were statements floating in from him from various secure zones in the air or underground . . . Even the president didn't seem sure of where to go.
>
> "He is at the very top of the United States," said Tammie Owens, a subway supervisor in a bright yellow uniform, who felt that a president, like the British royal family during the blitz, needed to reassure with his presence. "And the White House is where he should be."

Rosenberg, writing on September 14, 2001, didn't even bother, like Dowd, to disguise his contempt for Bush by using the old columnist trick of finding a "man in the street" to speak hatred of the target. Rosenberg, a hard Left television critic, penned one of the most obviously biased, hate-filled columns in all of modern newspaper history:

> Reagan and Clinton had what it takes to communicate to the country effectively through a medium that inevitably favors performers over informers.
>
> The nation's 43rd president does not. Three days of George W. Bush on television this week affirm that . . .
>
> [T]hroughout this terrible week in U.S. history, Bush lacked size in front of the camera when he should have been commanding and filling the screen with a formidable presence as the leader of a nation standing tall under extreme duress.
>
> Even his body language is troubling as when TV cameras captured him returning to the White House late Tuesday after being

shuttled about on Air Force One after an alert that the presidential residence and plane also had been possible targets of that day's terrorism. The Bush we saw, walking alone, appeared almost to be slinking guiltily across the lawn.

Bush seemed almost like a little boy at times—a kid with freckles wishing he were somewhere else—when instead a national anchorman was needed to speak believably with confidence about the state of the union during one of its darkest hours.

The incredible venom in these two columns wasn't unique to these two writers of the Left. They simply lacked the discipline to hide their bizarre worldviews, and startled readers got a glimpse of the real bias working with major media. Rosenberg has retired now, and he rocks on a porch somewhere forgotten and not missed, wondering no doubt how no one else in the country could see what he so clearly saw on September 11 and the days thereafter. Dowd has become a full-fledged crank, a source of sport among people who like to watch imbalanced people rave. Her column in *The New York Times* continues, a reminder of the real mind-set of the scribbling counterpart to the Left's talking heads and college-lecturing legions.

The attacks from these sources have never stopped coming, and the obstructionism of the Democratic electeds has never lessened, except for minor adjustments in the face of massive public outcry.

The venom on the Left, directed not at terrorists, but at the center Right had been noticed even before Howard Dean launched his 2003 campaign of resentment and alienation. Dean was the product of the Left's anger at the swelling of American resolve and the confirming of American exceptionalism. Though America was staggered by 9/11, President Bush rallied the country and struck back hard at evil in the world. The squaring off with evil and the resolute forcefulness not just with our enemies but also with our "allies" of the round-heeled sort have buoyed the president in the eyes of the nation, sometimes to astonishing highs in the polls, but even at his low point, to approval ratings higher than any of his three predecessors at comparable periods in their terms in office.

Bush's political success is a product of his leadership success, and he has had leadership success because he has been bold in attacking our enemies and unapologetic in declaring his intent to wage this war with complete commitment throughout his term in office.

Dean, of course, was almost the Democratic nominee because of exactly the opposite approach. He blamed Bush, not the terrorists, for the strain on our economy and the losses of the lives of American soldiers, sailors, airmen, and Marines. He blamed Bush, not Kim Jong Il, for North Korean bluster and threats. He blamed Bush, not the mullahs of Iran, for threatening the world with their nuclear ambition. Had Dean not displayed too much of his nuttiest side in December of 2003 and then imploded on national television on the night of the Iowa caucuses, he would have been the Democratic nominee. But even with him gone, his supporters did not change their worldview. They simply transferred their allegiance to John Kerry.

The shock of 9/11 and the choices the Democrats have made in its aftermath have put many people's party affiliation up for grabs. Longtime Democrats have looked up from the ashes of lower Manhattan and concluded that they have changed. In that change is the political upheaval under way in the country.

One such voter is known to my audience simply as "Robert from New York."

Robert was in Southern California on business when my radio show debuted on July 10, 2000. He called in and confidently predicted the defeat of George W. Bush by Al Gore.

Robert is Jewish, and he mocked my fall of 2000 appeals to Jews to vote for W. When Bush won, Robert predicted a one-term presidency and a failed one.

I spoke to Robert on the morning of 9/11. I began my three-hour broadcast minutes after the second plane hit the second tower, and many times since then I have had the odd experience of being told by people that I am part of their 9/11 memory because I told them about the attacks and the aftermath as they woke up or were commuting.

Robert called me that morning, after the towers had fallen. His office was a quarter mile from the World Trade Center, and the dust and soot obscured his view from his office. But the shock in his voice was as obvious as the television pictures from New York and Washington were horrific.

Robert changed, and he has remained changed. He is still a caller, especially when he travels in the West, but now he calls to praise the president and to express outrage at Democratic obstructionism. He believes that a major realignment is under way among Jews who understand the terrorists better than most, and he has no patience for people who want to debate the prescription drug benefit.

Sometimes he ends up shouting that people have to wake up, that we are in a war, and that the enemy is trying to kill us.

Robert's a 9/11 Democrat.

I believe there are millions of Roberts in America today, Democrats sick with worry over the threats to the country they love, and amazed, disappointed, and disillusioned with Howard Dean and Tom Daschle, Joe Biden and Ted Kennedy.

These people could not have ever imagined voting for anyone other than a Democrat before 9/11. Now they cannot imagine voting for a national Democrat.

But this is an excruciating process, one that means admitting error about first principles that have long been held dear.

Republican partisans cannot be indifferent to the difficulty of this process for Democrats taking leave of their long-held views of the world. Mockery of these who are leaving is a disastrous tack (though mockery of the Left reinforces the decision to leave being taken by millions).

Rather than taunt your friends in transition, provide them with arguments reinforcing their resolve, but in a patient fashion. Moving a Democrat into the Republican Party is a huge victory for an activist, but among one of the hardest things to accomplish. Usually it takes a lot of information and a persistent reminder of the stakes involved.

The best argument is, of course, national security. Not many Democrats believe in their hearts that Bill Clinton did a good job of protecting this country from the growing threat of bin Laden. They might have been willing to excuse his scandals when those were scandals that—

they believed—called into question only his personal integrity, not his professional competence.

But the failure to try to prevent 9/11—that is inexcusable. Only the self-deluding blame Bush and his team for the attacks, hatched and plotted years prior to his arrival in office. Al Qaeda sprang into life just as Clinton entered the national consciousness, and the bin Laden gang's power grew and became emboldened concurrently with Clinton's eight years in office. So, too, did the North Korean nuclear program. So, too, did Tehran's atomic ambitions.

The disastrous record of the Clintonites when it came to fundamental issues of protecting the country cannot be obscured for most of America.

This is where the argument over the next few months must center and, after the elections of 2004, must remain centered in 2006 and 2008 and beyond. All the posturing and hyper-partisanship of the 9/11 Commission's Richard Ben-Veniste and Bob Kerrey cannot obscure this basic and never-to-be-altered fact.

For as long as there is a terrorist/rogue state threat, for that long elections must be fought and won on the only issue that truly can be said to outweigh all others combined: how to protect the U.S.

Keep asking your Democratic friends (and your independent friends): Which party will better protect the U.S. from sudden and devastating attack?

Raise that particular question again and again.

The embarrassment that comes from abandoning some element of self-image is easiest to overcome when the prospect of death is staring you in the face.

CHAPTER 16

PEOPLE LIKE TO WIN (AND HATE TO HEAR THEY WON'T)

Voters who are leaving their party—transitional voters—are different from party regulars in one crucial way: regulars know they are going to lose some elections over a lifetime.

Transitional voters don't want to lose just as they jump from their old train onto a new one.

Which is one of two reasons why party leaders always keep on a game face even if the polls are negative.

Democratic Party National Chairman Terry McAuliffe is among the worst party chieftains in modern American political history. There's an excellent argument that he is the all-time champion of terrible party leaders. His every move has been wrong, his presence on television a constant reminder to Republicans why they loathed Clinton: the lying and the smarminess that accompany McAuliffe to every appearance are pure Clinton, but the McAuliffe version lacks Clinton's originality and talent. McAuliffe was installed by Clinton, and many assume his job was to assure that the party would have no one else to turn to by 2008, other than Hillary and, of course, Bill.

At times, though, McAuliffe can shock even the most jaded operative.

One example was when he appeared on *Meet the Press* with Tim Russert and McAuliffe's Republican counterpart, Ed Gillespie, on September 7, 2003. Russert asked McAuliffe to explain McAuliffe's many failed predictions of political success over the years.

McAuliffe explained that it was his job to lie: "I am the national party chairman. I am not going to go on television, you know, three days before an election and say, 'Oh, no, Tim. No, Mr. Russert, we're not going to win these elections.' My job is the chief cheerleader of the party. We're going to win everything. That's my job."

This bit of unexpected candor perfectly illustrates McAuliffe's many drawbacks as a party leader. He has no brakes, no internal guardrails. It is his job, in other words, to lie.

It is, in fact, the job of party leaders to keep both loyalists and transitional voters enthused. But not via lies. McAuliffe understands how important it is that candidates appear to be winning, but he violated the obvious rule that one can never lie. At the very least, even liars ought to understand that one cannot admit to lying.

McAuliffe preferred to admit to lying than to be seen by a nationally televised audience as stupid. Thus did his vanity further erode his already much diminished credibility.

McAuliffe's urgent need to build up losing candidates is consistent with letting transitional voters know they aren't leaping to their political doom. No one rushes to board a sinking ship.

The second reason to keep hunting for good news even when a campaign is faltering is to assure that the regulars do their jobs.

There are two classic examples of when news of an impending loss led to huge, same-day shifts in results.

In 1980, President Carter appeared early in the evening on election day—before polls had closed in the West—to concede defeat to Ronald Reagan. The effect was instantaneous and devastating to Democratic candidates still struggling to turn out their base. Stunned party volunteers just gave up and went home. Calls to remind regulars to vote never got made. Precincts never got walked. A loss became a blowout. Candidates learned to never again concede until voting ended.

In 2000, the networks learned never to call a race until they were sure of the result.

Going into the tight contest between George W. Bush and Al Gore in November 2000, all eyes focused on Florida. Most analysts agreed that Bush would need Pennsylvania or Florida to carry a majority of electoral votes.

The analysts were correct. Bush needed Florida, and he won it by only 537 votes.

But the networks almost delivered the state to Gore by declaring Gore the winner before polls closed in the conservative Republican panhandle of the state. Voters heading to the polls simply turned back and drove home. One estimate put the lost votes in the Bush column at more than 10,000.

Most Republican regulars also knew that Florida was crucial to the GOP candidate. Thus, the early and wrong call of Florida for Gore by the networks hurt GOP get-out-the-vote efforts across the country and may have cost Bush wins in Minnesota, Wisconsin, Iowa, New Mexico, and Washington State, where handfuls of votes gave the battles to Gore. In California, intense contests between the parties turned into blowouts as GOP get-out-the-vote volunteers simply disappeared.

In every phase of life, enthusiasm and energy are crucial ingredients of success, and electoral success especially depends upon the anticipation of winning. Voters in 2004, ready to defend the country from a Democratic Party that is mired in a mindless assault on the president and that has earned its reputation for weakness in the war against the terrorists, already know the right way to vote their concerns for the national defense. They need assurance that their choice is also the choice of a solid majority.

This is an easy assurance to give in 2004. The fundamentals of the case for reelecting George W. Bush are quite strong, even though Senator Kerry, Terry McAuliffe, and others work to keep up the appearance of competitiveness. In future years it may not be so easy to predict, but the deadly effects of pessimism shouldn't be underestimated.

CHAPTER 17

TRANSITIONAL VOTERS DON'T LIKE MOVEMENT ACTIVISTS OR FANATICS

I f you haven't figured it out yet, realignment depends on moving disenchanted Democrats and worried independents into the Republican column. There aren't enough Republicans to win on their own. Period. In every election they need the votes of Americans who don't call themselves Republicans.

To effect a genuine realignment, however, the GOP needs more than just one-time votes in 2004. The party needs a mental and emotional commitment to putting the Republicans in control and keeping them there for many years to come.

The GOP needs converts. Genuine converts.

Converts are ready in vast numbers to cross over to the GOP. The war has driven them away from the Dems and John Kerry. They may not be talking about this much, but they are aware that a vote for a Democrat is a gamble that Al Qaeda is destroyed and cannot rise again from the ashes of Afghanistan or Iraq.

Most of the work of conversion to the Republican Party was done by Democrats. Now the key is for Republicans not to mess it up by insisting on forcing the "almost converts" to stare at what they dislike the most about the GOP.

Those who have sold a house will know exactly what it means to "minimize the negatives."

Most houses come with negatives. Perhaps freeway noise is pretty close. Maybe the neighbor is a musician. Or the fourth bedroom is really small, or water temp in the shower may be adversely affected by flushing toilets or doing the laundry.

Savvy realtors or experienced sellers will do their best to minimize the negatives by playing music during an open house, showing the home when the neighbors are away, or putting a single twin bed and a small dresser in the tiny room. Certainly you don't put a sign in the hallway urging people to note that the freeway is two hundred yards to the south, the neighbors turn in at 4:00 A.M. most weekends, and the "bedroom" is really a den—and a small one at that.

As with home sellers, party leaders have to stress the compatibility of the party with the transitional voters. They know that in 2004, voters are on the move and are looking for reasons to vote for the national security and thus vote for President Bush and the Senate and House candidates who will support him in the war on terror.

Which is why you won't hear the president, the vice president, or presidential campaign spokesmen putting great emphasis on issues of great concern to movement activists, and certainly not the issues that drive the fanatics.

The hot-button issues repel as many voters as they attract. There are as many abortion rights absolutists as there are pro-life marchers. The numbers of Americans who worry about the proliferation of guns are huge, and even if NRA membership is larger, the offset between the two is not so great nationally as to allow indifference to the sensitivities of the antigun minority.

And while gays and lesbians and their immediate families may certainly number less than 10 percent of the electorate, there is no reason unnecessarily to drive these voters away. (There may be a necessary reason in the defense of marriage, but more on that later.)

Each of these "movement" issues and many others—property rights, antagonism toward "endangered species," off-road vehicle usage, oil drilling in Alaska, paycheck protection for union members—generate enormous amounts of commitment from relatively small numbers of voters. Each issue contributes crucial support blocs to a winning coalition.

But they also inspire the opposition to activity, and they unsettle some in the middle.

When blocs of voters in the millions are in transition, it doesn't make sense to block the roads. There is *no* sense in making these voters confront the issues with which they are most uncomfortable.

Imagine a young, Jewish mother of two living in Ann Arbor. She has always been a Democrat and always been a reliable vote for the Democratic candidate. She hung in with Bill Clinton through eight years and even bought the idea that his lying was about personal sexual misbehavior. She's pro-choice and antigun, pro–public schools and pro-environment.

But she's almost certain to vote for George W. Bush because she knows what 9/11 meant.

It meant that millions in the world had grown to hate the U.S. and that they had fanatics at their disposal ready to sacrifice themselves in suicidal zeal to kill civilians.

It also meant that the Clinton team—in office for eight years coinciding with the rise and move to operational readiness of Al Qaeda—had not taken the threat seriously.

Not after the first World Trade Center bombing.

Not after the bombings of our two embassies in Africa.

Not even after the attack on the USS *Cole*.

She is unwilling to let the Democrats run the nation's defenses again. Maybe she is not convinced that Iraq was a necessary war, but she is certain that being on the attack in the war against terror is much, much better than being on the defensive.

She's ready to vote for Bush.

Or at least she was when I visited with her in late October 2003.

Between now and the election, and in the elections beyond, she needs to be left alone to follow her natural inclination. She does not need a parade of pro-lifers knocking at her door, asking her to change all of the political views she has held through her adult life. The GOP needs her vote. We don't need her enrolled in the NRA. She may still want to ban drilling in the North. So what?

Only a fanatic would rather lose her vote than accept a differing view within the coalition reelecting Bush or adding to the GOP majority in the U.S. Senate.

But that's the problem. Some fanatics would, indeed, rather lose the election than allow the transitional voters of 2004 to arrive without signing the party platform in blood.

Movement activists aren't quite so demanding. They'll look the other way with voters like my friend in Ann Arbor, just as long as the president massages their issue joints every so often. But that's a problem too.

This is the classic GOP convention drama, a made-for-the-bloodletting television network special, pitting opposite camps on a single issue at each other's throats, preferably in prime time, just as transitional voters tune in. Shouting matches are even better, and bloodcurdling oaths and counteroaths the best.

Driving the swing vote back into Democratic hands is a specialty of the Democrats. They play the old tunes about Republicans destroying Medicare and threatening Social Security because these are effective messages designed to scare and successful in scaring restless constituencies back into party loyalty.

Which is why three months before an election, the parties frown on big thinkers floating bold restructuring proposals that then have to be disavowed.

Campaign 2004 has the potential to change the fundamental balance of power in the U.S. for a generation. The Democratic Party has defined itself as far outside the mainstream. President Bush is understood as honest and resolute, in the center of American politics.

The country needs such a repudiation of the Democrats' pacifist caucus and its isolationist Left. It needs a thunderous rebuke delivered to John Kerry, one so loud that the message cannot be mistaken.

Because of that urgency, the GOP needs to close the deal with millions of people like my friend in Ann Arbor. The movement activists have to agree to back off in 2004 and to trust the president and the campaign leadership.

The stakes are too high to demand special attention and self-defeating gestures.

It's a war. Demanding to be stroked in the middle of a war demonstrates a selfishness that is incomprehensible and that calls into question the genuine motivation of those who demand a special nod and wink.

CHAPTER 18

PARTY REGULARS DON'T LIKE MOVEMENT ACTIVISTS AND FANATICS, AND MOVEMENT ACTIVISTS AND FANATICS NEED THE REGULARS

I have tried to set up the sequence of these last few chapters to make this one self-explanatory.

Party regulars aren't particularly ideological. They like to win because everyone likes to win. They are Republicans for a lot of only mildly ideological reasons. Some are Republicans for no reason other than their spouses or parents or best friends were Republicans.

Some are Republicans because Ike, Rocky, Jerry Ford, and Bob Dole were good, solid Republican guys—smart guys who'd been around the block a few times and wouldn't screw up the country too much.

Some are Republicans because they golf with Republicans. These regulars are not ideological, but they are very reliable. And they don't like the noisy activists with buttons and signs. They can't imagine discussing abortion, much less marching to end it. They are still reading *Time* magazine and don't see the bias. They thought Clinton was a low-rent, white-trash, fast-talking lightweight, but he'd won and the impeachment stuff seemed a little crazy to them.

All told, these folks are bedrock Republicans, and they don't like the activists at all.

The regulars love W., and they don't even know why. They'll call him tough, no-nonsense, or hard-headed.

Which is their way of saying he's a lot like Dole, Ford, Rocky, and Ike.

As with the transitional voters, the regulars don't need a lesson on how to live a good moral life. They don't need lectures at all. They need to be listened to and respected and, in fact, flattered.

Only the self-destructive party regulars will go out of their way to denounce country-club Republicans as country-club Republicans.

If the regulars get interested enough to talk politics, however, then they need to understand that they'd be nowhere without the activists. There aren't enough regulars to get a candidate to 20 percent, much less 50 percent plus one. And although the regulars can raise a pile of dough when so inspired, the activists keep the fires burning with cause-based donations and the zeal to buy the books, and thus promote the success of conservative authors like Ann Coulter and David Limbaugh.

The regulars often feel a wholly unmerited contempt for the activists, not realizing that the brains and advanced degrees favor the activists more often than the regulars, even though the balance sheet favors the regulars more often than the activists.

They are locked in an alliance from which neither can escape without total injury to the aspirations of the other.

Keep thinking sales. It is all about selling, and if you lose sight of that, you lose elections.

You cannot sell anything by emphasizing its worst features. You don't advertise the most complicated element of a product or its least likable aspect. Not if you want to sell anything, that is.

And you don't turn political parties over to fanatics. Not if you want to win, that is.

On November 2, 2003, a year and a few days before the looming presidential election, two of the nation's preeminent political reporters—*The Washington Post*'s David S. Broder and Dan Balz—provided a summary of the state of play in the nation's political Olympics:

> Three years after one of the closest and most bitterly contested
> elections in U.S. history, the nation is again polarized over the
> performance of the president. Bush's Republican supporters see
> him as strong and decisive, a man of good character and moral
> convictions. His Democratic detractors believe that, at home and
> abroad, he is leading the country in the wrong direction.

The polling data accumulated by the *Post* showed an advantage for
President Bush, but the "independent vote" was narrowly split:

> Bush begins the campaign year with an overall approval rating of 56
> percent, according to the new *Post*-ABC News poll. The number is
> good by historical standards and masks sharp differences between
> Republicans and Democrats. Eighty-seven percent of Republicans
> approve of how Bush is handling the presidency, while 24 percent of
> Democrats approve—a 63-point gap in perceptions. Independents
> narrowly approve of his performance, splitting 52 to 47 percent.

The numbers have not changed dramatically in the nine months
since the poll was taken at the start of this election cycle. The country has
shifted to the right since the election of 2000, but the struggle for the
votes of people in the middle of the political road is fierce. The polariza-
tion is real, but it is also welcome. It is allowing the country to make a
clear choice between clear alternatives.

The choice has been clear for some time. As noted earlier in the fall of
2003, United States Senator Zell Miller, a lifelong Democrat from Georgia,
announced that he would support the reelection of President Bush. The
announcement stunned Democrats across the country, and not just because
of Miller's visibility and unimpeachable credentials as a Democrat.

It was the language Miller used to describe the rationale for his decision that stunned Democratic Party operatives hoping to unseat an
incumbent president.

Miller called Bush "the right man at the right time," and he regarded the next five years as crucial to the future of the country. Miller declared that he couldn't trust any of the nine Democrats then running for the presidency, and that included the nominee Howard Dean.

Miller comes from the center of the old Democratic Party, and the activists who powered the Dean campaign—and the sharp turn to the left that the campaign forced upon all the other Democratic candidates— shocked Miller into an early declaration of aisle-crossing.

The sudden appearance of his party's fanatics in positions of power surrounding Dean drove Miller away.

Fanatics always drive away the regulars. Regulars do not trust them. Unlike the movement activists who merely upset and discomfit the regulars, the fanatics outrage the regulars and force them to flee.

Which is why parties that win learn how to hide the fanatics from the public's eye, not put them on parade.

In the campaign of 2004, the Democrats have put their fanatics on parade. The fanatics of the Left congregate at MoveOn.org and DemocraticUnderground.com. They march in antiwar rallies, and they contributed to Dean and Kucinich and Sharpton. At www.moveon.org they allowed ads comparing Bush to Hitler to run on their Web site. At another repulsive Web site of the Left, Army Ranger Pat Tillman was denounced as a "dumb jock" after his death in Afghanistan. The bile of the Left has poisoned a significant slice of the Democratic Party.

These fanatics positively hate President Bush, and they make no effort to embrace the traditional tone of debate and the courtesies of campaigns.

They have their genesis in the hard Left of the '60s and '70s, and the next generation of party fanatics will be drawn from the mobs that move from city to city to break windows and disrupt gatherings of various international trade groups. The environmental and abortion rights interest groups also have contributed a cadre of hard Left activists whose tactics and language unsettle the middle, not only of their own party, but of independents as well.

The sudden and vocal appearance of these fanatics is good news for the GOP. There are hundreds of thousands of such folks, but there are tens of millions of observers who think they are shocking and alarming.

The fanatics are having an effect on the Zell Millers of the world, and they will push more and more of the independents into the president's column as the next few months pass.

In the years ahead they may completely capture the Democratic Party, which will cause its marginalization for decades to come.

There is nothing the GOP can or ought to do about this. Center-right strategists and enthusiasts can neither advance nor inhibit the rise of the fanatics in the Democratic Party. To attempt to interfere is to court disaster.

But—and this is crucial—the GOP has to learn from the experience of the Democrats that fanatics cannot be indulged or encouraged. The regulars and the activists have to agree to manage the thin numbers of the wild-eyed so that they cannot capture and distort the party's message.

Here's a lesson to learn from the Democrats: just because a candidate declares for president doesn't mean he or she has to be treated like a serious candidate.

Kucinich, Sharpton, and Moseley-Braun never had a prayer of garnering their party's nomination, but fear of the fanatics led party leaders to give these three extremists stage time and face time with the nation. This in turn led to respectability for simply absurd positions, especially those of Kucinich. And valuable time was wasted in every debate and joint appearance indulging the marginal candidates.

The GOP, especially as it approaches the campaign of 2008, must have in place rules that prevent similar marginal candidates, who attract the support only of fanatics, from using up space and oxygen in the debate about the post-W party.

Fanatics can provide money and energy in campaigns, and grassroots volunteerism in off years.

But that energy must be funneled into responsible activity and behind mainstream candidates. Those who can't adjust can exile themselves to the fringes represented by the Libertarian candidates. Parties are better off without the 5 percent of the 5 percent who end up causing train wrecks and, as with the Democrats of 2004, getting hold of the controls during the primary season and thus driving the entire Democratic Party into the ditch on the left edge of the road.

CHAPTER 19

THERE AREN'T ENOUGH TARGETS THAT YOU HAVE TO SHOOT AT YOUR FRIENDS?

Howard Dean shot himself in the foot many times in the campaign of 2004, most famously in his "I Have a Scream" speech after his dismal showing in Iowa, but the first time his competitors for the Democratic Party nomination began to shoot at him was November 5, 2003, at the CNN "Rock the Vote" debate.

Just prior to the debate, Dean had called on the party to seek the votes of southerners who displayed the Confederate flag. This was too great an opportunity for Dean's competitors to pass by, and the other Democrats lined up to treat Dean like a piñata at a birthday party.

It was wonderful fun to watch, so much so that I even watched the replay. There is nothing quite so pleasing to a partisan as the sound of a civil war across the aisle.

Then when John Kerry surged ahead and won Iowa and New Hampshire, Dean and the other Democrats turned on Kerry. I rolled tape and will be replaying the great sound bites throughout the fall.

Not that Republicans have resisted the temptation to launch their own internal slugfests. The Bush-McCain rumble of 2000 was a nasty one, and Democrats still attempt to exploit the worst confrontations of that contest, especially those that occurred around the time of the South Carolina primary.

Sometimes the intraparty smack-downs cannot be avoided. Despite a raft of polls showing that he couldn't win the California recall campaign, for example, California State Senator Tom McClintock ran in the recall and forced many conservatives to speak candidly about his shortcomings as a candidate for fear that his rock-ribbed conservatism could attract enough votes to disable Arnold without winning, thus throwing the race to the hopeless Cruz Bustamonte. McClintock's stubbornness in the face of electoral futility obliged many conservatives to treat him roughly, and it was unpleasant.

I know because I was one of McClintock's most severe critics. Never before had I been obliged to hammer on a Republican in the manner I hammered on Tom, and I hope similar circumstances do not occur again.

Ronald Reagan was right about his Eleventh Commandment: "Thou shalt not speak ill of fellow Republicans."

The Gipper coined that maxim because the opportunities are endless in politics to pick fights with your allies. Reagan recognized that such fights are self-defeating and almost always provide the Democrats and the Left with ammunition to use in general elections.

Just as Republicans will surely be using the attacks on Kerry by other Democrats when the race between Bush and Kerry sharpens in the fall of '04.

Candidates locked in primary contests and their supporters cannot avoid at least a little combat with their party colleagues. This is inevitable in the competition for votes. These clashes ought to be about differences in policies.

Outside the arena of primary elections or a rare situation like California's recall, however, it is almost always reprehensible to go after a fellow party member.

Republicans love to savage their own. Not long after Trent Lott was obliged to step down as leader of the GOP in the U.S. Senate, his successor, Bill Frist, came under fire from movement conservatives for not attacking the Democrats on their filibuster of Bush's judicial nominees.

Frist, of course, was new to his job and was working in concert with the White House. Eventually, in November of last year, he launched a masterful assault on Democratic obstructionism. The "thirty-hour" debate showcased the extremism and lying on the Democratic side and energized the GOP base.

Frist got deserved credit, but the attack on him from the Republican activists that wounded him during the summer couldn't be undone.

Partisans never help their cause by attacking their own representatives. *Never*. Only fanatics can convince themselves otherwise.

Saturday, December 6, 2003. *The Washington Post* runs a front-page story: "Conservatives Criticize Bush on Spending." It is authored by reporter Dana Milbank—easily the most anti-Bush of the regular White House reporters. Milbank has made phone calls to prominent figures in the conservative movement, trawling for attack quotes. He reeled in a big catch:

> *The Wall Street Journal* editorial page accuses Bush of a "Medicare fiasco" and a "Medicare giveaway." Paul Weyrich, a coordinator of the conservative movement, sees "disappointment in a lot of quarters." Bruce Bartlett, a conservative economist with the National Center for Policy Analysis, pronounces himself "apoplectic." An article in the *American Spectator* calls Bush's stewardship on spending "nonexistent," while Steve Moore of the Club for Growth labels Bush a "champion big spending president."

The Milbank hit piece, disguised as an article on dissent within the conservative ranks, continued for fifteen more paragraphs, each one another dart aimed at sowing division within a highly unified base as the election season gets under way. The reality is that outside the Beltway, the Republican Party is locked in near unanimous support for the president because, as a whole, they love the man and his policies. But still the self-anointed spokesmen for the conservative cause dutifully lined up to take a whack at the president in the pages of *The Washington Post,* proving once again that in the nation's capital, it isn't about winning or even moving in the right direction; it is about being noticed.

The desire for recognition often overwhelms judgment. The campaign of Pat Buchanan in 1992 led to the defeat of the first President Bush and his replacement with Bill Clinton. Calamities followed, all of them traceable to Pat Buchanan's overinflated sense of himself and his grievances. Buchanan went on to become one of America's best-known political cranks, and America went into an eight-year slide that ended only with the collapse of the World Trade Centers and the deaths of thousands.

Selfish grandstanding has its costs and consequences.

Not that the tendency to self-inflicted wounds is limited to Republicans.

On the same day that conservatives were bashing Bush in the pages of *The Washington Post*, a liberal columnist for *The New York Times*, Nicholas Kristof, was blasting Howard Dean as full of "angry bluster," as a figure who "frightens centrists," who "warms the hearts of the party's core but leaves others cold," whose "cockiness would exacerbate [the] suspicion" that "America's heartland" holds for "Eastern elites." Kristof slammed Dean as needing a "Berlitz course in self-deprecating folksiness," and for peddling a lame "excuse for dodging Vietnam."

Thank you, Mr. Kristof, for that entry in my clip-and-save file. Not that he was wrong, of course, because he wasn't. Dean was all of that and worse. But it is wonderful to be able to quote the Left criticizing the Left when one is trying to persuade the center and the undecided. Even when Dean dissolved in his own bile, the Dean Dongs who thronged to him remained, and the harsh treatment that Kristof and other eastern elitists dealt out to them will not be forgotten soon.

No doubt Democratic Party strategists were just as cheered to read the quotes of conservatives blasting Bush as I was to see Kristof swinging away at a fastball named Dean. Especially if Dean returns to the fray in a quest to become the nominee in 2008.

The publicity addicted always have an excuse for their efforts to wound their own among the nation's elected officials. The conservative activist Paul Weyrich, quoted in the Milbank piece, suggested he was just getting started in a long effort to reform the Bush administration: "I've helped to start revolts against many administrations over the years," he bragged, even as he admitted that "the level of outrage just isn't there where you could oppose the administration."

Well, then, why skitter about loading the cannons of the Left if you recognize there's no support for your criticism? Some, like Weyrich are committed ideologues. But other activists need outrage to fuel their direct mail fund-raising—it is as simple as that. There is nowhere near enough discontent with the president to raise a real rebellion, but fund-raising doesn't require anywhere near that number of discontents. In fact, successful direct mail needs a response rate in the single digits.

There is absolutely no reason not to communicate policy differences to an administration with which you are allied. The Bush administration especially has worked the activist vineyards in an effort to stay connected with its base and to remain as responsive as possible to their concerns. Weyrich has been an effective messenger from the Right to the Center over the years, but only when pursuing his goals without harming the party.

Still, there is no satisfying direct mail dependents. They will find some reason on which to dissent and to publicize that dissent. It is a ruinous selfishness, but it is there.

All of the criticisms leveled at Bush in the Milbank piece could have been leveled at Democrats who forced the higher levels of spending that came with Medicare reform. The best deal that could be had introduced much-needed competition into the system and delivered a promised prescription drug benefit. The law's passage was a huge win for the president and the Republican Party. It was denseness on a rare scale to blast away at the best possible bill that could be had. Some conservatives voted against the bill in both the House and the Senate, but many more voted for it. Those who could not bring themselves to support the bill kept their peace after the roll was called. You win some and you lose some, but you don't gnaw on your own leg in public.

Most of these voices will fall quiet in the two months before the vote. That's better than carrying on their fund-raising during the final sprint, but it would be best if they hadn't salted the mine with clip-and-carry quotes eleven months earlier.

Everything gets saved these days. Everything is recorded. Everything is ammunition, and the ammunition provided by your party's faithful is far more lethal than that manufactured on the other side.

There are plenty of targets across the way. Until they are all thrown back and defeated—and we are far from the day when the Left in America is impotent and ruined—it is foolish to damage your party in the name of your own ideals.

PART IV

MONEY

CHAPTER 20

GIVE

Money is the mother's milk of politics."
This very famous, very accurate quote came from Jesse Unruh, a Democratic power broker in California for many of the years before, during, and after Ronald Reagan's governorship.

Unruh gushed about the importance of money *before* money became obviously important. In the old days, the political pros knew it took a lot of cash to run campaigns and to operate political parties. But only the pros knew it.

Today, everyone knows it, or at least everyone who knows anything about American politics at the start of the twenty-first century.

Consider some examples:

Gray Davis raised and spent $70 million on his reelection campaign for the California governor in 2002.

John Thune raised and spent $5,989,043 in losing a race for the U.S. Senate in South Dakota, also in 2002. The Democrat who fended off Thune's challenge, Tim Johnson, spent $6,152,991. There were only 334,438 votes cast for these candidates!

Congressman Bob Beauprez raised and spent $1,827,119 in winning a U.S. House of Representatives seat in Colorado's Seventh District, also in 2002. Beauprez won by 121 votes out of 163,457 votes.

The story is the same everywhere. Close elections are marked by large expenditures, dollars that have to be raised from individuals.

This book focuses on federal elections—those for the presidency, the U.S. Senate, and the U.S. House of Representatives.

The laws that control the federal races are pretty simple:

Every American citizen can contribute $4,000 to every candidate for any federal office except the presidency: $2,000 for the primary—even if there is no opposition—and $2,000 for the general election.

For presidential candidates, you can contribute only $2,000 per individual if, like President Bush, the candidate will be accepting federal funding for the fall campaign. A married couple can thus provide President Bush with $4,000. If you have three children, you can send in another $2,000 in the name of each of those children. You can contribute via www.georgewbush.com this very moment. You can even charge it.

Every American can thus contribute $4,000 total to any U.S. Senate candidate—incumbent or challenger—$2,000 for the primary, and $2,000 for the general election.

You can thus give up to $4,000 to John Thune, a fine guy, running for the U.S. Senate seat in South Dakota. He's running again, this time against the Senate's Democratic leader, Tom Daschle, a hard Left opponent of the president, the chief architect of the Left's policy of obstructionism, with the creepy manner of a cartoon mortician.

It looks like John Thune is a good bet to win that seat and unseat Tom Daschle *if* he gets enough money. You can contribute online at www.johnthune.com.

Richard Burr is a fine Republican congressman looking to leave the House and join the most exclusive club in the world, the U.S. Senate. He's running for the seat currently held by Senator John Edwards, who is not seeking reelection. Edwards wanted to be president, so he launched a presidential campaign (which did not succeed), but to give it a shot, Edwards felt he had to leave the Senate behind, thus "opening" a seat to competition. (It is always harder to beat an incumbent running for reelection than it is to beat another outsider.)

North Carolina is generally a pretty conservative state, but Erskine Bowles is a very wealthy guy who is running for Edwards's seat for the Democrats. Bowles can spend a whole bunch of his own dough, and he has proved willing to do so. He spent more than $13 million ($7 million was his own money) losing a Senate race to Elizabeth Dole in 2002. He'll likely raise and spend at least as much in 2004 against Burr.

Burr needs a lot of donations. You can make one online now at www.richardburrcommittee.com.

There are also competitive Senate races in Alaska, Arkansas, California, Colorado, Florida, Georgia, Illinois, Louisiana, Nevada, North Dakota, Oklahoma, and South Carolina.

Eleven of the fifteen Senate seats considered competitive in 2004 are currently held by Democrats. Colorado, Illinois, Oklahoma, and Alaska are the exceptions. GOP front-runners Jack Ryan in Illinois, Kirk Humphreys in Oklahoma, and Lisa Murkowski in Alaska can use your help right now. (The GOP nominees in Colorado, Nevada, and North Dakota were not clear when this book went to press.) You can contribute online at www.jackryan2004.com, www.humphreysforsenate.com, and www.lisamurkowski.com.

I have listed the available Web addresses of most of the GOP's nominees in the crucial contested races in Appendix F. Check my weblog at www.HughHewitt.com throughout the fall for suggestions on where contributions are most needed.

There aren't many competitive races for seats in the U.S. House of Representatives because both parties have developed highly scientific approaches to drawing congressional district boundaries and usually the lines favor the incumbents so overwhelmingly that it takes extraordinary events to shift many seats.

The composition of the House and the division of its 435 seats among Democrats and Republicans matter a great deal, of course, but average voters and even very involved partisans find it hard to keep track of which of these races will emerge as competitive until the very last few weeks before an election.

Which is why the National Republican Congressional Committee (NRCC) does a lot of national fund-raising. The NRCC collects the dollars and allocates the resources based on need and opportunity to win as the clock runs down every other November. If you care passionately about the composition of the House of Representatives, then give via the NRCC and do so online at www.nrcc.org.

Similarly, if you want your dollars used for maximum impact on the U.S. Senate with minimum time spent studying where to put them, invest via the National Republican Senatorial Committee (NRSC) at www.nrsc.org.

Let's get to the big picture.

Political contributions are like investments in the stock market.

A contribution to an individual campaign is like an investment in an individual company. A contribution to the NRCC or the NRSC is like a contribution to a mutual fund—you let investment professionals make the choice of which companies will be bought and sold.

I prefer to contribute to candidates, not committees, but I have the time and interest to spend investigating the candidates.

Hard fact: most candidacies are doomed. I have no idea who is going to be running against Patrick Leahy in Vermont this year, but unless some sort of a miracle occurs, Leahy gets a free ride and his opponent will have trouble breaking 40 percent of the vote. No matter how much I dislike Leahy—and it's hard to describe my level of contempt for Leahy—I won't waste money on Leahy's opponent.

Similarly Democratic Congresswoman Loretta Sanchez is easily among the more annoying members of Congress. She's not particularly dangerous, just dense and giggly. She's in a very, very safe district, however, and I won't be contributing to her Republican opponent.

The professionals running the NRSC and the NRCC are very hard-nosed about such matters. They won't waste money on long shots. Which is why it's a safe bet to invest in the GOP via those committees.

But if there are a number of very competitive Senate races—and there are this year, and there are most years—I try to figure out who would serve the Senate best and the GOP strategically. Not all candidates are alike when it comes to potential to affect the country through ideas and profiles. So I try to send my money to the men and women who will bring the most to the Senate.

Sometimes it does make a difference in the House who is elected from a particular area. I mentioned Bob Beauprez, for example, the fine freshman congressman from Colorado's Seventh District.

Bob Beauprez is a great conservative and a wonderful family man, a small businessman, and a longtime party activist. He deserved the seat. He brings a lot of outstanding qualities to the House.

Plus, in 2002 Beauprez was running against a blowhard, a brass-knuckled Democratic pol who labeled Dick Cheney a "chickenhawk" and then refused to defend or explain his outrageous comments.

Though the race for the Seventh District in Colorado didn't ultimately decide the balance of power in the House of Representatives, it did strike an emotional chord with me, so I went to bat for Beauprez by urging people to contribute to his campaign. As with investing, some candidates, like some companies, just capture your heart.

In 2002, I fell in love with the candidacies of John Thune of South Dakota and Norm Coleman of Minnesota and, to a lesser extent, Saxby Chambliss of Georgia, Jim Talent of Missouri, and John Sununu of New Hampshire.

All five of these gentlemen are extremely capable and very smart. All five are great conservatives. Four of them won. John Thune was, I firmly believe, robbed by election-day thievery in South Dakota. As noted, Thune lost by 524 votes out of 334,438 cast.

I gave the max to John Thune, but he didn't win. My investment wasn't wasted, though. John's campaign pushed the Democratic incumbent in South Dakota, Tim Johnson, to the wall and forced then Democratic Majority Leader and fellow South Dakota Senator Tom Daschle to hemorrhage resources in South Dakota that might have been spent in Minnesota, Missouri, Georgia, and New Hampshire where Coleman, Talent, Chambliss, and Sununu did win.

While Daschle was busy saving Johnson (and spending scarce resources from the national Democratic coffers like crazy to do so), Coleman, Talent, Chambliss, and Sununu were marching to the wins that retook the U.S. Senate for the GOP.

Because John Thune's race was competitive, an investment made perfect sense, even if it didn't yield a win. Similarly, 2002 saw the easy reelection of my friends Congressmen Christopher Cox and David Dreier of California. Because both men were certain to win, investing in their campaigns made no sense, even though both are able congressmen.

By now even the newcomer to politics ought to have figured out that money matters a lot, and where you invest yours matters as well. So let me summarize with some rules for political contributions:

1. Money matters a lot in politics, so be prepared to give intelligently. Don't waste your money.

2. Give to the president first and to the max. The presidency matters most of all.

3. Give to individual candidates for the U.S. Senate only if you have had time to study the races and know for certain that your candidate (a) has a chance of winning, but (b) isn't going to win in a blowout.

4. If you do have time to do your research, give to individual Senate candidates with whom you most closely agree and who have a long future in politics.

5. Give to the NRSC and NRCC on a regular basis, especially in off years. Politics requires machinery and machinery requires money. These are the pros. Keep them in the field.

6. Almost never give to an individual congressman, other than the one who represents you.

7. Do not give large amounts to the congressman who represents you unless it is one of the very few races in the country that is genuinely competitive.

8. Almost never give to any candidate for any state legislature. The only exception is a personal friend. These are wasted dollars. Friends and special interests should fund campaigns for state legislative offices.

9. *Never* give to a Democrat. Even if it's your parent, sibling, or child. Love him, but don't help him. Be there for him when he loses.

10. With two exceptions, never, never, never give to a "cause."

This last rule will not make me many friends in the "cause" community, but the fact is that most causes raise money so that their bureaucracies can have jobs. The first of two exceptions to this rule is the

NRA, which plays politics to win and plays on the right side. But the rest of special interest groups waste millions in scarce resources.

The parties, not the special interests, matter. Give to the candidates, not the people who lobby them.

The second exception to Rule 10 is a work-related PAC. This is an unusual situation that allows employers to have an impact on politics. So take advantage of the opportunity to make your business effective, *provided* your business PAC gives *only* to Republicans. Don't be pressured into helping the Democrats just because some pinhead in your company's bureaucracy thinks "it makes sense to have friends on both sides of the aisle."

With these rules in mind, let's turn to the more interesting subject: How much should *you* give?

CHAPTER 21

GIVE UNTIL IT HURTS

W agon Boy" is well known to the audience of *The Hugh Hewitt Show*. Michael Smith is a relative newcomer to the world of political contributions. Until the election cycle of 2002, he didn't bother to give in large amounts.

But 9/11 had many effects on a lot of people. One of those widespread effects was the recognition that it had become urgent to become involved in politics because the political process would decide whether the serious people, the Republicans, would be in charge of the country's defenses.

The single most effective thing a citizen can do to influence politics in America is to give money to the candidates pledged to the policies that will protect the country.

That means the most important thing a citizen can do to serve his country in 2004 and the years thereafter is to give money to the reelection effort of George W. Bush and the Republicans who support him in the U.S. Senate and the U.S. House of Representatives.

Wagon Boy "got" this early in 2002. And his nickname comes from the fact that he is driving a beat-up old station wagon rather than a restored Mustang because his restoration budget went to the coffers of folks like John Thune, Norm Coleman, Saxby Chambliss, Jim Talent, and John Sununu.

What difference did the election of these five men make?

In early November of 2003, a memo from the Democratic staff on the

Senate Intelligence Committee found its way into the hands of broadcast journalist Sean Hannity. The memo detailed the Democrats' plan to politicize the work of the Intelligence Committee in an effort to bring down George W. Bush.

Here is the text of that memo:

We have carefully reviewed our options under the rules and believe we have identified the best approach. Our plan is as follows:

1) Pull the majority along as far as we can on issues that may lead to major new disclosures regarding improper or questionable conduct by administration officials. We are having some success in that regard. For example, in addition to the president's State of the Union speech, the chairman has agreed to look at the activities of the Office of the Secretary of Defense as well as Secretary Bolton's office at the State Department. The fact that the chairman supports our investigations into these offices and co-signs our requests for information is helpful and potentially crucial. We don't know what we will find but our prospects for getting the access we seek is far greater when we have the backing of the majority. (Note: we can verbally mention some of the intriguing leads we are pursuing.)

2) Assiduously prepare Democratic "additional views" to attach to any interim or final reports the committee may release. Committee rules provide this opportunity and we intend to take full advantage of it. In that regard, we have already compiled all the public statements on Iraq made by senior administration officials. We will identify the most exaggerated claims and contrast them with the intelligence estimates that have since been declassified. Our additional views will also, among other things, castigate the majority for seeking to limit the scope of the inquiry. The Democrats will then be in a strong position to reopen the question of establishing an independent commission (i.e. the Corzine amendment).

3) Prepare to launch an independent investigation when it becomes clear we have exhausted the opportunity to usefully collaborate with the majority. We can pull the trigger on an independent investigation at any time—but we can only do so once. The best time to do so will probably be next year either:

A) After we have already released our additional views on an interim report—thereby providing as many as three opportunities to make our case to the public: 1) additional views on the interim report; 2) announcement of our independent investigation; and 3) additional views on the final investigation; or B) Once we identify solid leads the majority does not want to pursue. We could attract more coverage and have greater credibility in that context than one in which we simply launch an independent investigation based on principled but vague notions regarding the "use" of intelligence.

In the meantime, even without a specifically authorized independent investigation, we continue to act independently when we encounter foot-dragging on the part of the majority. For example, the FBI Niger investigation was done solely at the request of the vice chairman; we have independently submitted written questions to DoD; and we are preparing further independent requests for information.

Summary

Intelligence issues are clearly secondary to the public's concern regarding the insurgency in Iraq. Yet, we have an important role to play in revealing the misleading—if not flagrantly dishonest methods and motives—of the senior administration officials who made the case for a unilateral, preemptive war. The approach outline above seems to offer the best prospect for exposing the administration's dubious motives and methods.

Zell Miller, a Democratic senator, denounced this memo as a "first cousin to treason." He did so because the memo clearly and undeniably conveys that the Democratic staff is using the intelligence oversight process to wound the president politically. Senate Democrats were thrown back in disarray as the public's disgust with their tactics became manifest.

The Democrats had implemented some of the plan outlined in the memo even before the memo was exposed, but they hadn't implemented most of it. Had Tom Daschle been the majority leader instead of minority leader, and had Democrat Jay Rockefeller been the chair of the Intelligence Committee and not just its ranking minority member, and had the Democratic staff that cooked up the "near treasonous" plan been in the majority with the power of subpoena and hearings, the damage to the national security would have been immense. Putting the Dems into the minority in the fall of 2002 meant a great deal to the country's national security.

The contributions of people like Wagon Boy in 2002 had kept the bottom-feeding staff members of the Democratic senators serving on the Intelligence Committee from perverting the committee's work and thus prevented injury to the war effort.

Democrats deeply resent what they brand as attacks on their patriotism, but the recklessness with which these staffers advocated politicizing the most sensitive committee in Congress provides an accurate gauge of the wildness that has overwhelmed Democrats generally. Regaining power by any means matters more to them than safeguarding the nation.

Keeping them in the minority, and indeed crushing their numbers in a repudiation of the anti-America extremists in their midst and within their coalition, is absolutely vital to the country's security.

This can be accomplished only through the election process. Democrats have to be dealt a series of devastating electoral setbacks in 2004, 2006, 2008, and 2010 if they are ever going to sober up and exile from the ranks the sorts of people who drafted that memo and the sorts of senators who hired them and protected them.

Shortly before World War I destroyed an entire generation of Europe's young people, a partisan viciousness overwhelmed England. William Manchester, writing of that era in his first volume of the life of Winston Churchill, wrote, "enemies were implacable. Friendships became exhausted, reservoirs of goodwill drained, public men used up." One participant, Lord Champion, remarked of the years between the wars that "party animosity reached a degree of virulence which is hardly conceivable in the present generation."

The sharpening of domestic partisanship usually means that great issues are being decided: issues of war and peace; issues of life and death.

The partisanship in America in a post-9/11 world underscores that the two parties have radically different views of how the world works and the direction in which the country should head.

It is no secret that I think John Kerry and the Democrats as a whole have set upon a course that will endanger the country and could lead to the deaths of thousands, if not hundreds of thousands, of Americans at the hands of terrorists.

That means that elections of the next few cycles are not just about tax policy and global warming, about accountability for public schools or agricultural subsidies or steel subsidies.

These next few elections are about staying alive and free.

That means they are worth a lot of my money, even though all I am buying is what every American should want: national security.

It would be easier and cheaper to know nothing about politics and not realize the stakes or the clear differences between the parties.

I would love to have back with interest the dollars my wife and I have put into various candidacies over the past two decades and especially the past five years.

I am sure Wagon Boy would rather be driving his restored Mustang.

But once you "get it," it is impossible to forget it.

Once you have figured out that your contributions can and do make a difference—a real difference—in the direction of the country and the makeup of the leadership running the war, then you have to give.

Either that, or admit to yourself that you put your personal comfort ahead of the national security.

Wagon Boy made the right choice. You should as well.

As you watch brave soldiers, sailors, airmen, and Marines fight the war on the terrorists and the nations that support them, and as you read the stories of the hundreds who have died in that war or the stories of the thousands who have been injured, realize there is nothing you can do that remotely approaches the sacrifices they or their families have made.

But you can make sacrifices to assure that the war is fought vigorously to a successful conclusion. Those who feel the desire to "do something"

should get involved in politics. It is the most effective and important contribution a civilian can make to the war effort.

Many of the president's critics blasted his tax cut proposals and their
successful implementation in the aftermath of 9/11. These critics believed
that Americans needed to be called to "sacrifice" in the aftermath of the
surprise attack on America.

The tax cuts were not, however, about "rewarding" people, but about
reviving the economy from its sluggishness in the aftermath of the collapse
of the stock market bubble, and the ferocious decline in the value of stocks
that began in early 2000 and that Bill Clinton did nothing to arrest. The
recession that followed, which began just as President Bush took office,
was a harsh one, and the economy needed stimulus, not rhetoric.

So the tax cuts were pushed through over Democratic objections, and
they have worked extraordinarily well.

But the vast majority of Americans would like to help the war effort.
They would like to contribute something—indeed, a great deal—to the
cause for which men and women in the armed services are giving so much.

There is no need for war bonds or victory gardens, for tire recycling or
tin drives. We should not raise taxes and hurt the recovery just for show.

But people can and should give of their wealth to the political and
charitable causes that will help win the war on terror.

Reducing the power of the Democratic Party at the federal level
helps win the war against terror. That simple fact drives Democratic partisans crazy, and they immediately screech that this is a challenge to
their patriotism.

The clear-eyed need to repeat again and again that it is not necessary
to destroy the power of the Democratic Party, because the Democratic
Party is treasonous. Destroying the power of the Democratic Party is
necessary because the Democrats are reckless, do not take enough time
to understand the threats abroad, and will not spend enough money to
defeat those threats abroad; they cannot be trusted to take preemptive
action to stop attacks on Americans before they occur.

Which is why you must give money to defeat Democrats—because
they will not do what is necessary to defend the country.

When you help elect Republicans, you help win the war on terror.

It is that simple, and the argument for giving to Republicans is that stark. So how much?

Start with this crucial understanding: no contribution is insignificant. The first dollar anyone contributes to any campaign is a huge dollar because it is symbolic of a decision to move to a different level of citizen participation.

Even if you are stretched to the max, give a dollar to the NRSC as a way of saying to yourself that you understand the stakes.

Be realistic that a $10 a month contribution is a big deal in politics. If you are giving $120 a year to political candidates of the NRSC or NRCC, you are part of a very small slice of the American population that has moved into serious activism. The party's senior leadership knows that the $10 a month gift is the key to healthy machinery.

Everyone who is reading this book can afford $10 a month. If you haven't given that much, you haven't done so because of procrastination or the belief it doesn't matter.

This is the great frustration of candidates: they know it matters but cannot convince ordinary voters that small contributions do add up.

Ironically it was Howard Dean who broke through to his supporters and convinced them that the $10, $25, or $50 contribution makes a huge difference. President Bush was not far behind, however, and small contributions to www.georgewbush.com have grown throughout the last two years as a result of a spreading recognition that the interest has made possible genuine broad-based funding of campaigns.

So small and regular giving matters a great deal.

The next question is: Should you be more than a small and regular contributor?

Evangelical Christians are familiar with the concept of tithing. For those of you new to the concept, let me summarize it this way: God is owed a tenth of everything you make.

"Owed," mind you. The first 10 percent of everything *belongs* to God for use in building His kingdom. Genuinely grateful people give above the 10 percent mark.

Now the vast majority of evangelical Christians don't tithe. The average annual donation to a church by a family is a few hundred dollars, not a few thousand. But the standard is often discussed by pastors as a means of inspiring believers to examine their faithfulness and to reach higher than they have in past years.

I think a 2 percent standard in politics can prompt the same evaluation and inspiration functions as the tithing obligations. There is no biblical mandate to contribute any amount to candidates, of course, but having a guideline against which to judge your commitment is a good thing.

So if you make $50,000 a year (earned income and investment income combined), I think you ought to be giving $1,000 to the political process.

If you are at $100,000, then give $2,000; at $250,000, then $5,000. In fact, the more you make, the more quickly you ought to give. The country's been very, very good to you. Don't wait to give a tiny bit back.

These are serious sums of money, especially since they carry zero tax deductibility, and you get *nothing* in return except an occasional glass of moderately priced wine and some finger food at a fund-raiser.

There is no sugarcoating the fact that investment advisors will think political contributions are crazy. They can probably show how disciplined investment of money you put into politics could buy you a condo in the desert or an annual ski vacation.

You genuinely will get nothing tangible for your money. Contributing to political campaigns is *not* about getting an edge or buying influence.

It is about keeping the country in competent, responsible hands. That is certainly worth the 2 percent.

The biggest obstacle to political giving is the fact that so few people do it, new givers often feel like chumps. The disconnected don't contribute, and many even mock the idea of giving to a candidate.

This is why appeals for political contributions are rarely successful if they are made without first establishing the stakes. Why bother giving to Candidate A if there is no difference between the Republicans and the Democrats? Only after the vast differences between the parties are established can an individual reasonably be expected to dig deep and give hard-earned money.

Folks who don't want to spend time, energy, or money on politics often disparage the parties as being essentially the same. Such comments are just admissions of ignorance, but they do provide their authors with a convenient excuse not to put themselves out or to involve themselves. Lazy people often come up with excuses for themselves. Minimizing the differences between the parties is a hall pass from responsibility.

Every great American leader since Washington has been a partisan—a combatant in the party wars of his or her day.

They knew that the collisions of the major parties produced the ideas and the mandates needed to govern the country.

And all of them depended upon the contributions of supporters to advance their candidacies and ultimately their ideas for the country.

It hasn't changed since 1789. You simply get to decide whether you will join the debate and the struggle for power. The first serious step begins with opening the wallet.

First to the president via www.georgewbush.com. Then to any of the campaigns listed in Appendix F. And keep going down the list until it really does begin to hurt your consumption plans. At that point you will have genuinely sacrificed on behalf of the best interests of the country.

CHAPTER 22

GIVE SOME MORE

I wouldn't spend so much time on money if it didn't matter so much.

But it does, so I do.

Even if you have never given a dollar in the past, and you don't even want to give a dollar in the future, consider opening the safe for the race of 2004.

Realigning elections carry consequences for fund-raising for years to come. Special interests put a lot of dough into politics, but most of them do so for nonideological reasons. When they wish to be heard on Capitol Hill during crucial legislative debates, it is a lot easier to get that hearing if they are speaking from the position of a group that has an established record of helping the majority party succeed through regular contributions.

It is possible to get a hearing for interest group views if those interest groups have never put a dime into politics, but it is much, much easier to ask for time and attention when they have given time and attention—and dough.

Some on the left and the right view this reality as proof of the corruption of politics. That's absurd, and the grown-ups know it. Votes are very rarely "sold," and even big contributors regularly walk away from the legislative fray deeply disappointed. And, of course, individual contributors never even get the "hearing" that special interests desire.

But special interests do contribute heavily to political campaigns, and most special interests contribute more to majority party candidates than to minority party candidates.

There are some exceptions. Big labor will never stop giving the bulk of its contributions to Democrats, and the NRA will always favor the GOP.

But a lot of special interest money just follows the power, and if realignment cements the GOP legislative majorities into place in 2004, the money advantage should begin to follow the legislative advantage.

That is not true today because of the overwhelming advantage that organized labor gives the Democrats.

Every paycheck that every union member receives for every pay period represents a contribution of a few dollars to Democratic candidates.

Unions have the right to deduct money to campaign war chests directly from their members' pay envelopes.

In the last chapter I mentioned the incredible value of a regular, small contribution. The unions have millions of such contributions, each giving a few bucks every couple of weeks, all of it going to the Democrats.

The numbers are staggering. As late as March 2004—with more than seven months to go in the 2004 federal election cycle—the unions had already spent heavily. The Boilerman's Union had contributed $524,000—$491,500 of it to Democrats. The International Brotherhood of Electrical Workers had ponied up $953,200—$918,500 of it to Democrats. The Machinists/Aerospace Workers had given $901,000—$886,000 to Democrats. The United Autoworkers had plunked down $710,000—$703,600 to Democrats. There are many other unions, so the picture should be clear.

This torrent of money has kept the Democrats competitive for years, but with postrealignment it will diminish substantially in importance as most other special interests will shift their contribution patterns to reflect decisive Republican majorities.

If those Republican majorities appear in November 2004.

Which is why this is the one year when digging deep makes the most sense.

There will always be a need for political fund-raising and donor bases. Even if the Democratic Party gets the whomping it deserves and the country needs it to get in 2004, the Dems will regroup and reorganize, one hopes, around a responsible foreign policy. But 2004 is the year in which individuals can make the most significant contribution of their lives.

So dig deep. The giver who actually finds himself postponing some other purchase in order to help build the national security has done the right thing.

CHAPTER 23

CELEBRATE JUNK MAIL

I have in my desk a letter from Bill Clinton.

It isn't a real letter from Bill Clinton. Rather, it is one of those mass-produced begging letters that the direct mail machines of the American political process generate by the tens of millions every year.

This one is addressed to "Dear Friend," and it seeks contributions on behalf of the Democratic Senatorial Campaign Committee. Bill Clinton writes, "So I'm counting on you to join me in fighting to TAKE BACK THE SENATE by contributing to the DSCC."

I pull this out whenever any new piece of news arrives that makes such a lofty goal even more remote. Louisiana Democratic Senator John Breaux, for instance, announced his intention to retire from his seat on December 15, 2003. That must have been another wrist-slitting day over at the DSCC, which has seen incumbent Democrats call it quits in Florida, Georgia, South and North Carolina, and then Louisiana—all states that went for Bush in 2000 and are likely to do so again in 2004, making it very hard for Democrats to hold those seats. No wonder the DSCC needs money and Bill Clinton is helping. They are looking at a wipeout, thanks to the combination of Democratic obstructionism in the Senate and the party's lurch to the Far Left margins of today's politics.

But I treasure Clinton's letter despite the ludicrousness of its message. The letter is evidence that the Dems don't know to whom they are mailing and they are still using the scattershot techniques that have proven so inefficient in years past. DNC Chair Terry McAuliffe has taken to bragging about the size of the e-mail list the Democratic National Committee now employs, but all the spam in the world can't help a party if it's being sent to recipients who treat it with all the respect of an appeal from some self-proclaimed ex-cabinet member in Nigeria seeking "Urgent Assistance" from any American with $600 and a lot of gullibility.

Direct mail follows anyone who subscribes to political magazines or who makes a contribution of any amount to any political effort. Campaigns and periodicals alike compile their lists of donors or subscribers and then sell them to whoever wishes to pay the freight. The lists are then used to circulate new appeals for different campaigns or different periodicals. Then they are sold again. And again. And again.

This is just the way it works, and it is a good thing, especially if you are receiving persuasive appeals from GOP candidates and amazingly misdirected mail from Democratic operatives and causes.

Don't give money to any direct mail appeal, by the way. Never. Always be proactive in donating—searching out candidates and contacting them. Responding to direct mail appeals puts your money at risk of being wasted far from the front lines of political combat.

But take time to read all the letters because they provide glimpses of the issue sets that both sides are working.

Bill Clinton's letter on behalf of the DSCC is heavy with worry over the "loss of 2 million jobs," the loss of "$5 trillion in the stock market," and the "$2 trillion deficit." Clinton's appeal asserts that "corporate executives have been rewarded for their dismal economic performance with record pay. And the wealthiest one percent of Americans have received an average tax cut of more than $53,000 every year since 2001."

In short, the Dems have nothing to sell but envy and lies. There is no program, no appeal to rally behind some new vision or different approach. Their direct mail depends upon the same old, same old. The warnings about the "Republican money men [who] are beating the bushes for campaign contributions from oil and gas companies, the National Rifle Association, drug companies and other special interests" have taken on an almost ritual-like tone.

The Democrats are out of intellectual gas, and their mail shows it.

GOP mail, by contrast, talks of battles that need to be won and Democratic blockades that need to be broken. It is the language of purpose and the rhetoric of goals accomplished and even more goals ahead. It is good stuff because it is forward looking, positive, upbeat.

Again, please don't write checks in response, but you can learn your arguments from such appeals, and you can anticipate the arguments from the other side by reading their papers.

But don't proclaim that the flood of appeals has turned you off to contributing.

I routinely hear this complaint from callers or e-mailers: "Hugh, I gave to www.nrsc.org as you suggested, but now I get an appeal every other day from some other group. I am sick of it."

Sick of it? Sick of receiving evidence that your side is well organized and in the hunt for more support? Sick of winning elections? Sick of majorities on both sides of Congress for the first time in fifty years?

It is shortsighted to moan about junk mail filling up your box. Those letters and bulletins and bogus polls are the lifeblood of the apparatus that we need to maintain majorities committed to the defense of the United States and its economic prosperity. Even the arrival of trash mail from the folks seeking to raise taxes and lower defenses gives you an opportunity to celebrate their silliness.

Junk mail is a badge of participation, a testament to your engagement in the crucial process of selecting national leadership. Don't shake your head when the next form letter arrives. Take a good, long look at it and its arguments.

And then head to the Web and give to the candidate of your choice. More mail will follow because you have once again done your job.

CHAPTER 24

OPENING YOUR HOME

O ne of the very few upsides to being awake through the night with the sort of cold that won't let you sleep is the opportunity to catch up on late-night C-SPAN. Flipping through the Tony Robbins infomercials—interesting—and the fitness plan infomercials— not interesting—and the Time-Life CD collection infomercials for the "Folk Years" collection or "120 Songs of the Seventies" brings you to C-SPAN's two channels eventually.

Early this year I was in that position, and I settled on a lecture to campaign workers by Grace Cummings, executive director of the Faith and Politics Institute. Although the institute is bipartisan, Grace was clearly an experienced Republican fund-raising executive, and she was walking her charges through the specifics of campaign finance organization.

The means available to campaigns to raise dollars are few: candidate phone calls; big-ticket events featuring an honored guest and many levels of contribution; direct mail; and the tried-and-true test of every campaign's organizational ability, the house party.

Ms. Cummings took a lot of time to emphasize the importance of this sort of event to her audience. A house party is just that: a meet-and-greet-and-ask by the candidate that occurs in the confines of a private home, usually aiming to raise at least $1,000, typically in $25, $50, and $100 contributions.

This is the ground game of a campaign, the three-yards-and-a-cloud-of-dust variety. There isn't anything remotely sexy about this aspect of fund-raising to the candidate or the staff, but to the ordinary activist, it is a great measure of commitment and a huge signal of dedication to the cause.

Opening a home to a candidate and inviting thirty to fifty acquaintances, business colleagues, or neighbors to hear him give a talk on politics is about as close to Tocqueville as the average American gets these days. On a percentage basis, only a tiny percentage of 1 percent of the electorate attends such an event, much less throws one, but you should consider doing so, especially in a year as pivotal as 2004.

If you have a viable candidate for the United States Senate running in your state, call the campaign and ask to be connected to the coordinator of house parties or, if there is no such animal, to the director or deputy director of fund-raising. Give your name and address, and explain your interest. Then make a list of people you'd like to invite. Well-organized campaigns will provide you with a draft invitation letter and detailed suggestions on the actual event.

Here's the kicker: most people love to come to such a thing if they have any interest in politics at all, especially if a soon-to-possibly-be United States senator is coming. (Lawyers especially are easy marks, for most of them dream of being federal judges someday, but so too are most professionals.) And if you get a decline, so be it. The very act of inviting an individual to attend is an interesting and very different bit of life, and a marker of seriousness about politics.

Grace Cummings kept coming back to the house party because her audience needed to hear that viable campaigns never miss an opportunity to hold such events. They serve the purposes of connecting a candidate to a new group of people, developing the small-donor file, and bringing in steady revenue. But all the plans fail if homes can't be found with hosts willing to throw open the doors and invite their friends into the political arena.

So take a deep breath and call the key campaign in your state. Let the organizers know you and your home are available if they need you.

CHAPTER 25

THE 527 THREAT

Whenever government attempts to control the flow of money into politics, those who wish to influence politics through money invent new means to that end. Reformers have kidded themselves for years that the influence of money could be diminished. The Supreme Court of the United States has encouraged the reformers in their dream by blessing a variety of tools that the reformers have embraced, including contribution limits. But every time the rules change, the smart folks figure out a new way to allow the rich folks or the organized little folks to put their money on the table.

This isn't a bad thing, by the way. It is the glory of democracy that our candidates require the support of tens of thousands of folks with cash and the willingness to donate it. One of the revolutions of the Dean campaign—before it imploded—was to introduce the idea of Internet contributions to the base of the Democratic Party. Dean had come close to tapping out his supporters when he blew up, but he made it stylish to give via the Internet. So stylish, in fact, that it will be very difficult for the Left to try to crush this process via regulation in the future since the Dean camp thinks it invented it.

The reformers, however, have left a huge loophole in their latest rewrite of the rules governing campaign spending: the 527 Committee.

The number 527 refers to a section of the Internal Revenue Code— the vast network of laws and rules governing the status of all financial organizations in the U.S. The 527 Committees are simply political groups organized under the rules of Section 527.

These committees have been important for a number of years, but when Senators John McCain and Russ Feingold pushed through a new law regulating campaign fund-raising in late 2002, the 527s took on huge additional importance.

Simply put, "McCain-Feingold," as it is called, outlawed soft money given directly to the Democratic National Committee or the Republican National Committee. Prior to McCain-Feingold, soft money couldn't be used to run ads against candidates, but it helped the national parties in major ways, and big donors liked to give directly to the DNC and RNC.

When McCain-Feingold outlawed soft money, the 527s remained, already in place, ready to accept the donations that otherwise would have flowed to the national committees in the form of the now banished soft money. The new law changed some of the rules for 527s, but until just before an election, the 527s can run negative ads against any candidate they like—and spend unlimited amounts of money doing so. There are even some loopholes governing the last sixty days when attack ads are allegedly banned from the airwaves. Because candidates can spend only what they raise, if a well-funded 527 takes aim at a candidate, that candidate is in deep trouble. He won't be able to match the combined resources of the opposition candidate and those of the 527s.

Both Republicans and Democrats have opened 527s, but the Democrats are much more proficient fund-raisers when it comes to 527s. The nonpartisan Center for Public Integrity (www.publicintegrity.org) described the Democratic dependence on 527s in a lengthy press release and study published on September 25, 2003, which reads in crucial part:

> As a new Center for Public Integrity analysis shows, Democrats and their allies funneled hundreds of millions of dollars through backdoor committees designed to influence key elections. In the 2002 race, the Democratic Party's silent partners spent more than $185 million—more than double the money spent by Republican organizations.

The Center's report shows that the Democrats and Democratic-leaning organizations made great use of a special type of political committee that can raise unlimited amounts of money to influence elections. These committees, known as 527 organizations after the part of the Internal Revenue Code that defines their tax status, can claim tax-exempt status as political committees while at the same time avoiding regulation by state or federal authorities. In fact, 527s may raise unlimited amounts of money from virtually any source and can spend those funds on just about any election-related activity except contributing directly to federal candidates. Since a law mandating disclosure passed in 2000, such groups accounted for just under $450 million in spending. Committees run by Democratic parties and candidates, along with their labor, environmental, abortion rights and trial lawyer allies, have spent nearly two-thirds of that total.

Nor has campaign finance reform eased 527 committee fundraising. So far, in 2003, these groups reported raising around $25 million, about 40 percent of that going to two groups formerly affiliated with the two national parties.

Two 527 committees belonging to the American Federation of State, County and Municipal Employees ("AFSCME"), a union of government workers, spent a combined total of almost $38 million in the past three years, the most of any organization. To put that in perspective, the figure is about $7 million more than the organization has given to federal candidates, PACs and parties—over the last 14 years.

Overall, AFSCME and its labor allies were big donors to Democratic Party committees, together the top recipients of 527 spending. Among individuals, actress Jane Fonda was the largest donor, giving $13 million mostly in support of abortion rights, and at least eight other individuals contributed more than $1 million each.

The center's study, funded by the Pew Charitable Trust, another non-partisan organization, focused on the spending by 527s from the 2002 cycle—before these committees became even more important! Although contributions to 527s had neared $40 million by the close of 2003, the committees had barely begun to raise the money they are expected to collect and spend in 2004. It is not unrealistic to expect that 527 spending will top a half billion in 2004.

This should concern Republicans, not Democrats. Marry the win-at-all-costs ethics of the Dems with the deep ideological and personal hostility many wealthy Democratic donors feel toward President Bush, and the conditions for a volcanic explosion of 527 funding are in place.

The Center for Public Integrity study highlighted the contributions of Jane Fonda in the last cycle: more than $13 million by Fonda alone. I wonder where Fonda's sympathies will lie in the Bush-Kerry race?

Understand that there are many people far wealthier than Fonda who have decided that George W. Bush has to go. That's the problem.

In an age of billionaires, the reformers capped the amount that individuals could give to candidates, but left open a means for unbalanced, wealthy egomaniacs to spend as much as they want to go after a particular candidate.

Which brings us to George Soros and Harold Ickes—the perfect storm for Republicans: A billionaire many times over with an ax to grind, and a brass-knuckled, utterly ruthless hard Left operative.

The first President Bush lost his presidency when a billionaire decided it was time for a change. But at least Ross Perot declared himself a candidate and took his charts and his wallet into the very center of the American political arena.

George Soros is nothing like Ross Perot. Soros, born in Hungary, made much of his approximately $7 billion trading currencies, and he has declared that defeating George W. Bush is "the central focus of my life."

By the end of 2003, Soros had already surpassed Fonda's single-year giving total, having plunked down $10 million for the 527 America Coming Together, another $5 million with a partner into the coffers of the hard-Left MoveOn.org, and a pledge of $3 million to former Clinton aide John Podesta's think tank, the Center for American Progress.

Consider the possibility that Soros is willing to contribute just 10 percent of his fortune to the defeat of President Bush. The 527s can certainly handle $700 million, even if they can't air attack ads on television with such money.

Then there's the Media Fund—another 527, this one created by Ickes, "a major power in the Democratic Party," according to the *Los Angeles Times*, "a broker whose media money could make the difference in the 2004 election."

"I've been heartened by the number of people who think George Bush should find other employment," Ickes told the *Times*. "We expect well over $100 million. We're shooting for $190 million. It's a very big goal."

Almost every objective account of Ickes is full of references to his temper, his nastiness, his venom. But they are also full of tributes to his political instincts and his drive. The *Times* reported that Soros is also contributing to Ickes's effort.

These are just two of the 527s—America Coming Together and the Media Fund. And all those others that existed in the 2002 cycle when Dems blew away the GOP with 527 funding are likely to be back as well.

Desperation is likely to open Democratic wallets as never before. If, as is expected, the GOP's majority in the House and the Senate increases, expect a serious effort to curtail the abuses of the plaintiff lawyers and the environmental extremists. Returning balance to tort law and to the regulation of private property does more than threaten the ideas of these special interest groups—it threatens their very livelihood.

If any serious effort to halt runaway lawsuits materializes, plaintiffs' lawyers will lose billions overnight. They can be counted on to defend the crazy system of runaway juries and no cost for frivolous lawsuits via hefty contributions to the 527s.

And what would happen to the fund-raising of the environmental lobby if a Republican Congress not only reformed the environmental laws of the country but also ended up increasing clean water and air and protecting habitats for endangered species more efficiently and completely than the failed strategies of the command-and-control Left? Not only would the direct mail money dwindle and the "public interest" jobs disappear, so too would the sense of moral superiority.

A lot of the Left is driven by money, and these folks will fight to keep the money flowing.

And a lot of the Left is driven by the desire to be somebody via the exercise of power over others, and the GOP is arrayed against such meddlesome bossiness dressed up as do-goodism.

So expect a tidal wave of funny money crashing into the president's reelection campaign. And be prepared to talk about it.

I am not a fan of the Center for Public Integrity's legislative agenda. The center doesn't believe in the free speech absolutes that I hold dear, and it has unbalanced the playing field through its advocacy, pushing an agenda that unwittingly ended up giving Soros and other hyperwealthy activists a huge advantage over ordinary contributors. People willing to give a few thousand find themselves capped, while the multibillionaires can run wild, and the Center is partly responsible for this uneven playing field.

But the Center does a fine job of following the money. So acquaint yourself with the Center's Web site, and be sure to check up on the Media Fund and America Coming Together. Make a point of letting your coworkers, neighbors, and the talk radio audience know how much these groups have raised and spent as Election 2004 draws near. There is an effort underway to have the Federal Elections Commission issue regulations governing the 527s, but even if those rules appear in early or mid-summer, already the 527s will have destroyed the intent of McCain-Feingold for this presidential campaign.

The decision by deep-pocket hard Left Democrats like Soros and their brass-knuckled agents like Ickes to try to destroy the president via independent expenditure committees will not play well with the electorate—if the electorate knows the score. Don't count on the news media to track this flow of hidden dollars into the campaign fund, or on

Kerry-favoring talking heads to denounce this most unpopulist and unprogressive of efforts.

But patient attention to easily available facts and repetition through the open airwaves will do a wonder of good.

And if you are one of the wealthy who finds the Soros declarations to be unsettling, then track down the best of the GOP-allied 527s and even the playing field. The Center's "Silent Partner" section of its Web site lists all of the 527s. There are some large GOP-supporting entities. Do a little investigation and write the checks.

But first max out to candidate committees, the National Republican Senatorial Committee, and the National Republican Congressional Committee. As I urged in earlier chapters, give until it hurts and then give again.

CHAPTER 26

DON'T EXPECT
TO BE THANKED

One of the most successful Bible studies in America is run by Greg Matte at Texas A&M in College Station, Texas. It is named Breakaway (www.breakawayministries.org). More than four thousand college kids show up for Greg's study on a weeknight throughout the school year. Anyone who knows anything about college kids should realize what an impressive figure that would be, even on the campus of a Christian university or college. Texas A&M is secular, of course, and its reputation for preferring parties over Bible study is pretty secure.

So when I spoke at a conference that also featured Greg, I took advantage of the chance to hear him deliver a talk on service.

Now this book is a secular book about politics, but political operatives and activists can and should learn a lot from anyone with a demonstrated record of effective communication with a hard-to-reach demographic, and young people are notoriously hard to reach.

The day I heard him, Greg Matte was talking to two thousand college kids. Greg was delivering a pretty tough message: "service" isn't really "service" when done in the expectation of recognition and praise. This is a pretty basic message of Christianity, but it needs repeating and emphasizing often. The theology is simple: believers in Christ who are undertaking care of the hungry, the sick, the imprisoned, among others, should be doing so as an expression of gratitude for their salvation through the atoning sacrifice of Jesus on the cross, not because they enjoy being thanked.

People being people, Greg lectured, almost never act from such a pure motive, however. They are almost always looking for the pleasure that comes from recognition or gratitude.

Greg's talk that day was a pretty comprehensive overview on how to combat the need for recognition, and I want to transfer his message from theology to the arena of political activism.

Simply put: don't expect to be thanked. You won't be, at least not regularly, and if you expect otherwise, you will be disappointed.

If you cultivate indifference to recognition for your efforts and thank-yous for your contributions, your activism will not flag.

Lots of donors to political campaigns write checks in order to meet the president, the vice president, or another elected official. They want a picture for the wall or a story for their club. Political operatives know this and labor mightily to make sure thanks are extended and recognition conferred.

But almost always there are contributors for whom a picture is not enough, and some donors and activists demand thanks and recognition out of proportion to their contribution. As I argued in the past few chapters, small donations are hugely important to a campaign, but not if the care and feeding of the donor cost more than the donation itself. Even a $2,000 maxed-out donation can quickly consume more in attention and time than the donation provided.

The donors of time or money who demand the least in attention are the most valuable donors of all. They are the low-maintenance, high-value activists.

Be one of them. Don't write a check or organize an event in expectation of thank-yous.

And certainly don't do it in expectation of an appointment or an invitation to a state dinner.

Do it because we are in a war and the responsible party needs to win.

PART V

MESSAGE DELIVERY

Every man that lowered our flag
was a Democrat . . . Every preacher that said
slavery was a divine institution was a Democrat.
Recollect it! Every man that shot a Union soldier
was a Democrat. Every wound borne by you
Union soldiers is a souvenir of a Democrat.

—Robert Green Ingersoll, attorney general of Illinois,
campaign speech, 1890

CHAPTER 27

KNOW YOUR STUFF: THE KEY FACTS

Every election cycle pivots on a few issues. These issues end up dominating the last ten weeks of a campaign because, by the mysterious process that flows from the combined impact of millions and millions of conversations and hundreds of thousands of hours of television and radio programming and tens of thousands of columns, stories, and editorials, the public's attention turns to one or two or, at most, a handful of key debates.

In 2000, the cost of prescription medicine dominated part of the crucial months of September and October, and the size and scope of tax cuts also mattered, as did the debate over Al Gore's exaggerations.

In 2004, the crucial debates will be over the conduct of the war on terrorism and the condition of the economy.

No matter what the year or the set of issues, though, activists need to line up and memorize the key facts. The following chapters stress the mechanics of "message delivery," but all presuppose that you know what the message is from the start. The credibility of any message depends on the credibility of the messenger, and the messenger's credibility depends on a confident and accurate command of facts.

One of the joys of my radio work, and it happens frequently, is the call from a Lefty that begins with an easily identifiable misstatement of fact.

One caller in December of 2000, a passionate Dean Dong, was rolling along in loud denunciation of the president, and no doubt carrying a few listeners along with him.

Until he asserted that unemployment in the United States was as bad as it had been in the Great Depression. Of course, the unemployment in the U.S. at the end of 2003 was just under 6 percent. At the height of the Great Depression, it was almost 25 percent. The caller had revealed that he didn't know what he was talking about.

I immediately seized on this whopper and used it to erase any credibility that Dean's man had built for himself. By the time the call was finished, the audience had to have understood that this Dean supporter's enthusiasm for Dean was suspect because it was built on falsehoods. When you get basic facts wrong, it's not just the argument you built on those facts that collapses; your entire trustworthiness has been slaughtered. Either you are a liar or you are as dumb as a post, but either way, listeners aren't going to put their faith in you.

Which is why, in this and every election cycle, you ought to make a list for yourself of the half-dozen crucial facts you want to repeat in every argument and then stick with them. Don't exaggerate and don't embroider. Try to answer every question from your fact set, if necessary by changing the question you have been asked into a question that can be answered via one of your key facts.

One final illustration.

The collapse of Howard Dean's candidacy may well have begun on the day he appeared on the most influential of all political talk shows: *Meet the Press*, hosted by Tim Russert. I joke with my audience that this program ought to be called *Meet the Cuomo Aide* because Russert earned his political pedigree by working for Mario Cuomo (just as Chris Matthews earned his by working for Jimmy Carter and George Stephanopoulos earned his by working for Bill Clinton—what's Ari Fleischer doing these days?), but there's no denying the influence of Russert's program.

Russert threw Dean a softball: How big is the American military? If Dean had answered accurately, he would have shown that he was prepared. Had he answered with unexpected detail—About 480,000 soldiers in the army, Tim; the navy's got about 300 ships, and its total enlistment is around 410,000; the air force has about 368,000 airmen flying, among other things, about 180 long-range bombers and hundreds of F-15s, F-16s and, of course, the F-117 Nighthawks; and let's not forget the Marine Corps; never forget the Marines, Tim, and their 175,000 Devil Dogs— Dean would have hit a home run.

But Dean botched it. He answered between 1 and 2 million after protesting that knowing such things really didn't matter. He didn't know even the basics. He *should* have known. In a time of war, the man who would be commander in chief should know the *facts* about the military he desires to lead.

Facts matter. So know yours. For example, the number of uninsured in the country is around 44 million, up slightly since President Bush took office. The number of abortions performed since *Roe v. Wade* is also around 44 million—a staggering number. The projected federal deficit in 2004 will total about 3.5 percent of the nation's wealth, compared to 6 percent in 1983, and 30.3 percent in 1943! John Kerry opposed the B-1 and B-2 stealth bombers, the M1 Abrams tank, the Patriot missile, the Aegis cruiser, and all land-based ballistic missile defense.

"Facts are stubborn things," John Adams exclaimed famously, "and whatever may be our wishes, our inclinations, or the dictates of our passions, they cannot alter the state of facts and evidences." Armed with facts, all the wild assertions of the Left crash harmlessly about. So get them down. Cold.

CHAPTER 28

THE MEDIA
TILT WAY LEFT,
SO LIVE WITH IT

J onathan Alter is a reporter/columnist for *Newsweek*. In the November 3, 2003, issue of the magazine, Alter wrote a column asserting that "of course" Donald Rumsfeld "probably should have been fired last summer for incompetence" in the planning for postwar Iraq. He went on to urge that Rumsfeld develop "empathy" for his opponents: "Empathy would mean talking to the Iranians and the North Koreans to see if they might dismantle their nuclear programs in exchange for U.S. promises not to invade, which was the essence of the deal that spared the world a nuclear war during the Cuban missile crisis."

In the same issue, Eleanor Clift, a reporter/columnist for *Newsweek* and a well-known Lefty, contributed to an article by *Newsweek* reporter John Barry that intoned that Rumsfeld's "critics in the Capitol and even in the Pentagon are questioning his performance in the months since the major fighting ended: the lack of relevant postwar planning, the shortage of troops on the ground in Iraq, the failure to find weapons of mass destruction."

Also in the same issue of *Newsweek*, reporter/columnist Howard Freeman warned that the president's popularity was in danger, that he couldn't afford "to lose John McCain, the avatar of independents who defeated Bush in the 2000 Republican primary" in New Hampshire, and that Bush's "political challenges are growing . . . rapidly."

These three stories threw darts at the Bush administration, even though the president's poll numbers remained far above those of Bill Clinton at a similar point in his presidency and even though no serious bookie thought that the November 2004 race would be the same sort of nail-biter as the 2000 contest had been.

The Beltway journalism establishment was just going through its predictable assault on a popular conservative president, in the uncoordinated but highly ideologically driven game of "get Bush," that the Beltway media have been about since Campaign 2000.

The imbalance in this single issue of *Newsweek* is not shocking. It's not even a mild surprise. It's just the way things are. And just the way things will be for many years to come.

The elite media are overwhelmingly left wing. And the honest members of the elite media admit it.

Which is why the best response to media bias is not outrage, but patient, persistent exposure of the bias via the Web and blogs. Via talk radio. Via the few outlets like Fox News Channel that will carry a well-researched story about media bias.

In the fall of 2003, a writer for the *Los Angeles Times*, William Arkin, investigated a leak given to him, he said, by a Pentagon source. The leaker pointed to Lt. Gen. Jerry Boykin as a fundamentalist Christian, and Arkin set about collecting tapes of talks that Boykin had given in churches.

Some examples from those tapes sounded horrible to ears not used to the particular language of an evangelical testimony. Arkin persuaded his bosses at the *Los Angeles Times* to allow him to provide the story to the folks at NBC first, and on a Wednesday night the networks carried some clips of Boykin. The next morning, the *Los Angeles Times* ran a story on the front page about the general's speeches, and Arkin penned a column for the paper on the same day, denouncing the general as a religious zealot.

I got hold of Arkin and put him on my radio show. He admitted to the manipulation involved in giving the *Times* story to NBC, and he also promised to provide me the transcripts of Boykin's faith talks, which he never did.

After I did some background investigation on Arkin, I discovered that this writer had called himself a "former military intelligence analyst" but had served in the army only from 1974 to 1978, and had only a BS from the University of Maryland. In addition to these rather thin credentials, Arkin had spent twenty years in D.C. working for an assortment of very Far Left "think tanks" or activist groups, including the Institute of Policy Studies and Greenpeace.

Arkin was nothing more than a long-serving member of the professional Left. He'd set out to take down a member of the Bush defense team and had gotten in a good lick or two before the media mob moved on to another story.

Fair journalism might have wondered about Arkin's motives before he got the attention and the employment from NBC and the *Los Angeles Times*. But then NBC and the *Los Angeles Times* wouldn't be reflexively left wing if they were at all self-critical about their biases.

Arkin's attack on Boykin was blunted somewhat by my counterattack on Arkin's "credentials." The day after my report on Arkin's "credentials" ran, Brit Hume introduced the summary of my findings on the Fox News Channel. The counterstory at least provided some small cover to Boykin and his friends in the Pentagon and the administration.

It is always crucial to expose left-wing media bias, even when some damage has already been done by that bias.

Think sports. Even when the good teams give up a couple of early scores, they don't throw in the towel.

As a longtime Notre Dame football fan, I wish USC had given up the game after the first half of the Irish-Trojan 1974 game. Notre Dame led 24-0 at halftime, but USC came back to crush the Irish behind Anthony Davis's talent and triumphed 55-24.

As a longtime Ohio State football fan, I am glad the Buckeyes played relentlessly in the Fiesta Bowl in January 2003. They came back to tie the game in regulation and then beat Miami in overtime.

As a long-suffering Indians and Browns fan, I wish the Marlins had quit before the ninth inning of the seventh game of the 1997 World Series, or that John Elway and the Broncos had said, "Too bad, we'll wait until next year," in either 1987 or 1989.

The other side scores points. Sometimes they are the result of cheap shots, and in politics that's a lot of the time when the media are involved.

Activists don't get mad. They even the score.

If serious activists began to use the blogosphere to chart journalists' work and publish via the Net the accountability those biased journalists deserve, the media would slowly change.

It is worth the effort to call talk radio with specific instances of media bias and to tip friendly journalists with some information. It isn't an easy or a quick fight to restore balance to elite media, but it is possible to win and well worth the effort.

In the fall of 2003, CBS pulled its proposed miniseries, *The Reagans*. It did so because word of the movie's distortions and hate-filled attacks on Reagan had leaked, and the Internet and talk radio combined to bring pressure to bear on CBS. CBS blinked because the spotlight got thrown on the script and the activists patiently spread the word.

It was a significant event in the evolution of elite media. It can be repeated. Activists need to continue to find clear opportunities to expose the Lefty bias of elites. Each time these elites are forced to withdraw or retreat, a huge victory is won.

Time is on the side of the truth.

CHAPTER 29

CONTROLLING THE INFORMATION FLOW, PART 1: THE RISE OF THE NEW MEDIA

Every campaign depends upon communicating the message that one candidate is better than all the others. That is the goal of every statement by the candidate or his team, and every newspaper, television, radio, or Internet report either adds to or detracts from that core message. Every story is a "good" or "bad" story depending on whether it conveys the idea of "better" or "worse." There will literally be millions of stories in the course of every presidential campaign, and each one of them will advance or detract from President Bush's reelection or John Kerry's upset win.

That's why vast teams of campaign consultants spend so much time "shaping the message," and why candidates at every level try to "stay on message." For every setting there is a particular message, but each particular message is part of the great übermessage of "better" or "worse."

Because most elite media are biased against the Republican candidate in almost every race, Republican candidates begin every campaign with a disadvantage because their message of "better" doesn't get equal play with their opponents' message of "better." That doesn't mean they start behind in terms of polls or money or electability. They just have a handicap, like a thoroughbred having to carry more weight in a particular race because of his past record of excellence. As the book and movie *Seabiscuit* so vividly illustrated, that champion horse almost always had to carry extra weight just to make the contests with lesser horses sporting. Almost all horse racing "handicaps" the better horses with an extra burden in order to create closer, more thrilling contests.

The GOP has this handicap, though it has lessened in recent years with the rise of talk radio and some balancing in cable land with the emergence of the Fox News Channel and a couple of center-right voices, like CNBC's Dennis Miller and MSNBC's Joe Scarborough, at other cable networks. Still, message delivery has to be carefully managed, and painstaking attention to detail is required. Repetition, especially, is called for.

When in early December of 2003, Howard Dean let fly with his crackpot theory that the Saudis might have warned President Bush about the attacks of 9/11, it was at first ignored. The exchange occurred on an obscure show on National Public Radio, with host Diane Rehm. Recall that Rehm asked Dr. Dean: "Why do you think he [Bush] is suppressing that [Sept. 11] report?"

Dean responded: "I don't know. There are many theories about it. The most interesting theory that I've heard so far—which is nothing more than a theory, it can't be proved—is that he was warned ahead of time by the Saudis. Now who knows what the real situation is?"

Though I comb the papers and the Internet each morning and read the *Hotline* —the political junkie's online news summary available only to subscribers who pay a hefty fare—I missed the Rehm-Dean exchange entirely until *The Washington Post* columnist Charles Krauthammer noted it in a column on December 5. Immediately I asked my producer, Duane, to download the audio of the interview from the NPR site, and I began playing it repeatedly as evidence for the second leg in my three-legged description of Howard Dean as "angry, unstable, and truth challenged." I played the exchange perhaps fifteen times on that first Friday, and I posted the text of the exchange on HughHewitt.com as well as asked key radio show guests like Fred Barnes and Morton Kondracke about their assessment of the exchange.

On the following Sunday, Chris Wallace asked Dean about the original exchange, and the former governor backpedaled a bit but refused to make the necessary apology for trafficking in crackpot theories. Then on Monday I replayed the exchange in which Dean suggested that President Bush might have been warned about 9/11 by the Saudis. Howard Kurtz of the *The Washington Post*, perhaps the country's most influential media commentator, without prompting from me declared it a crackpot theory and slammed Dean for using an old political dodge to put it into circulation. The next day, Tuesday, December 9, New Hampshire's leading newspaper, *The Manchester Union Leader*, ran one of its famed front-page editorials with the headline: "Dean's Smear: Will It Be Ignored?" The editorial began,

Anyone who would insinuate that President Bush knew in advance of the September 11 attacks on America would normally be dismissed as a charter member of the lunatic fringe.

But when that person is the leading candidate for the Democratic Party's Presidential nomination, it is a different situation.

The paper continued:

It was a Democratic President of whom it was claimed that he knew all about the attack on Pearl Harbor. Has FDR's party now stooped so low as to countenance a similar irresponsible charge against the current President by one of its own presumed leaders? For shame if the answer is yes.

The lurch by Dean into tinfoil-hat land dogged him throughout December and into early January, and contributed to his Iowa meltdown, but only because it had been repeated enough in diverse enough settings that the electorate knew that it happened. Had Krauthammer not brought it into the open via his syndicated column, neither I nor Chris Wallace and perhaps not even *The Manchester Union Leader* would ever have used our various forums to call national attention to the exchange. Had Dean not stumbled in early January, he wouldn't have imploded in Iowa on caucus night with his famous roll call of the states punctuated by his strangled Muppet scream.

This is an illustration of the principle and power of repetition. When a story conveys either a powerful plus or a powerful negative, that story needs repeating as long as the news cycle will carry it. Each repetition brings an expanded audience and deepens the impact on any hearer getting the message a second time. This is basic advertising, but it is crucial in politics. Again and again basic messages must be delivered, even if they begin to grate on the nerves of those who have heard them before.

My listening audience recognized the negative power of Dean's baffling embrace of the lunatic theory of the Saudi early warning system, and the Dean supporters began calling, first, to attempt to spin the Dean comments and, then, to denounce my repeated play of them. There is no greater sign of a powerful message than its denunciation by the opposing side. Dean's people, more than anyone else, knew that he could not survive a reputation for bizarre conspiracy thinking, so they rallied to the phones to try to blunt the message immediately. Too late for my show, and far too late for Krauthammer. Dean hadn't corrected his own display of nuttiness, and you don't get a second chance in presidential campaigns.

CHAPTER 30

CONTROLLING THE INFORMATION FLOW, PART 2: THE USE OF TALK RADIO

Why does an ad on a nationally syndicated talk radio show cost so much? A minute on *The Rush Limbaugh Show* or the *Sean Hannity Show* costs thousands; on my show or Michael Medved's or Laura Ingrahm's or Dennis Prager's, the minute costs hundreds. On a local talk show, the cost can be as low as $10 or as high as a few hundred bucks.

Why such a range, and why can the rate get so high?

Advertisers pay for audience. The bigger the audience, the more the show can charge per minute of ad.

This elementary principle drives all of advertising in every medium: print, radio, television, billboards, and the Internet. People trying to sell products pay to reach eyes and ears. Talk radio commands a lot of ad revenue because it delivers a large audience.

How large is difficult to calculate. Unlike television ratings, which can be deduced via electronic gizmos attached to television sets, radio depends upon a wholly unsatisfactory process: listener-maintained diaries. Listeners are asked to write down their listening choices and send the diaries into a reporting service that tallies the numbers.

Unfortunately most people can't be troubled to do this, and high-income people especially reject the idea of doing this. So ratings are mere guesses, and they significantly underreport the tastes of the educated and the upper middle class.

Even a system that substantially undercounts moderately to highly educated people nevertheless reveals that millions of Americans are tuning in to talk radio programs every week. A University of Michigan study from 1996 found that more men than women listened to talk radio, that the listeners were older, earned more than the average American, were more educated than the average American, and were more likely to pay attention to government—but how many listeners are there?

The American Radio News Audience Survey, conducted by the Radio and Television News Directors Foundation, indicated that Americans between the ages of eighteen and sixty-four listen to an average of three hours of radio every weekday, and that close to "one-half of all radio listening involves news or talk content." Thirty percent of the radio audience are classified as "light" or "heavy" listeners to talk radio. A full 14 percent of the adult population are considered "heavy" listeners to talk radio.

Talkers Magazine, a trade publication, uses a very unscientific methodology to conclude that Rush Limbaugh has a weekly audience of more than 14 million. The exact size of Rush's vast audience cannot be determined with precision, but it seems clear that it is the largest, regularly recurring audience in America today for a political show. Nothing else comes close. All of the cable news networks' prime-time shows combined do not equal Rush's daytime audience.

That's why ads that run on his show cost so much—he delivers a huge audience, and an educated, affluent, politically active one at that.

So does Sean Hannity. So do I. So do Glenn Beck, Laura Ingraham, Michael Medved, Bill O'Reilly, Dennis Prager, Michael Reagan, and Michael Savage. Every nationally syndicated political talk show host assembles an audience in the millions every week.

Most local hosts have good-sized audiences as well, and most of those audiences have large numbers of affluent, educated listeners interested in news and politics.

These audiences represent a large portion of the American electorate, and a portion that can fairly be understood to be opinion shapers. Because the consumers of talk radio are themselves relayers of the opinions and facts they hear, the actual audience of each of these shows is much larger than those who actually tune in.

How often have you heard someone say, "I heard Rush say . . . ," or "Sean Hannity was interviewing a senator today . . . ," or "Hugh Hewitt had a caller today who said . . ."?

How many times have you regaled someone with an anecdote you heard on a talk radio show?

Talk radio is one of those force multipliers that matters so much in modern communication—an original platform that comes with an echo chamber built in. We can never know how far the messages carry, but they carry very far indeed.

Which is why the advertising is so expensive.

And why the criticism from the Left is so harsh, and why the envy of the Left is so deep.

Of course, you have heard the Democrats complaining about talk radio. Bill Clinton started it with an explicit attack on Rush during Clinton's first term. Clinton's fabled political antennae failed him on that count because in attacking Rush, he brought Rush huge attention and an even greater audience.

Despicable commentary attempted to link talk radio to nutty and dangerous extremists in the aftermath of the Oklahoma City bombing, but not even a slur of that proportion could slow down the growth rate of the format. Prior to the rise of the Internet, the blogosphere within the Internet, and the Fox News Channel, the center-right audience had nowhere to go but talk radio. And they went there and they stayed.

Democratic Party professionals knew what this meant, but they had no counter. So the hysteria grew from election to election, and now the denunciations of the "right-wing hit machine" are so routine as to have no weight in the public's mind. Hysterical complaints diminish in impact even as patient recitation of facts increases the impact of those facts. Truths settle in when they are persuasive. Rants fade.

My colleagues have always been quick to welcome any attempt by the Left to launch their own programs because such efforts are all the proof anyone needs that radio shows succeed because they draw audiences that sell ads. When the Left tries and repeatedly fails to succeed in the format, it underscores the bankruptcy of the argument that "right-wing talk" is some sort of conspiracy. It is just the market. And Dems grow quite glum when the black-and-white numbers of ad revenues and audience growth demonstrate that market forces favor the center-right coalition and thus the GOP. The liberal Air America had a huge free-media assist at its launch, and still it struggles—another bit of evidence as to why liberals hate talk radio: they lack the talent and the audience to support shows that favor the Left.

The facts of the cost of advertising and of repeated Democratic attacks on the medium should also tell you that your participation in the great conversation is important.

My first program director, Los Angeles station KFI's George Oliva, told me to never forget that the vast, vast majority of the audience never calls, and that blinking lights signifying callers don't necessarily mean good radio. As my colleague in San Diego, Mark Larson, has frequently said, a psychic hotline show can always keep the phones blinking, but there is no audience for such stuff.

But the interesting callers do matter a lot to the show, and you can consider a good call to any radio show as a contribution to the reelection of whichever candidate you are promoting. Remember, though, that a bad call is like a contribution to your candidate's opponent.

I welcome calls from the Left, especially the passionate Left. These callers tend to be irrational and excitable. Americans don't much like wild-eyed folks from either end of the political spectrum. They unsettle us. We like our leaders to be commonsense, rational, purposeful folk, though we like some humor thrown in. Howard Dean's weird intensity was very off-putting for most Americans, and his Iowa meltdown sent his campaign into a tailspin. President Bush's amiability, by contrast, is quite reassuring.

Members of my audience love to listen to the wild-eyed, but they don't want to vote for them. When Dean Dongs called, I was as happy as could be. They helped the center-right by scaring the center Left toward the center.

But there is also an opportunity for the center-right to use the platform of talk radio at every level to send messages that need to be sent.

If you call a talk show and are given even a few seconds to speak, you can advance the center-right agenda.

If you don't choke, that is. Most people simply choke.

What do I mean by choking? Arriving unprepared and nervous, most callers stumble over the greeting, become self-conscious over their error, and then mumble some sort of half-sentence that leaves me or any other host wondering what they are trying to say. Opportunity wasted. Call ends (and depending on the host, with or without some mockery thrown it).

Here's what you have to do.

Ask yourself, *Why call?* If the answer is to help reelect the president, for example, then arm yourself with at least one statement of fact that can't be refuted and a source for the fact. Example: "The Department of Labor announced that the country added 150,000 jobs this month. That means Bush's tax cuts are working!" Once you have made the statement, your call is a success, no matter what happens next. A key fact has been launched. It will be absorbed by the vast audience. It will circulate and recirculate. If you get a chance to repeat it in the course of the conversation, great, but no matter. Mission accomplished.

Same thing with this example: "Saddam is in prison, and he can no longer invade his neighbors or murder his innocent citizens or keep children in jail. He can no longer subsidize suicide bombers or run rest homes for terrorists like Abu Nidal. Bush took him out." Chances are, you are going to get that much in before being interrupted. Such messages matter.

Sure, hosts will interrupt you, mock you, scold you. But your message gets through. If the message is persuasive, that's all that matters.

Don't call with crazy arguments or personal attacks on opponents. They sound stupid when voiced by amateurs. Sure, Dr. Dean was a big target, but you wouldn't think of fixing your own car, so don't try to do my job. Instead, speak the positive on the radio, and do it again and again.

If you pick up the phone and call with a message of support for the president but one preceded by a statement of fact concerning his record, you have assisted the effort to persuade a country of the correct course it ought to follow. The Bush-Cheney 2004 campaign didn't have to buy a thirty-second ad to get that message across, and you didn't have to write a check to do so.

Of course, the Left can try to do the same thing and frequently does. These are the fabled "seminar callers" that Rush exposed years ago, the "plants" of the talk radio world, and I love them. Seminar callers pass themselves off as "friends" or "allies" but want to give a seminar on the failings of the officeholder or candidate they purport to support.

Inauthenticity is easily exposed. Liars are easily discovered. Truth is a superior force to falsehood. And the resort to trickery is a fundamental admission of an inability to present a case.

Democratic callers who want to score points off George W. Bush are welcome on my show and most of my colleagues' shows. They are not a serious threat to the audience when it comes to persuading the audience because they don't generally arrive with a statement of fact like the one outlined above. Any host familiar with the facts of American political life welcomes the ill-informed caller, but doesn't screen out the well prepared either. Battles of ideas can't be won unless they are joined.

But no matter what supporters of John Kerry or other Lefties do, you should realize that your investment in preparing for and calling a show with an audience is an investment in the effort to persuade America that its cause is just and its present leadership competent, solid, and courageous.

These messages need to get through. They matter almost as much as contributions and votes, but they are not risk free and require some effort. In Appendix I, I have listed the Ten Key Talking Points for 2004. Use them if you are uncertain of other points, but in any event, call.

Every single call to every single radio show is an opportunity to advance the politics of peace through strength and economic security through growth. Don't miss your opportunity to contribute to that effort.

CHAPTER 31

CONTROLLING THE INFORMATION FLOW, PART 3: THE LETTERS PAGE

T his is the chapter where cynics roll their eyes. It is the exhortation to write "letters to the editor." You know, the daily shotgun of one or two dozen letters that appear opposite the unsigned editorials.

For years party professionals have urged would-be activists to send their written thoughts on crucial subjects to the papers in the regions wherein they live. For years some have answered the call. Most have not.

I am in the latter category. If it isn't 750 words or more, I'm not interested. Increasingly I'm not interested in newsprint generally because circulation is falling and the influence of papers plummeting. But I have alternative means of communicating open to me that most readers don't.

For a long stretch, letters to the editor were all a citizen had. In the age of blogging, talk radio, and e-mail list-servers, any activist worth his salt can communicate with hundreds or thousands and not have to trust to the sympathies of the letters' editor.

But the pros still advise the volunteers and the activists to take the invitation seriously to send in their two cents' worth to the local paper. The 2003 success of the Dean campaign was built on many pillars, but that organization always stressed such letters.

The best letters are short, contain a key fact or two, and reiterate important messages that have already been articulated by GOP leaders. If a particularly contentious legislative issue is coming to a head, for example, the writers are best advised to listen for the themes articulated by the president, Senator Frist, or Speaker Hastert and then to revise those themes in their own language and send them away.

Typically the letters will never see the light of day. But if one hundred are submitted, a few will get through. Even the most imbalanced editorial page—say, that of the *Los Angeles Times*—will admit a few opposing voices onto the letters page.

The sophisticates sniff at such efforts. The pros know these columns are short but sincere epistles to a significant audience. Like waves on rocks, they do have effect, even if imperceptible.

So pick up a pen and do your part.

CHAPTER 32

CONTROLLING THE INFORMATION FLOW, PART 4: USING THE BLOGOSPHERE

W hen a caller to my show begins by asking, "What's a blog?" I know two things. I know he hasn't been listening long since I discuss blogs almost every day. And I know he is a low consumer of information.

High consumers of information spend a significant part of every day searching for information on whatever subject concerns them, whether it is politics, economics, stock prices, the weather, sports, or fashion. No matter what the core interests, high consumers of info are in the hunt every day and sometimes many times a day.

High consumers of info, by the way, are typically at the top of their fields because information advantage is a key to success in almost every field.

Moderate consumers of information have set up their lives to receive regular and substantial infusions of information about the topics they care about. Perhaps they take a paper or two, watch a couple of shows, listen to the radio. They are not clueless, but neither are they passionate about staying ahead of the information curve.

Low consumers of info drift along. If some information hits them in the head, it registers. If not, it doesn't.

Blogs are very much a part of the world of high-information consumers because they are the children of the Internet age. If you spend much time on the Web, you know about blogs.

Blog is short for "Web log"—an online site with time-dated postings, maintained by one or more posters, that features links and commentary. That is the most basic definition. But it is like saying a car is a means of transportation featuring four wheels.

There are literally millions of blogs, with more being established every day. Many are started and abandoned, but most are maintained for at least a few months. My own blog, www.hughhewitt.com, was launched in early 2002 and averages more than 10,000 visitors a day. It passed its 2 millionth visitor in early 2004 and will pass 3 million by the conventions of 2004.

HughHewitt.com is a relatively new and moderately successful blog. I use it to bring my readers' and listeners' attentions to stories that I judge to be important, and to circulate my commentary on those stories as well as any other subject on which I choose to opine. HughHewitt.com is my own opinion page with a readership greater than most small town dailies.

My blog is part of the political blog universe in which there are thousands of entries. The most important center-right blogs, given the volume of visitors and the "echo" they produce in the blogosphere at this writing, are www.instapundit.com, www.lileks.com, and www.andrewsullivan.com, but there are perhaps fifty that matter a great deal in the world of politics. I include a current list of a few center-right blogs that beginners might want to sample in Appendix H. You need to start reading these blogs, and you need to start your own if you wish to be an effective participant in the world of politics and in the cause of destroying the power of the Democratic Party. Blogging is one field of contest between liberals and conservatives, one field of competition between Democrats and Republicans.

It is not the most important field by far, but it does matter. The blogosphere—which is the name given to the entire Internet community of blogs—is part of the infrastructure by which political ideas are developed and communicated. Blogs are like small radio stations or small circulation newspapers: they are influencers of opinion.

The better the blog, the more readers it attracts. The more readers, the more widespread the dissemination of the opinions contained on the blog.

It is that simple.

The political region of the blogosphere is credited with two major stories in recent years—the toppling of Trent Lott as majority leader and the ouster of Howell Raines as editor in chief of *The New York Times*.

Both claims have been disputed, but both have their defenders. In each instance, stories were developed on various blogs and grew in importance via repetition and elaboration until the mainstream, elite press took note and began to follow the stories with vigor. Media frenzies developed—firestorms, really, or what I took to calling "opinion storms." When such an opinion storm develops, almost every corner of media gets involved, and the stories take on a life and momentum of their own.

In the case of Howell Raines, the blogosphere provided a home for two of his most acidic and talented critics—Andrew Sullivan, who writes at www.andrewsullivan.com, and Mickey Kaus, who writes Kausfiles for the online journal *Slate* (www.kausfiles.com). When word began to break that a young *New York Times* reporter, Jayson Blair, had lied about his sources and his stories, Sullivan and Kaus jumped on the story and drove it farther almost daily. Soon other Web sites were in the hunt, and a chorus of indignation arose, which flowed into other newspapers and throughout the institutions of American political power.

Each day brought new details, and Sullivan and Kaus became must-reads for everyone interested in the scandals at the *Times*. Both writers speculated whether big boss Raines—an imperious and hard Left–leaning aristocrat—could survive the revelations about the slipshod way in which he had managed not only Blair's career but also the entire news operation. Others joined in the speculation, and a critical mass of opinion was generated that the great beacon of American journalism could not regain its reputation as long as Raines remained. When his resignation arrived, it seemed in retrospect as though it had been inevitable.

But it hadn't been inevitable. Most observers agree that absent a blogosphere to fuel and drive the story, Raines would be editing the paper to this day. But with daily updates on these two sites and scores more, hunkering down was simply not an option.

Senator Trent Lott of Mississippi must still be wondering what hit him. One day his leadership of the GOP in the "world's greatest deliberative body" was unchallenged, and the next he was under fire for a toast he had offered the retiring Strom Thurmond, the one-hundred-year-old senator from South Carolina who had once run for the presidency on a segregationist platform.

In making the salute to Thurmond, Lott had stated in passing that a lot of people thought the country would have been better off if Strom had won his quixotic race for the White House in 1948. While certainly a ham-handed way of paying tribute, the remark was not initially understood by the media to be an endorsement of Thurmond's long-ago repudiated segregationist views.

But the blogosphere, principally in the form of *National Review*'s group blog, The Corner, asked tough questions about Lott's rhetoric and, in doing so, cued a gang tackle of Lott. After these conservative writers exposed Lott's weakness among folks who ought to have been supporters, reporters swooped in from every corner of the country to speculate on what Lott meant and didn't mean. Lott retreated into a "no comment" mode and then began to offer up apology after apology, but the fire lit by bloggers kept burning brighter and brighter. When President Bush added his criticisms to those of practically every commentator in the country, Lott's support in the Senate broke, and in days he announced he was stepping down as majority leader. Senator Bill Frist of Tennessee replaced him, and the national Republican Party had a new and far more sympathetic national spokesman, given Bill Frist's credentials as an accomplished heart surgeon.

Again, without a blogosphere, there would have been no momentum behind the story. Trent Lott would still, in the minds of many, be the GOP's majority leader.

Speculation about what might have happened had the Internet not spawned its blogs is beside the point. The world of blogs—24/7 news and commentary coupled with a fierce accountability and instant fact-checking—exists. Both parties have entered this election season with a commitment to managing the blogosphere.

There were blogs at both www.georgewbush.com and www.dean-foramerica.com. Both sites also maintained a lengthy "blogroll"—a list of hundreds of other blogs recommended for visits. The blogrolls are lengthy because inclusion is easier than exclusion, and the degree of differentiation is so advanced that it just pays to make sure every conceivable "friendly" is included. The Dean campaign embraced the blogosphere in a way no other campaign ever had, and the benefits to Dean were immense, though fleeting. Here is how *The New York Times Magazine* captured the impact of the blogging phenomenon on the Dean campaign in a December 7, 2003, profile by Samantha M. Shapiro:

This national network of people communicates through, and takes inspiration from, the Dean Web log, or blog, where official campaign representatives post messages a few times a day and invite comments from the public. The unofficial campaign interacts daily with the campaign in other ways as well. When Jeff Horowitz, a full-time volunteer, needs help compiling news articles that make the staff's daily internal press briefing, he e-mails a request for help to a list of supporters he has never met, asking them to perform Internet news searches at certain times and then e-mail him the results. "Ten people will volunteer to give me a news summary by 8 A.M.," Horowitz explains. "People in California, which means they have to get up at 4 A.M." A number of campaign staffers are in regular contact with Jonathan Kreiss-Tomkins, 14, who lives in Sitka, Alaska. Growing up on a remote Alaskan island, Kreiss-Tomkins has become especially adept at finding pen pals and online friends, and he now uses that skill on behalf of the Dean campaign, recruiting supporters through the Internet and then sending lists of e-mail addresses to the campaign.

Dean's opponents have begun to mimic the trappings of his campaign. Many of the Democratic candidates now have blogs. Even President Bush has one, though comments from the public— an essential element of Dean's blog—are not allowed. The Dean campaign tracks online contributions with the image of a base-ball bat (at one point, the Web site added a new bat for every $1 million raised); shortly after the Dean campaign raised its first million dollars, John Kerry's campaign took up the Web icon of a hammer. But Dean's Internet campaign dwarfs those of his rivals. In the third quarter of 2003, Kerry raised in the vicinity of $1 million online; Dean raised more than $7 million. A typi-cal post of the Kerry blog receives, on average, 18 comments, while Dean blog posts generally receive more than a hundred. The Dean Web site is visited with roughly the same frequency as the White House Web site.

Shapiro's tone was breathless, and it was probably her first assignment covering a presidential campaign. Every presidential campaign is full of volunteers who believe they have invented a new kind of campaign, one full of genuine passion and commitment. In truth, the Dean campaign was the Ford campaign with text messaging, e-mail, and cell phones. But it had adapted the new technology, and once a technology is in play, everyone needs to master it.

Perhaps you saw Tom Cruise's recent epic, *The Last Samurai*. Forgive me if you didn't because I have to comment on the movie's end. The very honorable samurai charge Gatling guns, and they lose. Decisively. New technologies do that to old technologies.

The Internet is not a brand-new technology, but political organizing via the Internet is, as is the dissemination of information via blogs. Given that blogs are here to stay, with enormous power and even greater poten-tial, what should an activist do?

Why, master the technology, of course.

That means, first, reading the major blogs regularly for a good period of time to understand what sets some apart and gains audiences for them.

Then, having figured out the basics, launch a blog via whatever platform, like "blogspot," that is then dominant. Posts all over the Web explain the mechanics of getting started, but the message of this chapter is this: get started. Joe Carter at www.evangelicaloutpost.com wrote a great series of posts on getting started.

It is crucial for the center-right to maintain a constant flow of new bloggers into the blogosphere because sheer numbers matter and because genuine talent will rise out of the mass of bloggers. I have on my Web site a blogroll, and within that blogroll I have a section devoted to the Young Justice League of America, my name for a collection of under-twenty-five bloggers with real talent accompanied by the senses of irony and humor that are essential to blogosphere success.

I have carved out this area and routinely promote it because if center-right ideas are to prosper, they need carriers much younger than I am to press them forward in the years ahead. At one time opinion punditry was confined to a handful of aging center Left columnists and talking heads who fought their way up the media food chain.

No more. Now anyone with an Internet connection and some basic skills can join the fray. The talented ones gain readers and, with readers, influence. The smart bloggers who have been at it for a few years do what they can to promote the good, young talent.

A decade from now the bloggers who dominate today's traffic-monitoring sites will almost all have declined or ceased to exist. New voices will have arisen. If the center-right puts a production system into place now and nurtures it with encouragement and attention, it will have the infrastructure to continue to dominate the information dissemination phase of campaigning.

High consumers of information are always going to be out there prowling for data and opinions. The party that organizes to meet that demand wins in the long run. Blogging is an essential part of that effort.

CHAPTER 33

WINNING CONVERTS

political realignment like the one we are experiencing is the consequence of dramatic events such as the attack on America and the sudden, widespread recognition that we are in a war that challenges our survival as a free society. Such explosive moments demolish old arrangements and coalitions, leaving them arrayed in dramatically altered states.

Jewish Americans, for example, voted overwhelmingly for Al Gore in 2000. Most observers expect significant defections from this demographic to the president's column in 2004 as a result of his firm support for Israel and his commitment to winning the war on terror.

As is spelled out elsewhere, Catholics and blue collars are also leaving the Democratic column in numbers that could not have been predicted in 2000.

The big events of terrorism and war scramble and then reassemble the political map. But it is individual persuasion that cements the new coalition into place.

If every Republican activist cemented a transitional voter into the GOP, the new majority would be assured a generation or more in power.

How is this done? Lots of ways, but there are two most effective techniques.

Give a transitional voter a book.

Or give a transitional voter a magazine subscription.

Better yet, do both.

The moment you sense disgust with the Democrats on the part of a Democrat, see a shift to the right by an independent, or hear a favorable opinion voiced of George W. Bush by a longtime critic, that is really the invitation to drive a lever into the crack in that voter's opinion wall and push with great energy. Hectoring won't work. But the very sophisticated flattery of a book will.

Which book? Well, this year there are three.

There's this one. It lays out the case for voting GOP and does not demand a month-long commitment from the reader. It'll go down easy if I've done a good job.

And there's Rich Lowry's *Legacy*, a wonderful review of the failures of the Clinton presidency, devastating in its accumulation of details and anecdotes.

There's also John Podhoretz's *Bush's Country*, an excellent summary of George W. Bush's first three years in office.

If you give to someone Lowry's, Podhoretz's, and my books, and the recipient reads all three, he will not vote Democratic again if he is open-minded at all.

But some folks aren't book readers. They'll spend ten minutes reading politics or maybe even a half hour, but never much more than that.

For them, your best bet is a subscription to *The Weekly Standard*.

I have contributed to this magazine and write a weekly column for its online edition, so I'm biased.

But *The Weekly Standard* is center-right, wonderfully written, eclectic, and persuasive. If it is put into the hands of an open-minded person, it will reinforce that individual's opinions and instincts with facts and analysis.

Bill Kristol, Fred Barnes, Terry Eastland, Stephen Hayes, Matt Labash, Claudia Winkler, Jonathan Last, J. Bottum, David Tell, and the rest put out forty-eight issues a year that track the latest headlines. A subscription costs $40. Giving such a gift to a thinking friend is a genuine gesture of respect and affection.

These are confusing times, and the tidal wave of information is growing larger, not less. When you see an opening, take it. Especially if the flexible mind belongs to an opinion leader or to a young adult.

The average American will get fifteen presidential votes. Influence an eighteen-year-old and you've influenced more than a dozen election cycles.

You are not the best advocate for the GOP. But you can summon those who are the best advocates to your side.

A warning. Some authors and columnists ought not to be given to the transitional voter. Ann Coulter is great for the true believer looking for a romp in his own worldview, but even the titles of her books, *Treason* and *Slander*, repel the undecided rather than attract.

We are lucky to have Ann going hand to hand with the knucklehead Left on the cable knife fights, and giving college audiences a jolt of un-PC intellectual adrenaline. But she and writers like her are not the stuff of conversion.

A tone and a tempo need to be used when a voter has begun to question his basic assumptions. Don't overplay your hand.

CHAPTER 34

SUPPORT THE
PEOPLE WHO SUPPORT
YOUR POLITICS

When people tell me they love my radio show, I often respond by asking, "Did you buy your car from William L. Morris Chevrolet (www.morrischevy.com), refinance your mortgage with Roger Schlesinger (1-877-304-4844), shop online for health food and vitamin products at www.vitaganza.com, buy life insurance from James Johnson Life Insurance Agency (1-800-400-9434). These people keep me on the air. If you want me on the air, patronize the people who put me there.

This is one expression of a crucial and elementary principle of politics: help the people who help your people.

Sulla was a Roman general and politician who chose to become a ruthless dictator a few years before Julius Caesar came to power. His tomb is inscribed with a famous epitaph: "No friend has done me a favor, nor enemy an injury, that I have not repaid in full."

Simple stuff. Chilling in the context of a dictator with life-or-death power, but simply persuasive in the context of American politics.

You like what Rush, Sean, Michael, Laura, Dennis, and I have to say? Then listen to the list of our sponsors and patronize them.

You like what the president is doing? Then subscribe to magazines and papers that support him.

You don't like the fact that the *Los Angeles Times* is a tip sheet for the hard Left caucus of the Democratic Party? Then cancel your subscription and buy *The Orange County Register* or the *Los Angeles Daily News*.

Pay attention to what corporations and their executives do with their political dollars. It is pretty easy to figure out the white hats and black hats in politics. If it is important enough to vote, it is just as important not to undo your vote by sending money to a company that is working with every Lefty in town, in the state, or at the national level. Buying Ben & Jerry's Ice Cream in the years when its owners were still the nutty socialists who founded the company was arming the Left with funds to destroy the economy.

Let's stipulate that most car dealers are neutral on matters of politics. So why not ask before you arrive on the lot? Or why not ask your local GOP Party leaders if there are any car dealers who have helped the party?

Take my friend Jeff Morris, a sponsor of my show. Jeff has been standing up for the Boy Scouts against the PC police of Ventura County for nearly a decade. When the United Way of Ventura County cut off the funding of the Boy Scouts because of the Scouts' policy against allowing gay men to be scoutmasters, Jeff spearheaded a very successful effort to replace the lost funding. In fact, they ended up raising far more money for the Scouts than the United Way pulled.

Jeff's stand took guts. Before he became a sponsor of my show, I had Jeff on the program to highlight his activity. Then he turned around and sponsored my show. Then I bought my next car from him, even though his dealership is more than one hundred miles from my home. (Nowadays, with Internet pricing and interstate delivery, distance matters not at all.)

That's one example of reciprocity from among thousands.

Again, if it matters enough to vote, it should also matter to do more obvious things to reinforce that vote.

Maurice Knott is a fine older gent living in retirement in Orange County, California. Maurice loves my books. He buys dozens of them for his friends. I say, "God bless Maurice Knott!" I wish that everyone else understood the power of such loyalty.

If you are a corporate type, let me ask you: What did you spend on legal bills last year? A lot, right? That's to be expected. Good lawyers are worth every penny.

But what happens to that money after it goes through the firm and into the individual partners' pockets? I know a great number of excellent lawyers who are very left of center. They make their bones representing home builders, as I have for many years, but then turn around and contribute good-sized chunks and cash to Democratic Senators Barbara Boxer and Dianne Feinstein. Why not find a firm that doesn't help elect enemies of your bottom line? Most people can't be bothered to take the time to find a firm helping conservatives through donations, but they are quick to moan about legislation that allows plaintiffs' lawyers to abuse the builders again and again.

Some object that this accountability is "unfair" or "un-American." Nonsense. Shareholders would say it is responsible corporate governance.

Each and every transaction we enter into has a political dimension, right down to whether or not we bought Ben & Jerry's Ice Cream when the two guys running it were wing nuts.

Many Americans refused to buy French wine in the aftermath of France's obstructionism in the run-up to the liberation of Iraq. It was an easily understood and deeply felt bit of consumer payback. It was just as easy to buy California wine, so why reward France when it was possible to achieve the same end without doing so?

As with everything in politics, moderation should govern the principle of rewarding friends and punishing enemies. In May of this year, my radio network dispatched me on a cruise of the Mediterranean, which made the network money. The cruise stopped in Marseilles. I went ashore but didn't spend money. As I said, moderation.

But clearly we make decisions every day that can reinforce our political values, just as there are choices that can undermine those values. It is best to return favors and to keep close track of the politics of the ones with whom you do business.

CHAPTER 35

SUBSCRIBE TO THE MAGAZINES THAT USUALLY SUPPORT THE GOP

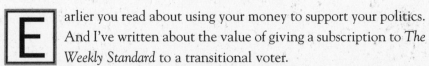

E arlier you read about using your money to support your politics. And I've written about the value of giving a subscription to *The Weekly Standard* to a transitional voter.

This chapter is different. Regardless of what you do with your dough or whether you have ever met in the past or will in the future meet a transitional voter, please subscribe to *The Weekly Standard*, *National Review*, *Commentary*, *The American Spectator*, and *World*.

These magazines are the research arm of the center-right in America. They employ the investigative reporters and polemicists who provide the facts and analysis that the center-right needs to make its case and to influence the news cycle.

A great number of the debates over the politics generally and the conduct of the war specifically take shape first in the pages of newspapers, on television, and in the political press.

Most newspapers and television staffs are hostile to the center-right. Without the work product of the center-right political press, the GOP would be severely hampered in the information war.

These magazines depend on subscriptions and ad revenue to survive.

They have pretty small audiences, in the tens of thousands. If political activists subscribed in anywhere near their real numbers, these publications would flourish and employ more staff and produce more stories full of more facts useful to winning more elections.

The political press is a crucial part of the engine that powers the center-right. Help maintain the engine. Here's where to call for subscriptions:

- *The Weekly Standard:* 800-283-2014
- *National Review:* 815-734-1232
- *Commentary:* 800-829-6270
- *The American Spectator:* 800-524-3469
- *World:* 800-951-NEWS

The great news about these calls is that you get a great product in return.

PART VI

"DANGER, WILL ROBINSON, DANGER!"

We all like to hear a man speak out on his convictions and principles, but at the same time, you must understand that when you're running on a ticket, you're running on a team.

—Richard Daley

CHAPTER 36

ABORTION, GUNS, AND THE ENVIRONMENT

T his isn't a policy wonk book. It is about winning elections in a time of war when bad electoral results can disable a war effort and result in the deaths of hundreds of thousands of Americans. Because the focus is on winning elections, it is necessary to look at particular issues from the perspective of whether they advance the cause of electing candidates who will defend the country vigorously and effectively. Three issues in particular can sink Republicans if handled poorly: abortion, guns, and the environment.

ABORTION

Each year I teach the Supreme Court's abortion cases to law students. I do so with the intent that they learn the law in order to be equipped to pass a state bar exam that tests them on the subject.

No matter how professional the approach or dispassionate the tone, always this class is tense with emotion. For three decades abortion has been widespread in the United States. Tens of millions of women have had abortions, and each year tens of thousands of marchers commemorate January 25, 1973, the day when the United States Supreme Court struck down the laws of any state that had placed serious obstacles on a woman's right to secure an abortion.

I am a right-to-life Republican who hopes someday to see the Supreme Court admit that its case law in this area is incoherent and its many attempts at "solving" the abortion problem have been false starts. This is a complex issue that requires legislative answers, not judicial decrees. Only when voters believe that their view has been heard and their votes felt will the deep bitterness over judicial imperialism in this most sensitive area subside.

The only way for the issue to be returned to legislative control, however, is for the federal courts generally, and the United States Supreme Court specifically, to be populated with genuine constitutionalists—jurists who understand and abide by the principle that our government cannot endure unless elected representatives decide all of the major issues of our society.

The appointment of such judges requires the election of Republicans at every level of the government, but especially in the presidency. Thus, the *real* pro-life voter will always vote Republican and will do so without threats and demands and loud condemnation of nominees who are insufficiently attentive to their causes.

Pro-choice absolutists cannot expect to control the Republican Party. As a matter of math, the GOP is a pro-life party. If abortion rights is the only issue of import to you, you ought to leave the GOP for the Democratic Party *if* you believe the issue must be decided by judges. If you are a pro-choice advocate who trusts in the legislative process, by all means stay.

To both factions within the Republican Party, an appeal: we are in a war, and your debate, crucial as it is, must take a second seat for at least a few years. It will be a debate of little consequence in the aftermath of a catastrophic attack on the United States.

There are shelves full of books on the abortion controversy. Very few people are of a persuadable view on the issue, which is why party politics ought not to try to persuade beyond the idea that elected representatives, not appointed ones, ought to be answering the questions of when and under what conditions abortions ought to be available.

I can hear the complaints even as I write this. They are the same complaints I have heard for a dozen years of broadcast journalism. But most of the electorate does not cast its vote based upon this issue, and the collective distaste for the conversation is now so pronounced that the side that forces the conversation is the side that loses ground.

There is a majority opinion that abortion is a very wrong, but necessary freedom in the early months of a pregnancy. There is a majority opinion that abortion after even three months is a profound moral failing and that it is reprehensible late in a pregnancy. The political dynamic of the country does not welcome a debate over those positions. Pro-lifers who wish and pray for courageous judges who will stand with legislative discretion are well and fully advised to work quietly—quietly—for the election of politicians who stand with the conservative opinion.

It really is that simple.

GUNS

My brother-in-law, a retired lieutenant colonel from the United States Marine Corps, owns three dozen weapons from the most lethal of legal weapons to a black powder rifle. George routinely competes in and wins skeet competitions. He's a serious collector and marksman and a safety nut. On the times he has taken me shooting, he has impressed me with his comprehensive concern for safety, and I believe him to be the norm for members of the National Rifle Association.

A fellow television professional of my acquaintance carries an unlicensed pistol in his glove compartment. He works late hours in the tough parts of Los Angeles. He has never fired his weapon in anger. He is also a Second Amendment guy.

My producer on *Searching for God in America*, a genuine PBS Lefty, took his .22 rifle to high school on hunting days and left it in his Idaho school's cloakroom along with all the other weapons. No big deal in the '70s.

Guns are part of the American fabric, and only a fool would tell any of the three people noted here that they can't have their weapons. Terrible accidents happen, and sometimes nuts go nuts with automatic weapons, and carnage and tragedy result.

But guns aren't going away. Ever.

No Republican should ever think about pushing a gun control agenda on the party.

But the gun absolutists have to realize that the prohibition on individuals owning machine guns and high-powered automatic weapons makes sense to a large majority of Americans. So if the GOP agrees with this consensus, the gun absolutists should sit down and shut up. By demanding a theoretical purity, they endanger a working majority.

Control of assault weapons is not the first step down the slippery slope. It isn't even a slope. It's called a broad consensus. Live with it, strengthen your side, and all will be well.

The time and money that gun absolutists spend attacking GOP politicians who embrace the consensus position are wasted. Put the effort into strengthening the party across the board.

THE ENVIRONMENT

The first two issues that make up the political Bermuda Triangle are full of statistics of interest.

There have been more than 44 million abortions in the United States since the 1973 decision in *Roe v. Wade*.

The rate of abortion peaked in 1990, when more than 1.4 million abortions were performed, and in 2003 the Centers for Disease Control estimated that approximately 860,000 abortions occurred.

There are an estimated 235 million firearms in the United States. Slightly more than 40 percent of U.S. households have a firearm within them, and 28 percent of Americans are gun owners.

There are about 1,100 accidental deaths due to firearms each year. About 18,000 people kill themselves with guns each year, and about 14,000 victims are murdered with firearms each year.

You get the picture. The universe of data for both abortion and guns is broad and fairly agreed upon, though some groups might quibble with particular data sets.

This is not the case with the environment. *The environment* is itself a hugely ambiguous term that can mean clean water or clean air, global warming or wetland loss, fuel efficiency or ozone depletion, endangered species controversies or the use of pesticides.

But there is one indisputable fact about the environment: as a political issue, it works for the Democrats. Because Democrats have been rather shameless in their exploitation of the fears of the average modern American, the Democratic Party has successfully painted the GOP as anti-environment.

There's not much sense complaining about this and bringing up Teddy Roosevelt, the GOP hero who started the national park system. The apparatus of the Left when it comes to environmental propaganda is vast and powerful, and the symbols appropriated by the Left are also powerful—from baby seals to majestic vistas and breathtaking glimpses of deep ocean mystery.

The GOP does what it can to counter the nonsense and the scare-mongering of the Left, and to point out the horrible failures of collectivist environmentalism, but the press is arrayed against the Republicans on this issue and there's not much hope of cracking the united front of media and hard Left environmental activism. The environment is a substitute for religious faith for many, and no reformers or prophets ever pursued their vision with greater conviction or ferocity than environmental activists.

A long study on "swing voters" from the January 2004 edition of *The Atlantic Monthly* concluded that the environment was "one of the few 'wedge issues' available to Democrats, and an issue pollsters believe is the primary motivator for six percent of the voters."

Both bad and good news can be found in that conclusion, which is consistent with my experience from all my years as a broadcast journalist and as a natural resources lawyer for property owners.

The bad news is that voters who are motivated by the environment are not going to vote for the GOP in large numbers. It will take a defining and high-profile initiative like TR's to establish the national park system to redefine the GOP in this area. Although such an effort would be great policy and politics—$10 billion for new imperiled habitats acquisition, for example—it still would not likely be decisive with this 6 percent.

The good news is that it is *only* 6 percent. The vast majority of Americans want only reassurance that, as is true and will remain true, the Republican Party will protect the national consensus on clean air and water and preservation of the national parks. Over the past ten years the endangered species horror stories have grown so numerous as to have drained any electoral power from appeals to save the cave bugs, fairy shrimp, and Delhi sands flower-loving flies, but the public still wants rhetorical buy-ins from GOP candidates on the consensus that smog is bad and clean water is good.

The GOP could go wrong in pushing for "efficiency" in this area. The environmental laws are notoriously inefficient and do not deliver on their loftiest goals, but Republicans cannot be maneuvered into pushing such debates.

Reform of the nation's environmental laws lies with the Left. It's a "Nixon to China" thing, and the GOP is simply not well positioned to lead in this area. Some efforts are under way on the left, with brave scientists pushing the sort of hard science that makes the activists cringe, but whatever the temptation to rush in, the GOP must allow the Left to carry these efforts.

James Watt did a lot of damage to the GOP during his tenure at the Department of Interior, and while Bruce Babbitt was arguably the worst secretary of the interior in the history of the office—his species' policies cost billions and the fires he did not manage cost billions more, and both failures caused enormous environmental damage—Watt is the guy remembered as the environmental wrecker.

Because of Watt's bad press, there are no votes to be had here for Republicans. Because the GOP's natural allies among sportsmen, ranchers, and farmers already know the score and are already deeply committed to the GOP, they don't need much in the way of maintenance reassurance, and it certainly doesn't have to be high-profile massaging. As with guns and abortion policy, there aren't any undecideds left. Dick Cheney on a quail hunt is about all our side needs to see every year.

The Bermuda Triangle of issues exists, and here's its effect: purists who demand that the GOP take loud stands on any of these issues are demanding tribute at the expense of votes.

Why would they do such a thing?

In some cases, it is desperation.

Some pro-life activists cannot stop thinking about the human toll, both on the unborn and on the women who regret their choices and live with guilt.

Some gun owners fear that the slippery slope is real, and the Left will never be satisfied with a ban on assault weapons, and will immediately demand a new regulation after the ink on the latest gun grab is dry.

And some property owners worn down by callous bureaucrats or driven to distraction by nutty environmental activists spouting off silly science just want to even the score.

These are the sincere but misguided folks who can do a lot of political damage.

The insincere ones have built careers on their activism, and for them, stirring the pot on these issues is as much about cash flow from direct mail and book sales as it is about changing policy.

The latter use the former to force destructive debates into nominating conventions, then debates that are exploited by the Left and the Left's friends in the media to reopen old wounds and drain away votes, even as the debates energize the Left's base.

The bottom line is what matters: elections that are fought when these issues are the central issues are elections that the Republican Party loses.

And elections that the Republican Party loses are elections that bring horrible results for those in the pro-life, pro–Second Amendment, pro–property rights camp.

Sometimes the hardest thing to do in politics is . . . nothing.

Since the issues that dominate 2004 and the elections over the horizon are so favorable for the Republican Party, it is simply crazy to push for elevating the profile of the issues that could threaten the certain majorities ahead.

When next you hear an activist demanding strong platform language on one of these issues or judging a candidate by his fealty to this or that statement of principle, take him aside and try to explain the reality of progress versus the comfort of feeling that you have fought the good fight.

CHAPTER 37

THE EDGE OF THE KNIFE: IMMIGRATION, JUDGES, GAYS, AND GOD

I n the last chapter I outlined the three issues that Republican Party activists should be very slow to raise as central issues in any campaign.

In a time of war, the focus ought to be on the war, national defense, and homeland security. The electorate credits the Republicans and President Bush with a huge advantage over the Democrats on these issues, so every minute spent talking about other issues is a minute not spent focusing the electorate on the crucial question: Which party is better positioned to defend the United States against devastating attack and to pursue and defeat our enemies before they strike again?

It is in the nature of politics, however, especially when politics is influenced greatly by a media overwhelmingly hostile to the Republican Party, that national campaigns are fought over issues other than the central issue, no matter how disciplined the effort to maintain focus. Inevitably reporters will demand answers on other subjects, and while candidates and commentators might try to steer the discussion back to the issue of national security, even the most skilled campaigns have to be prepared to wage the contest on other issues.

The last chapter argued that Republicans don't want to fight for votes on the issues of abortion, guns, and the environment.

For obvious reasons, Democrats should not want to fight elections on the issue of taxes, though, inexplicably, every Democrat who wanted to challenge George W. Bush in 2004 campaigned in the primary season on a pledge to raise taxes, and none more vigorously than John Kerry, whose proposed tax hikes would disable the economy.

Beyond taxes, there are four issues that, if approached carefully with discipline and skill, can reap huge benefits for Republicans.

But they are also dangerous issues—edge-of-the-knife issues. It is easy to slice yourself as well as an opponent with these issues. As an activist, you'll want to think them through and to especially listen for cues from national party leaders on whether and how to raise these subjects with that all-important group: the swing voters.

In the last chapter I referred to an article on swing voters from *The Atlantic Monthly's* January 2004 issue. It was one of scores of articles on the subject that arrive like clockwork every election year. Pundits and pollsters are looking for swing voters every cycle on the theory that if they stampede in one direction, the election is over before it has begun:

> As the American electorate becomes even more polarized, the number of undecided voters and the number of states in which the two parties will truly compete have diminished considerably. Two decades ago as much as a third of the electorate was deemed to be in play, and there were grand debates, particularly in the Democratic Party, about whether the best way to win "swing" voters was to pursue a southern strategy or to target the Rocky Mountains . . . Strategists in both parties have narrowed their focus to no more than 10 percent of the electorate (some have narrowed it even further) and both parties plan to seriously contest only about fifteen states in November.

This theory is rejected by Republican strategists and played up by Democratic strategists who wish to conceal as long as possible the fact that a major realignment has occurred and will continue to accelerate because of 9/11. But caution is always a virtue in elections, as Thomas Dewey taught everyone in 1948. It thus pays big vote dividends to pay attention to the issues that can move swing voters in the direction of the GOP's emerging majority.

As there are three issues that can disable the Republican cause, so there are four—in addition to taxes—that can help the GOP: immigration reform, judicial selection and service, gay marriage, and God.

God, of course, is not an "issue" for the faithful, and since I am an evangelical Christian, I am aware that casting God as a subset of issues can offend believers. I do so only to continue the tone of candor in the book. This is how strategists talk, and the faithful ought to understand how they are understood. My apologies to the offended.

Now on to the particulars.

IMMIGRATION REFORM

As the next chapter details, the percentage of American citizens of Latino descent is large and growing. That percentage is already a plurality in California, and it may well become the dominant ethnic group in other states as well. These citizens are a hugely important electoral bloc.

The number of noncitizens who entered the U.S. illegally and remain here illegally is estimated at 8 to 14 million. The sheer size of the spread between the high and low estimate telegraphs part of the problem: illegal immigration affects the country in huge ways, and we can't even begin to chart these effects in full measure because we don't have the data.

But we know this: illegal aliens cost the public purse a lot of money, and a dam that leaks as badly as our border is a national security threat.

We also know that there is a huge demand for the labor performed by illegal aliens. I live in Southern California, where vast numbers of illegal aliens perform back-breaking work in the fields and in low-paying service industry jobs. Only zealots deny that the American economy could function efficiently and with its current productivity without this labor force, and only zealots refuse to admit that there are many categories of jobs for which there are few, if any, citizen volunteers—such as migrant farm labor.

Participants in the debate over what to do about the vast illegal alien population should recognize that the far larger population of citizens of Latino descent listen to this debate very carefully, and often hear extreme voices fueled by racist demagoguery mixed with legitimate and serious concerns over the costs and consequences of the illegal population. The voting pattern of citizens of Latino descent turns in part on what they hear being said and by whom they hear it said.

Citizens of Latino descent are sharply split on the best approach to the illegal population. Some want amnesty. Others want rigorous enforcement backed up by expulsion of illegals who are apprehended and punishment of employers who employ them.

But almost all citizens of Latino descent whom I have spoken with and interviewed on and off the air over a dozen years are extremely sensitive to anti-Latino rhetoric and race demagoguery.

President Bush has asked Congress to begin to grapple with the facts of the massive illegal population. He has done so with extraordinary sensitivity and candor, and his standing within the community of citizens of Latino descent is quite high. His refusal to embrace harsh rhetoric has earned him some critics on the right who ought to reread Chapter 19 carefully. His opposition to a new amnesty has earned him critics on the left and among all leading Democrats (certainly John Kerry, who favors a new amnesty).

Policy on illegal immigrants is the most difficult issue in American politics on which to communicate without giving offense or sparking outrage, but the GOP has to master this skill or forfeit the majority it currently enjoys. The demographic realities of America compel serious political activists to grasp this fact and learn this issue while adopting the president's tone.

There is no alternative. See the next chapter.

JUDGES

This issue is a winner for the GOP because the Democrats have played a radical and outrageous hand and adopted an extremist agenda that, while satisfactory to its elites and elites in media, deeply offends most fair-minded Americans who hear of it.

Simply put, the Democrats in the United States have agreed to change more than two hundred years of Senate procedure. Never before in the history of the U.S. Senate have nominees to the intermediate level of the federal courts—the very important United States Court of Appeals—been filibustered.

A filibuster is a parliamentary trick to prevent a vote from occurring that can be decided by a majority of senators. When there are fifty-one or more votes for an issue, those who are about to lose the vote resort to filibuster.

A rule in the Senate says a final vote on a judicial nominee must be preceded by a vote to end debate, and a vote to end debate requires sixty votes.

There are only forty-eight Democrats in the Senate, and thus all Republican nominees to the appellate court would win their confirmation vote. As a result, Democrats refuse to end debate on the qualifications of these nominees, and as a result, up-or-down votes have been denied Charles Pickering, Miguel Estrada, Janice Rogers Brown, Priscilla Owens, Carolyn Kuhl, and William Pryor. Six different distinguished lawyers have been filibustered. Each of them would be confirmed if a vote was allowed.

Prior to 2003, there had never been a successful filibuster of even a single appellate court nominee.

In one year of Democratic radicalism, Senate Democrats launched and maintained six filibusters.

Senate Democrats have taken this position for a lot of reasons. Internal memos from Democratic staff on the Senate Judiciary Committee were made public in 2003 that conclusively proved the Democrats were pursuing their radical agenda against women, minorities, and nominees with deeply held religious beliefs. These are appalling descents into bigotry of the worst sort, but Senate Democrats are growing increasingly desperate as a long stay in the minority seems increasingly inevitable to them. As their power crumbles, their recklessness increases. (This story has not recieved much attention because the Democratic staff memos may have been obtained via underhanded tactics.)

Republicans need to keep a focus on the radical nature of the Democrats' filibusters, and they need to keep it simple: never in the history of the United States has a minority of senators obstructed floor votes on judicial nominees who have been sent to the floor by the Senate Judiciary Committee. Delays, sometimes long delays, have been imposed on nominees by both parties in the past, and some nominees of both parties have seen their nominations die in the committee.

But never has the rule of the majority of the Senate been undermined by a radical few.

This obstructionism is a key issue of 2004 and beyond. If Americans want a judiciary free of the radical influence of the hard-left wing of the Democratic Party, the Democrats' numbers in the Senate must be reduced to the point that their minority is just too small to obstruct the functioning of the courts as it has been doing these past few years.

Radical judges can declare the Pledge of Allegiance unconstitutional, say that gay marriage is a protected right, announce new rights for accused terrorists, or strike down vouchers for low-income kids because the recipient schools are faith based, but eventually the majority of Americans will elect presidents who will send nominees of a different sort who will become responsible judges. Judicial activism breeds its own correction in the election of presidents and senators pledged to correct judicial excess.

But that process requires the minority party—the Democrats—to play by long-established rules. The Senate's Democrats are cheating, and Republicans ought to campaign incessantly on that fact. If Democrats succeed in casting this as an issue of keeping "extremists" off the federal bench, however, their underhanded and constitutionally unprecedented tactics will be obscured.

GAY MARRIAGE

The vast majority of Americans understand and accept that the ranks of their fellow citizens include millions of gays and lesbians, and that these citizens are and should be equal in every respect to all other citizens. Gays and lesbians do and should pay the same tax rates and enjoy the same protections of law. The proposition that "all men are created equal, that they are endowed by their Creator with certain unalienable Rights" extends to all human beings, regardless of sexual orientation.

But a healthy majority of Americans believe that marriage is an institution, divine in origin, an institution that the state regulates closely and that the state should not extend to same-sex couples.

That majority may crumble over time, though I suspect it won't. But it is quite real and quite strong and deserves respect in 2004. On February 24, 2004, President Bush entered this debate decisively by endorsing an amendment to the Constitution that would preserve marriage as an institution between one man and one woman. He did the right thing.

Proponents of gay marriage know that solid majorities favor the president's view, so they push for judicial usurpation of the legislative job. This is what has happened in Vermont and most recently in Massachusetts. Judges have ordered radical restructuring in those states' laws of marriage.

Local officials in San Francisco and elsewhere simply started to issue marriage licenses to same-sex couples, in clear violation of existing law.

If these judicial decrees are interpreted by federal courts to be applicable in states other than Vermont and Massachusetts, a constitutional amendment will be necessary to prevent such imposition of radical beliefs on unwilling supermajorities. The process of preparing such an amendment should begin now in order to be positioned to submit such an amendment to the states in 2005 if necessary.

There is no more arduous legislative process than that surrounding a constitutional amendment. It is enormously difficult to achieve an amendment to the Constitution, which is a good thing. The political stability of the United States depends upon the stability of the constitutional order.

But if courts insist on radical rewrites of law and tradition in the United States, the people's directly elected representatives should put the issue to the states. If, as I suspect, there is a huge and enduring majority in favor of defending marriage as an institution reserved for heterosexual couples, the debate will be swift and affirming of the traditional understanding. After all, not once in the 228 years since the Declaration of Independence has either the federal Congress or any state legislature passed even one law that intended to declare marriage as a legal arrangement open to two individuals of the same gender.

President Bush has been careful to caution all Americans to conduct this debate in terms that recognize the dignity and rights of gay and lesbian

Americans. As with every other issue that causes controversy, radical voices can easily rise to prominence, destroying goodwill and injuring feelings as well as parties along the way. There is no need to win ugly or to make common cause with intolerance or simple hatred. Proponents of traditional marriage have to guard against the appearance among their ranks of antigay activists whose fury and passion are expressions of underlying agendas with which no Republican official wants to be allied.

"Defending marriage" is a powerful and necessary political appeal, but antigay bigotry will destroy the movement and the message.

GOD

Long before the Democrats became a party hostile to the public expression of faith and long before they became outspoken opponents of judicial nominees who possess, as Senator Charles Schumer (D-NY) put it, "deeply held beliefs," the Democratic Party had marginalized most evangelical Christians and orthodox Catholics within its ranks. The Democrats did this because evangelical Christians and orthodox Catholics simply don't vote in great numbers for Democrats.

It is a cliché of 2004 that the best clue to guessing a person's political party is to inquire as to his church or synagogue attendance. The most regular attenders are overwhelmingly likely to be Republicans. The most secular people and the atheists are overwhelmingly likely to be Democrats.

Democrats hate to talk about this trend because it spells certain electoral doom over the next few decades. The decline in religious attendance in America has stalled, and some see a new awakening under way, which would be bad news indeed for Democrats.

America is a deeply religious country. Sociologist Peter Berger famously remarked that if India was the most religious country in the world, and Sweden was the least religious country in the world, then the United States was a nation of Indians ruled by Swedes.

Well, maybe it used to be.

The Republican Party must continue to be a champion of the free exercise of religious belief. It must continue to champion the cause of the faithful as they seek to exercise the long tradition of public expression of faith.

The GOP should come to the aid of churches denied building permits and prisoners denied Bible studies.

The GOP should champion faith-based recovery programs and vouchers for inner-city schools that operate as extensions of a religious denomination.

And the GOP must protect the tax-exempt status of churches and the tax-advantaged status of pastors and preachers and rabbis and imams.

In short, the Republican Party must enthusiastically endorse and hold up the genuine tradition of America, which is of a robust religious presence in the public square.

When wacky judges declare the Pledge of Allegiance to be unconstitutional, the GOP should never stop talking about not just the judges who issued that decision, but also the out-of-control ambitions of other judges, the ACLU, the People for the American Way, Americans United for Separation of Church and State, etc., etc., etc.

When Barry Lynn, longtime executive director of Americans United for Separation of Church and State, denounces President Bush's repeated references to and from Scripture, the House and Senate should hold special sessions to debate and throw a spotlight on the proposition of whether such references are a continuation of long-established American tradition (they are) or a radical turn toward the crazy (a laughable assertion that marks anyone who makes it as either a fool or a liar).

And when nominees to the courts or any jobs are ridiculed or slandered on the basis of their "deeply held beliefs," the Republican Party from top to bottom should use every means at its disposal to defend those nominees, even if it requires uncomfortable moments with friends across the aisle.

The agenda of the Democratic Party, from gay marriage to the imposition of a constitutionally prohibited religious test on nominees for the federal courts, has become radical in its opposition to traditional religious belief. So radical, in fact, that simple affirmation of the Baltimore Catechism would make a judicial nominee radioactive, and sincere orthodoxy on the issue of when life begins makes a Catholic unconfirmable, even if he swears to apply abortion case law precedent.

The Democrats have embraced suspicion of sincere religious belief.

The GOP ought to accept the Democratic decision and campaign on it.

These are uncomfortable conversations for Americans with a deep tradition of tolerance and respect for all religious points of view. But the politics of the Left has driven traditional religious practice to the margins and demonized the faithful.

People of faith in the Democratic Party have to understand that their party has declared war on the public expression of their traditional faiths. These people have to choose. And the GOP ought to spare no effort to alert them to the necessity of that choice.

The issue of the defense of religious freedom is one that strengthens the GOP the more it is on display. The majority position in America is that people of faith should be respected and should never be discriminated against because of their faith. The Democrats have abandoned that tradition because of abortion rights absolutism on the part of its most powerful special interests. That was a radical choice by a party that had been built in part on the votes of Catholics who attended Mass, and one for which a huge political cost should be paid.

As 2004 opened, the Catholic bishops of America initiated a debate about how they ought to treat elected officials who routinely advocate laws diametrically opposed to church teaching. The bishops would probably stop short of urging votes against pro-choice legislators, but perhaps they will act to protect the right of devout Catholics to serve on the federal bench and in other positions of authority.

Even if the bishops don't act, American Catholics especially need to understand that the party of JFK has turned against the Catholic church. When that recognition occurs, the realignment of American politics will be enduring. But the argument must be carefully phrased to avoid the deeply repugnant challenges to an individual's sincerity of belief in God. The Democrats who attack traditional Catholic nominees are not atheists, simply opponents of traditional Catholic teaching. This is a huge and crucial difference.

The issues of immigration, judicial selection, gay marriage, and religious freedom present huge opportunities to move significant numbers of voters if they are addressed correctly, with attention to facts and not with easily ridiculed overstatements.

But Democrats know their peril on these issues, and they react fiercely when pressed. When many writers and activists called attention to the obvious anti-Catholicism of the Democrats' filibuster of Alabama Attorney General William Pryor, Catholics in the Senate reacted with fury. Tom Daschle and Patrick Leahy loudly called attention to their own Catholicism and argued irrationally that attendance at Mass somehow made a senator immune to charges of anti-Catholic bias in the judicial confirmation process.

Yet the ferocity of the response was belied by the vote of the large Catholic lay group Knights of Columbus to condemn the handling of Pryor and also by the condemnation of Pryor's treatment by the archbishop of Denver, Charles Chaput. Elite media and left-wing bloggers kept up the chant that the charge of anti-Catholicism was ludicrous, but repetition in 2003 and 2004 is waking the electorate to the controversy. The facts hurt the Democrats because Catholics especially know what's taking place in the Pryor debate, and they applaud the president's decision to appoint Pryor through a controversial recess appointment in February 2004.

It is a delicate debate, and a charge that the Catholic Democrats weren't "real Catholics" would have been wrong and disastrous, whereas focus on the anti-Catholic nature of the anti-Pryor campaign is effective. Attacks on the sincerity of personal faith, like attacks on the sincerity of personal patriotism, *always* backfire. The Roman Catholic heirarchy has begun to ask whether self-professed Catholics who vote for the agenda of the abortion-absolutists are entitled to recieve communion. Non-Catholics should be slow to declare these elected officials insincere, but quick to welcome the heirarchy's seriousness on the subject.

The caution to activists must be, when it comes to this quartet of issues, to listen carefully to the arguments as presented by national opinion and party leaders. Departing from the suggested script can do much more harm than good.

The messages discussed in this chapter are powerful and need to be communicated, but carefully and skillfully.

CHAPTER 38

A MAJORITY
THAT ENDURES

T he Republican Party has enjoyed three decades of over-whelming support from one easily identified demographic group: white males. President Bush enjoys that support still. As *Los Angeles Times* reporter/columnist Ronald Brownstein put it in December 2003: "President Bush's overwhelming strength among white men looms as a central obstacle between Democrats and the White House as 2004 approaches."

White men make up 40 percent of the current electorate. White women make up 40 percent of the electorate. The remaining 20 percent are a rainbow of ethnicities, with Latinos and African Americans making up the largest slices of that spectrum.

President Bush beat Al Gore by 24 percent in the votes of white men. His father beat Mike Dukakis by 27 points in this category, down from Reagan's and Nixon's 35-point shellacking of Mondale and McGovern, respectively. Given that Kerry's a virtual clone of Mondale and McGovern, expect President Bush to roll up a 35-point spread among white males.

The long-term demographic trends in the United States should keep the champagne corked, however. Americans of Latino descent are grow-ing as a percentage of the population, and President Bush, greatly admired by the Latino Americans of Texas, could claim only 35 percent of the

Latino vote in the 2000 election. He did even less well with Jewish Americans, garnering only 22 percent of those votes, and he netted a risible 8 percent of the African American vote.

One other slice of the demographic pie should interest you: President Bush received 47 percent of the Catholic vote in 2000, and Al Gore, 50 percent.

Both to assure a mandate for vigorous prosecution of the war and to establish a healthy base for future elections in which the issue of national security, while always present, may not be so obvious, the campaign of 2004 must—absolutely must—expand the president's percentages among the ethnic voting blocs that have not given him strong support in the past.

A party, the future of which depends upon huge majorities among white men, is a doomed party. That's a demographic fact. That's a political fact.

Which is why every partisan has to be involved in expanding the reach of the GOP in these voting blocs. Poll data are promising, but poll data aren't voting data. Don't be tempted into thinking the growth of these percentage shares is happening as a sort of mystical by-product of the sudden revelation of new priorities to differing ethnicities. Increased percentages depend upon effective communication with these groups of persuasive appeals to their self-interest.

Just in case you aren't buying this, review the data from the decade of the nineties.

During that decade, African Americans grew to a population of 34.7 million—an increase of 13 percent.

Latinos actually passed African Americans in terms of numbers, reaching 35.3 million—an amazing 56 percent growth spurt.

Asian Americans cracked the 10 million mark—hitting 10.6 million at decade's end—a 40.7 percent increase.

Contrast those numbers with the growth of white America: from 209 to 212 million over the years, less than 2 percent growth.

Again, if the GOP does not expand its appeal among citizens of color, especially the need for those newly dominant demographic subgroups to prize national security above all other issues, then the

Republican Party's renaissance will be brief indeed.

There are reasons for optimism. President Bush has emphasized education accountability, which resonates especially with families of limited incomes within these demographic groups that see public education as the ticket to better futures for their children.

And Americans did react to 9/11 in the same way, regardless of ethnicity. No demographic group can fail to appreciate the real perils in the world if the perils are effectively communicated.

The problem is that some voices on the right are irresponsible in their rhetoric about illegal immigration and affirmative action, and because of their volume and tone, they forfeit opportunity after opportunity to be heard by Latinos and African Americans especially.

While self-proclaimed experts on borders and quotas and culture rant away, voting citizens hear these rants as appeals to racist instincts, even when they are not intended that way. No Republican who identifies with the noisy right-edge margin on the illegal immigration issue or the harshest arguments concerning affirmative action will ever get a hearing from these groups, even from those members of the ethnic groups who believe strongly in secure borders or a color-blind society. African Americans and Latinos will never shed decades of suspicion over Republican policies if voices they understand to be Republican are continually talking in a tone that seems to communicate exclusion and contempt.

Which is why George W. Bush is trying to change the tone of the conversation on issues of symbolic importance to rapidly expanding segments of the electorate. Hard-right, teeth-grinding, growling, and fist-clenching extremists need to be shunned, or they will be destructive forces within the new majority, causing it to splinter even as it reaches for the ability to govern effectively.

California's history on these issues is instructive. Anti-illegal immigration activists qualified Proposition 187 for the ballot in 1994, then Governor Pete Wilson embraced it, and a decade of animosity was launched between California's large and growing Latino population—the voting-citizen-entrepreneurial-family-loving Latino population—and the GOP. Proposition 187 was the greatest electoral blunder of the generation, but its enthusiasts are still in the Golden State, still demanding another destructive spasm of fist shaking at the illegal alien population. Proposition 187 called for a variety of steps to be taken to deny benefits to individuals who had entered the country illegally and to mandate citizen cooperation in the identification of illegals, and the thrust of the measure was a generalized "get tough" sentiment.

It was a disaster. Even though it passed by a large margin, the angry symbolism of the vote stayed and festered within the ranks of citizens of Latino descent. They felt, and continue to feel, that the GOP wants no part of them.

The backers of Proposition 209 in 1996 chose a strategy that patiently explained that the use of race in the allocation of benefits was wrong, but they did so in such a fashion that few, if any, activists of the Left can raise a cheer by reminding crowds of 209. The cry of "no more 187s," by contrast, still resonates with Latinos in the Golden State.

Politics can't be held hostage by the most passionate and the loudest activists, especially on the issues that will drive away the political affiliations of the segments of the voting population that are growing most rapidly.

Keeping the majority that will keep the country defended requires rejecting and, if necessary, ejecting activists who refuse to pursue their agendas with tones and styles that allow majorities to endure.

PART VII

TONE AND FOCUS

It was not merely a one-issue but
a one-man election. As Lord Shaftesbury put
it in his diary, there was only one question,
"Were you, or were you not? are you,
or are you not, for Palmerston?"

—From Muriel E. Chamberlain's *Lord Palmerston* (1987)

CHAPTER 39

PERFECT PITCH

My nephew Patrick is an Eagle Scout, an accomplishment that remains shorthand for character and discipline. Patrick's brothers and sisters and scores of cousins have many other accomplishments that I admire greatly: Diana has been on long mission trips to faraway places under difficult circumstances; Will and Jamie have swum thousands of hours in pursuit of excellence; Matt skippers a ship in the U.S. Navy; David, Jay, and Stephanie work long hours building careers; and the list goes on as long as the family extends, which, like most American families, is long indeed.

But of all of these many accomplishments—marathons run, excellent grades obtained, hundreds of hours spent in service—only Patrick's achievement carries with it an involuntary political message. Somehow the American culture has changed to make the Boy Scouts a source of controversy in some eyes. Politics has invaded every aspect of American life, and there is no going back to the days when the private and the public were easily kept separate.

This spread of the political has caused a lot of resentment and bitterness. It is easy to see this with the Boy Scouts as bewildered parents and volunteers wonder aloud what in the world happened to allow the elites' routine demonization of this wonderful organization. Twenty-five years ago it would have been impossible to imagine the United Way moving to expel Boy Scout troops from their web of affiliated organizations, or a federal judge banning Scouts from the use of the public facilities the Scouts had actually built and maintained for decades, as happened in San Diego. The desire by elites to purge the Scouts from public life has become so intense that it requires real courage to oppose it, which is why my admiration for men like Jeff Morris, whose story is recounted earlier, in Ventura County, California, is so deep.

When Jeff Morris discovered that the local United Way was purging the Scouts from its roll of beneficiaries because of the Scouts' policy against allowing gay men to serve as scoutmasters, Jeff calmly but firmly took up the cause of calling the United Way to be accountable to its community and of raising the lost support for the local Scouts.

And he did it with a tone that is a model for these times. First he assembled the facts. Then he calmly outlined his objections. And then he organized a response.

That's the way to act in response to a politicized culture. Morris is not a screamer or a fist clencher. He's a prudent, organized, and effective activist. And my objective in writing this book is to clone Jeff Morris.

It isn't hard to find passion in American politics. There's plenty of passion all across the political process.

But it is hard to capture the energy of that passion and put it to constructive use.

I finished the manuscript for this book on Super Bowl Sunday when the Pats and the Panthers squared off. These teams had risen to the top of their profession because of talent and passion, of course, but also because of discipline. Their achievements were obscured because of the undisciplined excess of the halftime show's participants.

In politics, the hardest thing to master—to discipline—is tone. There is such a thing as perfect pitch in American politics, and when a leader gets it right, the results are astonishing.

George W. Bush is as close to perfect pitch as the Republicans have come since Ronald Reagan, and it is crucial that activists listen closely to the key in which he is communicating. It is crucial that they model their message on his and their activism on the example of Jeff Morris and thousands like him.

Because so many issues of the last few years spark outrage—the demonization of the Boy Scouts, the wave of illegal immigration, and of course, the brutal attacks on America and on innocents across the globe—the great temptation is to take that outrage onto the political stage and to let it appear as unrefined anger, even rage.

That temptation has to be revisited and conquered. Anger is the most self-destructive of all political impulses. The wreckage of the Howard Dean campaign is only the most recent of many monuments to the catastrophic consequences of mixing anger and politics.

Americans are not and will never be an angry people because the evidence of our abundance and our great and good fortune is everywhere on display.

It's impossible to ignore these blessings for long, and most voters know that, even with all of its problems and controversies, there is no better place on earth to live than America, no better age in which to exist than today.

We won the lottery. All of us. And anger in response to any of the particulars of our *internal* conditions repulses voters.

Anger toward our *external* enemies who would kill millions of us if they could does resonate.

But *never* anger toward fellow citizens over issues of political difference, even the issues that, in fact, anger us. As a matter of political survival, anger doesn't simply have to be managed. It has to be exiled.

This is the message of this chapter because anger can defeat every other advantage of this fall's election and every future contest.

Take your tone from the president and your tactics from Jeff Morris. Leave the ranting to Howard Dean and the MoveOn.org folks, now comfortably embedded within the John Kerry campaign.

This isn't a suggestion to be quiet or moderate. Far from it. As Chapter 40 shows, I hope, being loud and pointed when it comes to political arguments wins elections.

But being "for" something is also going to win over being "against" someone or something.

To repeat, this isn't a scolding or a demand for manners. As Chapter 40 indicates in its assessment of Patrick Leahy and Barbara Boxer, you don't have to pretend that fools are wise or that dummies are smart. And you can't afford to be gentle during campaign season. "This isn't complicated," the late Republican strategist Lee Atwater once confided to a friend. "When you got 'em by the throat, you take out a damn howitzer and blow their brains out."

You can be upbeat and optimistic, full of energy and hope, always willing to welcome anyone into the party. And at the same time, you can be determined to win.

That's the perfect pitch that wins elections. And we certainly need it now more than ever.

CHAPTER 40

THE STAKES

T he Victorians understood politics. The world in the second half of the nineteenth century turned on the policies of Great Britain, and the policies of Great Britain turned on a group of leaders of extraordinary ability in many fields, but especially in the field of politics. Palmerston, Disraeli, Gladstone, Churchill, Balfour, Chamberlain and, of course, Salisbury—four times the foreign secretary of England, three times its prime minister.

I have included in this book some famous and some not-so-famous quotations from the men who ran the last democratic empire the world is likely to experience. They were great men of the world, but also practical politicians, scrapping for a majority in Parliament so that they and their colleagues could advance their visions of how the world ought to operate, and Great Britain's place in that world.

All of them were well educated and deeply read—there were no imposters on the front bench of Parliament that today is led by Tony Blair, an able and courageous heir of this tradition.

They all knew the power of majority and the necessity of winning at the polls. Winston Churchill came of age during their last decades, and he observed them closely. Of one, Lord Rosebery, Churchill concluded of his failing as a politician, that "he would not stoop; he did not conquer." Churchill recorded of another, Gladstone—the great liberal of his age, the "Grand Old Man"—that it was his rule: "The first essential for a

Prime Minister is to be a good butcher." Gladstone's ardent opponent, Disraeli, is said to have been the most gifted speaker of his age, but Disraeli counseled that "a majority is better than the best repartee."

They all—Liberals and Tories alike—knew how to win. Joseph Chamberlain, who split from Gladstone and split the Liberal Party when he did so, did not hesitate to campaign with brass knuckles. "A vote for the Liberals is a vote for the Boers" was Chamberlain's slogan in the famous Khaki Election of 1900, an explicit equating of his political opposition with England's war enemy in a manner that would no doubt drive today's Left to howls and tears but brought victory to his Tory colleagues a century ago.

Chamberlain expected politics to be no holds barred. "Once, when Chamberlain was firing directly at Gladstone," historian Robert Massie recounted, "a mass of Englishmen charged him from their benches. Fists flew, hats toppled, and Chamberlain was quite unmoved. To him, politics was a kind of warfare; beliefs must always be passionate; there must be 'no fraternizing in the trenches and no wandering about in no-man's land.'"

Chamberlain wasn't unique, and the desire for full-throated debate and electioneering allowed England's voters to make clear choices and set clear directions. Transparent, pointed politics allowed England to maintain its security and to keep the world's peace for many decades.

In the aftermath of the Great War, though, a fog descended on England's political life, and Stanley Baldwin—the great fixer and trimmer—rose to power, and with him an ethic of blurring of partisan lines and a general lowering of the political volume. Politics became muffled, and in that quiet, complacent time, loud and jarring voices like Churchill's were shoved to the corners and counted as cranks. Appeasement, which was not yet a word of condemnation but a label on a policy proudly extolled and pursued, was every reasonable man's policy.

And the disaster followed, even greater than the one before.

When political life goes soft, danger comes in fast behind. Only through the sharp exchange of jabs and jolts do contrasts emerge and significant choices get made. The country doesn't need more Clinton triangulation. It needs clear choices, and in 2004 it has such a choice.

Lord Salisbury wasn't the most famous of the Victorians, though he was arguably the most successful. He looked like one of the fellows on the Smith Cough Drops box, if indeed those boxes are made today. He kept watch on a dangerous world for decades and, first with Disraeli, and then alone, maintained England's safety year after year. He was a deeply religious but deeply practical man, given to cutting quips and long naps. A 1999 biography of him, by Andrew Roberts, is titled simply *Salisbury: Victorian Titan*.

One passage of this book is worth reading closely, for it applies to the would-be leaders from the Left of today:

> The centenary of the French revolution fell on 14th July 1889, and France intended to commemorate it in style, commissioning a temporary 985-foot tower in the Champ de Mars designed by the engineer Alexandre Gustave Eiffel. The revolution and its aftermath had long exercised a morbid fascination for Salisbury, and he saw no reason to celebrate an event which would have hoisted him up on the first tumbril. He made a close study of it, collecting a large number of books and pamphlets, and references to it cropped up regularly in his journalism and speeches. Its lessons infused his political beliefs. "The witness of history is uniform to this," he wrote about it in 1860, "that Nemesis may spare the sagacious criminal, but never fails to overtake the weak, the undecided and the over-charitable fool." Men such as Jacques Necker, the Abbe Sieyes and the Marquis de Lafayette he saw as archetypes of the weak-willed liberals he so despised:
>
> > "They believed intensely in amiable theories, they loved the sympathy and applause of their fellow men, they were kind-hearted, and charitably fancied everybody as well-meaning as themselves; and therefore—so far as it can be said of any single man—they were the proximate causes of a civil convulsion which, for the horrors of its calamities, stands alone in the history of the world."

Lord Salisbury did not foresee that such leaders would come to power in his own country in the '20s and the '30s, and he could not have foreseen that such leaders would conduct the foreign policy of the world's only superpower in the 1990s.

But they did return, and they are trying to return to power again: would-be leaders who think they can wish evil away and moderate the deadly passions of the country's sworn enemies with speeches and proclamations. Bill Clinton and Madeleine Albright thought they could deal with Kim Jong II. He cheated them blind. Now he has nukes and threatens us weekly. The story never changes, but the costs keep getting higher.

Such leaders destroyed France in 1789, nearly destroyed England in the 1930s by leaving the country vulnerable to Hitler's aggression, and left America unprepared for the murderous assault of 9/11. Now the election of 2004 turns on the question of whether the electorate will believe that the blind can suddenly see, and the pacifiers have, overnight, become realists.

The reason that politics must become very tough indeed is that we cannot afford another run of such leaders. Really, we can't. The Clintons and the Carters and the Baldwins and the Lafayettes—the cost of their pageants is unacceptable.

George W. Bush is a serious man, surrounded by serious men and women, the sort of leader and the sort of helpers who will not be tricked or truckled, seduced or shamed, corrupted or hornswoggled.

But the same cannot be said of Kerry and Dean, Sharpton and Kucinich, Pelosi and Daschle, Albright and Berger, McDermott and Moran. They are, all of them, insufficient to the task of defending the United States.

If given political power again, they will get us killed. Again.

But they desire power again because power is a pleasant and intoxicating thing. The White House is a fine place to entertain. Contributions are far more easily garnered when your party is in the majority than when it is an insignificant minority. Doors are opened when you are important; you hold them open when you are not. There is money to be made in the majority. There isn't much point in being in D.C. when you and yours account for 40 percent.

There are among the Democrats many who genuinely hope to accomplish good things for the underclass, for those whom they view as oppressed, for the genuinely sick and poverty stricken.

But intentions are not results, and one hundred years of Barbara Boxer would never make her smart or even moderately well-informed, or her solutions effective. Even the sincere ones—not Boxer certainly, and not many generally—are deeply misguided about the world of economics, and even the very few with an idea or two with merit would be in service to a party deeply compromised on the national security that is the predicate for everything else.

There is no rational case for the Democrats because the Democrats are going to get you killed.

It is that simple.

So, please, revisit the chapters on effective activism. Reread the chapters on the necessity of making contributions early and often. And give this book to a friend.

Better yet, give ten books to ten Democrats, and then argue it out with them.

The country needs a renewed Democratic Party, one genuinely committed to the ideals of Truman and FDR—one that wants to hammer and tong it out with the GOP on taxes and other domestic programs. And the country needs Democrats willing to demand that the party change itself back into a freedom-loving, defense-spending, national security–recognizing party, shedding and then exiling the blame-America-first professors and the whacked-out nuclear-freezing, missile-defense-obstructing senators and congressmen from its ranks. When Patrick Leahy is denounced as the bizarre nut that he is, and Barbara Boxer and Patty Murray and, yes, Tom Daschle, are retired from public life, perhaps then the Democrats will have a case to make for majority status again.

But that's not this year. Or 2006. Or 2008.

Vote accordingly. Your life depends upon it.

PRESIDENT BUSH'S REMARKS AT NATIONAL DAY OF PRAYER AND REMEMBRANCE

The National Cathedral
Washington, D.C., September 14, 2001

THE PRESIDENT: We are here in the middle hour of our grief. So many have suffered so great a loss, and today we express our nation's sorrow. We come before God to pray for the missing and the dead, and for those who love them.

On Tuesday, our country was attacked with deliberate and massive cruelty. We have seen the images of fire and ashes, and bent steel.

Now come the names, the list of casualties we are only beginning to read. They are the names of men and women who began their day at a desk or in an airport, busy with life. They are the names of people who faced death, and in their last moments called home to say, be brave, and I love you.

They are the names of passengers who defied their murderers, and prevented the murder of others on the ground. They are the names of men and women who wore the uniform of the United States, and died at their posts.

They are the names of rescuers, the ones whom death found running up the stairs and into the fires to help others. We will read all these names. We will linger over them, and learn their stories, and many Americans will weep.

To the children and parents and spouses and families and friends of the lost, we offer the deepest sympathy of the nation. And I assure you, you are not alone.

Just three days removed from these events, Americans do not yet have the distance of history. But our responsibility to history is already clear: to answer these attacks and rid the world of evil.

War has been waged against us by stealth and deceit and murder. This nation is peaceful, but fierce when stirred to anger. This conflict was begun on the timing and terms of others. It will end in a way, and at an hour, of our choosing.

Our purpose as a nation is firm. Yet our wounds as a people are recent and unhealed, and lead us to pray. In many of our prayers this week, there is a searching, and an honesty. At St. Patrick's Cathedral in New York on Tuesday, a woman said, "I prayed to God to give us a sign that He is still here." Others have prayed for the same, searching hospital to hospital, carrying pictures of those still missing.

God's signs are not always the ones we look for. We learn in tragedy that [H]is purposes are not always our own. Yet the prayers of private suffering, whether in our homes or in this great cathedral, are known and heard, and understood.

There are prayers that help us last through the day, or endure the night. There are prayers of friends and strangers, that give us strength for the journey. And there are prayers that yield our will to a will greater than our own.

This world He created is of moral design. Grief and tragedy and hatred are only for a time. Goodness, remembrance, and love have no end. And the Lord of life holds all who die, and all who mourn.

It is said that adversity introduces us to ourselves. This is true of a nation as well. In this trial, we have been reminded, and the world has seen, that our fellow Americans are generous and kind, resourceful and brave. We see our national character in rescuers working past exhaustion; in long lines of blood donors; in thousands of citizens who have asked to work and serve in any way possible.

And we have seen our national character in eloquent acts of sacrifice. Inside the World Trade Center, one man who could have saved himself stayed until the end at the side of his quadriplegic friend. A beloved priest died giving the last rites to a firefighter. Two office workers, finding a disabled stranger, carried her down sixty-eight floors to safety. A group of men drove through the night from Dallas to Washington to bring skin grafts for burn victims.

In these acts, and in many others, Americans showed a deep commitment to one another, and an abiding love for our country. Today, we feel what Franklin Roosevelt called the warm courage of national unity. This is a unity of every faith, and every background.

It has joined together political parties in both houses of Congress. It is evident in services of prayer and candlelight vigils, and American flags, which are displayed in pride, and wave in defiance.

Our unity is a kinship of grief, and a steadfast resolve to prevail against our enemies. And this unity against terror is now extending across the world.

America is a nation full of good fortune, with so much to be grateful for. But we are not spared from suffering. In every generation, the world has produced enemies of human freedom. They have attacked America, because we are freedom's home and defender. And the commitment of our fathers is now the calling of our time.

On this national day of prayer and remembrance, we ask almighty God to watch over our nation, and grant us patience and resolve in all that is to come. We pray that He will comfort and console those who now walk in sorrow. We thank Him for each life we now must mourn, and the promise of a life to come.

As we have been assured, neither death nor life, nor angels nor principalities nor powers, nor things present nor things to come, nor height nor depth, can separate us from God's love. May He bless the souls of the departed. May He comfort our own. And may He always guide our country.

God bless America.

PRESIDENT BUSH'S ADDRESS TO A JOINT SESSION OF CONGRESS AND THE AMERICAN PEOPLE

United States Capitol

Washington, D.C., September 20, 2001

THE PRESIDENT: Mr. Speaker, Mr. President Pro Tempore, members of Congress, and fellow Americans:

In the normal course of events, Presidents come to this chamber to report on the state of the Union. Tonight, no such report is needed. It has already been delivered by the American people.

We have seen it in the courage of passengers, who rushed terrorists to save others on the ground—passengers like an exceptional man named Todd Beamer. And would you please help me to welcome his wife, Lisa Beamer, here tonight.

We have seen the state of our Union in the endurance of rescuers, working past exhaustion. We have seen the unfurling of flags, the lighting of candles, the giving of blood, the saying of prayers—in English, Hebrew, and Arabic. We have seen the decency of a loving and giving people who have made the grief of strangers their own.

My fellow citizens, for the last nine days, the entire world has seen for itself the state of our Union—and it is strong.

Tonight we are a country awakened to danger and called to defend freedom. Our grief has turned to anger, and anger to resolution. Whether we bring our enemies to justice, or bring justice to our enemies, justice will be done.

I thank the Congress for its leadership at such an important time. All of America was touched on the evening of the tragedy to see Republicans and Democrats joined together on the steps of this Capitol, singing "God Bless America." And you did more than sing; you acted, by delivering $40 billion to rebuild our communities and meet the needs of our military.

Speaker Hastert, Minority Leader Gephardt, Majority Leader Daschle and Senator

Lott, I thank you for your friendship, for your leadership and for your service to our country.

And on behalf of the American people, I thank the world for its outpouring of support. America will never forget the sounds of our National Anthem playing at Buckingham Palace, on the streets of Paris, and at Berlin's Brandenburg Gate.

We will not forget South Korean children gathering to pray outside our embassy in Seoul, or the prayers of sympathy offered at a mosque in Cairo. We will not forget moments of silence and days of mourning in Australia and Africa and Latin America.

Nor will we forget the citizens of 80 other nations who died with our own: dozens of Pakistanis; more than 130 Israelis; more than 250 citizens of India; men and women from El Salvador, Iran, Mexico and Japan; and hundreds of British citizens. America has no truer friend than Great Britain. Once again, we are joined together in a great cause—so honored the British Prime Minister has crossed an ocean to show his unity of purpose with America. Thank you for coming, friend.

On September the 11th, enemies of freedom committed an act of war against our country. Americans have known wars—but for the past 136 years, they have been wars on foreign soil, except for one Sunday in 1941. Americans have known the casualties of war—but not at the center of a great city on a peaceful morning. Americans have known surprise attacks—but never before on thousands of civilians. All of this was brought upon us in a single day—and night fell on a different world, a world where freedom itself is under attack.

Americans have many questions tonight. Americans are asking: Who attacked our country? The evidence we have gathered all points to a collection of loosely affiliated terrorist organizations known as al Qaeda. They are the same murderers indicted for bombing American embassies in Tanzania and Kenya, and responsible for bombing the USS *Cole*.

Al Qaeda is to terror what the mafia is to crime. But its goal is not making money; its goal is remaking the world—and imposing its radical beliefs on people everywhere.

The terrorists practice a fringe form of Islamic extremism that has been rejected by Muslim scholars and the vast majority of Muslim clerics—a fringe movement that perverts the peaceful teachings of Islam. The terrorists' directive commands them to kill Christians and Jews, to kill all Americans, and make no distinction among military and civilians, including women and children.

This group and its leader—a person named Osama bin Laden—are linked to many other organizations in different countries, including the Egyptian Islamic Jihad and the Islamic Movement of Uzbekistan. There are thousands of these terrorists in more than 60 countries. They are recruited from their own nations and neighborhoods and brought to camps in places like Afghanistan, where they are trained in the tactics of terror. They are sent back to their homes or sent to hide in countries around the world to plot evil and destruction.

The leadership of al Qaeda has great influence in Afghanistan and supports the Taliban regime in controlling most of that country. In Afghanistan, we see al Qaeda's vision for the world.

Afghanistan's people have been brutalized—many are starving and many have fled. Women are not allowed to attend school. You can be jailed for owning a television. Religion can be practiced only as their leaders dictate. A man can be jailed in Afghanistan if his beard is not long enough.

The United States respects the people of Afghanistan—after all, we are currently its largest source of humanitarian aid—but we condemn the Taliban regime. It is not only repressing its own people, it is threatening people everywhere by sponsoring and sheltering and supplying terrorists. By aiding and abetting murder, the Taliban regime is committing murder.

And tonight, the United States of America makes the following demands on the Taliban: Deliver to United States authorities all the leaders of al Qaeda who hide in your land. Release all foreign nationals, including American citizens, you have unjustly imprisoned. Protect foreign journalists, diplomats and aid workers in your country. Close immediately and permanently every terrorist training camp in Afghanistan, and hand over every terrorist, and every person in their support structure, to appropriate authorities. Give the United States full access to terrorist training camps, so we can make sure they are no longer operating.

These demands are not open to negotiation or discussion. The Taliban must act, and act immediately. They will hand over the terrorists, or they will share in their fate.

I also want to speak tonight directly to Muslims throughout the world. We respect your faith. It's practiced freely by many millions of Americans, and by millions more in countries that America counts as friends. Its teachings are good and peaceful, and those who commit evil in the name of Allah blaspheme the name of Allah. The terrorists are traitors to their own faith, trying, in effect, to hijack Islam itself. The enemy of America is not our many Muslim friends; it is not our many Arab friends. Our enemy is a radical network of terrorists, and every government that supports them.

Our war on terror begins with al Qaeda, but it does not end there. It will not end until every terrorist group of global reach has been found, stopped and defeated.

Americans are asking, why do they hate us? They hate what we see right here in this chamber—a democratically elected government. Their leaders are self-appointed. They hate our freedoms—our freedom of religion, our freedom of speech, our freedom to vote and assemble and disagree with each other.

They want to overthrow existing governments in many Muslim countries, such as Egypt, Saudi Arabia, and Jordan. They want to drive Israel out of the Middle East. They want to drive Christians and Jews out of vast regions of Asia and Africa.

These terrorists kill not merely to end lives, but to disrupt and end a way of life. With every atrocity, they hope that America grows fearful, retreating from the world and forsaking our friends. They stand against us, because we stand in their way.

We are not deceived by their pretenses to piety. We have seen their kind before. They are the heirs of all the murderous ideologies of the 20th century. By sacrificing human life to serve their radical visions—by abandoning every value except the will to power—they follow in the path of fascism, and Nazism, and totalitarianism. And they will follow that path all the way, to where it ends: in history's unmarked grave of discarded lies.

Americans are asking: How will we fight and win this war? We will direct every resource at our command—every means of diplomacy, every tool of intelligence, every instrument of law enforcement, every financial influence, and every necessary weapon of war—to the disruption and to the defeat of the global terror network.

This war will not be like the war against Iraq a decade ago, with a decisive liberation of territory and a swift conclusion. It will not look like the air war above Kosovo two years ago, where no ground troops were used and not a single American was lost in combat.

Our response involves far more than instant retaliation and isolated strikes. Americans should not expect one battle, but a lengthy campaign, unlike any other we have ever seen. It may include dramatic strikes, visible on TV, and covert operations, secret even in success. We will starve terrorists of funding, turn them one against another, drive them from place to place, until there is no refuge or no rest. And we will pursue nations that provide aid or safe haven to terrorism. Every nation, in every region, now has a decision to make. Either you are with us, or you are with the terrorists. From this day forward, any nation that continues to harbor or support terrorism will be regarded by the United States as a hostile regime.

Our nation has been put on notice: We are not immune from attack. We will take defensive measures against terrorism to protect Americans. Today, dozens of federal departments and agencies, as well as state and local governments, have responsibilities affecting homeland security. These efforts must be coordinated at the highest level. So tonight I announce the creation of a Cabinet-level position reporting directly to me—the Office of Homeland Security.

And tonight I also announce a distinguished American to lead this effort, to strengthen American security: a military veteran, an effective governor, a true patriot, a trusted friend—Pennsylvania's Tom Ridge. He will lead, oversee and coordinate a comprehensive national strategy to safeguard our country against terrorism, and respond to any attacks that may come.

These measures are essential. But the only way to defeat terrorism as a threat to our way of life is to stop it, eliminate it, and destroy it where it grows.

Many will be involved in this effort, from FBI agents to intelligence operatives to the reservists we have called to active duty. All deserve our thanks, and all have our prayers. And tonight, a few miles from the damaged Pentagon, I have a message for our military: Be ready. I've called the Armed Forces to alert, and there is a reason. The hour is coming when America will act, and you will make us proud.

This is not, however, just America's fight. And what is at stake is not just America's freedom. This is the world's fight. This is civilization's fight. This is the fight of all who believe in progress and pluralism, tolerance and freedom.

We ask every nation to join us. We will ask, and we will need, the help of police forces, intelligence services, and banking systems around the world. The United States is grateful that many nations and many international organizations have already responded—with sympathy and with support. Nations from Latin America, to Asia, to Africa, to Europe, to the Islamic world. Perhaps the NATO Charter reflects best the attitude of the world: An attack on one is an attack on all.

The civilized world is rallying to America's side. They understand that if this terror goes unpunished, their own cities, their own citizens may be next. Terror, unanswered, can not only bring down buildings, it can threaten the stability of legitimate governments. And you know what—we're not going to allow it.

Americans are asking: What is expected of us? I ask you to live your lives, and hug your children. I know many citizens have fears tonight, and I ask you to be calm and resolute, even in the face of a continuing threat.

I ask you to uphold the values of America, and remember why so many have come here. We are in a fight for our principles, and our first responsibility is to live by them. No one should be singled out for unfair treatment or unkind words because of their ethnic background or religious faith.

I ask you to continue to support the victims of this tragedy with your contributions. Those who want to give can go to a central source of information, libertyunites.org, to find the names of groups providing direct help in New York, Pennsylvania, and Virginia.

The thousands of FBI agents who are now at work in this investigation may need your cooperation, and I ask you to give it.

I ask for your patience, with the delays and inconveniences that may accompany tighter security; and for your patience in what will be a long struggle.

I ask your continued participation and confidence in the American economy. Terrorists attacked a symbol of American prosperity. They did not touch its source.

America is successful because of the hard work, and creativity, and enterprise of our people. These were the true strengths of our economy before September 11th, and they are our strengths today.

And, finally, please continue praying for the victims of terror and their families, for those in uniform, and for our great country. Prayer has comforted us in sorrow, and will help strengthen us for the journey ahead.

Tonight I thank my fellow Americans for what you have already done and for what you will do. And ladies and gentlemen of the Congress, I thank you, their representatives, for what you have already done and for what we will do together.

Tonight, we face new and sudden national challenges. We will come together to improve air safety, to dramatically expand the number of air marshals on domestic flights, and take new measures to prevent hijacking. We will come together to promote stability and keep our airlines flying, with direct assistance during this emergency.

We will come together to give law enforcement the additional tools it needs to track down terror here at home. We will come together to strengthen our intelligence capabilities to know the plans of terrorists before they act, and find them before they strike.

We will come together to take active steps that strengthen America's economy, and put our people back to work.

Tonight we welcome two leaders who embody the extraordinary spirit of all New Yorkers: Governor George Pataki, and Mayor Rudolph Giuliani. As a symbol of America's resolve, my administration will work with Congress, and these two leaders, to show the world that we will rebuild New York City.

After all that has just passed—all the lives taken, and all the possibilities and hopes that died with them—it is natural to wonder if America's future is one of fear. Some speak of an age of terror. I know there are struggles ahead, and dangers to face. But this country will define our times, not be defined by them. As long as the United States of America is determined and strong, this will not be an age of terror; this will be an age of liberty, here and across the world.

Great harm has been done to us. We have suffered great loss. And in our grief and anger we have found our mission and our moment. Freedom and fear are at war. The advance of human freedom—the great achievement of our time, and the great hope of every time—now depends on us. Our nation—this generation—will lift a dark threat of violence from our people and our future. We will rally the world to this cause by our efforts, by our courage. We will not tire, we will not falter, and we will not fail.

It is my hope that in the months and years ahead, life will return almost to normal. We'll go back to our lives and routines, and that is good. Even grief recedes with time and grace. But our resolve must not pass. Each of us will remember what happened that day, and to whom it happened. We'll remember the moment the news came—where we were and what we were doing. Some will remember an image of a fire, or a story of rescue. Some will carry memories of a face and a voice gone forever.

And I will carry this: It is the police shield of a man named George Howard, who died at the World Trade Center trying to save others. It was given to me by his mom, Arlene, as a proud memorial to her son. This is my reminder of lives that ended, and a task that does not end.

I will not forget this wound to our country or those who inflicted it. I will not yield; I will not rest; I will not relent in waging this struggle for freedom and security for the American people.

The course of this conflict is not known, yet its outcome is certain. Freedom and fear, justice and cruelty, have always been at war, and we know that God is not neutral between them.

Fellow citizens, we'll meet violence with patient justice—assured of the rightness of our cause, and confident of the victories to come. In all that lies before us, may God grant us wisdom, and may He watch over the United States of America.

Thank you.

PRESIDENT BUSH'S
STATE OF THE UNION ADDRESS

The United States Capitol
Washington, D.C., January 29, 2002

THE PRESIDENT: Thank you very much. Mr. Speaker, Vice President Cheney, members of Congress, distinguished guests, fellow citizens: As we gather tonight, our nation is at war, our economy is in recession, and the civilized world faces unprecedented dangers. Yet the state of our Union has never been stronger.

We last met in an hour of shock and suffering. In four short months, our nation has comforted the victims, begun to rebuild New York and the Pentagon, rallied a great coalition, captured, arrested, and rid the world of thousands of terrorists, destroyed Afghanistan's terrorist training camps, saved a people from starvation, and freed a country from brutal oppression.

The American flag flies again over our embassy in Kabul. Terrorists who once occupied Afghanistan now occupy cells at Guantanamo Bay. And terrorist leaders who urged followers to sacrifice their lives are running for their own.

America and Afghanistan are now allies against terror. We'll be partners in rebuilding that country. And this evening we welcome the distinguished interim leader of a liberated Afghanistan: Chairman Hamid Karzai.

The last time we met in this chamber, the mothers and daughters of Afghanistan were captives in their own homes, forbidden from working or going to school. Today women are free, and are part of Afghanistan's new government. And we welcome the new Minister of Women's Affairs, Doctor Sima Samar.

Our progress is a tribute to the spirit of the Afghan people, to the resolve of our coalition, and to the might of the United States military. When I called our troops into action, I did so with complete confidence in their courage and skill. And tonight, thanks to them, we are winning the war on terror. The men and women of our Armed Forces have delivered a message now clear to every enemy of the United States: Even 7,000 miles away, across oceans and continents, on mountaintops and in caves—you will not escape the justice of this nation.

For many Americans, these four months have brought sorrow, and pain that will never completely go away. Every day a retired firefighter returns to Ground Zero, to feel closer to his two sons who died there. At a memorial in New York, a little boy left his football with a note for his lost father: Dear Daddy, please take this to heaven. I don't want to play football until I can play with you again some day.

Last month, at the grave of her husband, Michael, a CIA officer and marine who died in Mazur-e-Sharif, Shannon Spann said these words of farewell: "Semper Fi, my love." Shannon is with us tonight.

Shannon, I assure you and all who have lost a loved one that our cause is just, and our country will never forget the debt we owe Michael and all who gave their lives for freedom.

Our cause is just, and it continues. Our discoveries in Afghanistan confirmed our worst fears, and showed us the true scope of the task ahead. We have seen the depth of our enemies' hatred in videos, where they laugh about the loss of innocent life. And the depth of their hatred is equaled by the madness of the destruction they design. We have found diagrams of American nuclear power plants and public water facilities, detailed instructions for making chemical weapons, surveillance maps of American cities, and thorough descriptions of landmarks in America and throughout the world.

What we have found in Afghanistan confirms that, far from ending there, our war against terror is only beginning. Most of the 19 men who hijacked planes on September the 11th were trained in Afghanistan's camps, and so were tens of thousands of others. Thousands of dangerous killers, schooled in the methods of murder, often supported by outlaw regimes, are now spread throughout the world like ticking time bombs, set to go off without warning.

Thanks to the work of our law enforcement officials and coalition partners, hundreds of terrorists have been arrested. Yet, tens of thousands of trained terrorists are still at large. These enemies view the entire world as a battlefield, and we must pursue them wherever they are. So long as training camps operate, so long as nations harbor terrorists, freedom is at risk. And America and our allies must not, and will not, allow it.

Our nation will continue to be steadfast and patient and persistent in the pursuit of two great objectives. First, we will shut down terrorist camps, disrupt terrorist plans, and bring terrorists to justice. And, second, we must prevent the terrorists and regimes who seek chemical, biological or nuclear weapons from threatening the United States and the world.

Our military has put the terror training camps of Afghanistan out of business, yet camps still exist in at least a dozen countries. A terrorist underworld—including groups like Hamas, Hezbollah, Islamic Jihad, Jaish-i-Mohammed—operates in remote jungles and deserts, and hides in the centers of large cities.

While the most visible military action is in Afghanistan, America is acting elsewhere. We now have troops in the Philippines, helping to train that country's armed forces to go after terrorist cells that have executed an American, and still hold hostages. Our soldiers, working with the Bosnian government, seized terrorists who were plotting to bomb our embassy. Our Navy is patrolling the coast of Africa to block the shipment of weapons and the establishment of terrorist camps in Somalia.

My hope is that all nations will heed our call, and eliminate the terrorist parasites who threaten their countries and our own. Many nations are acting forcefully. Pakistan is now cracking down on terror, and I admire the strong leadership of President Musharraf.

But some governments will be timid in the face of terror. And make no mistake about it: If they do not act, America will.

Our second goal is to prevent regimes that sponsor terror from threatening America or our friends and allies with weapons of mass destruction. Some of these regimes have been pretty quiet since September the 11th. But we know their true nature. North Korea is a regime arming with missiles and weapons of mass destruction, while starving its citizens.

Iran aggressively pursues these weapons and exports terror, while an unelected few repress the Iranian people's hope for freedom.

Iraq continues to flaunt its hostility toward America and to support terror. The Iraqi regime has plotted to develop anthrax, and nerve gas, and nuclear weapons for over a decade. This is a regime that has already used poison gas to murder thousands of its own citizens—leaving the bodies of mothers huddled over their dead children. This is a regime that agreed to international inspections—then kicked out the inspectors. This is a regime that has something to hide from the civilized world.

States like these, and their terrorist allies, constitute an axis of evil, arming to threaten the peace of the world. By seeking weapons of mass destruction, these regimes pose a grave and growing danger. They could provide these arms to terrorists, giving them the means to match their hatred. They could attack our allies or attempt to blackmail the United States. In any of these cases, the price of indifference would be catastrophic.

We will work closely with our coalition to deny terrorists and their state sponsors the materials, technology, and expertise to make and deliver weapons of mass destruction. We will develop and deploy effective missile defenses to protect America and our allies from sudden attack. And all nations should know: America will do what is necessary to ensure our nation's security.

We'll be deliberate, yet time is not on our side. I will not wait on events, while dangers gather. I will not stand by, as peril draws closer and closer. The United States of America will not permit the world's most dangerous regimes to threaten us with the world's most destructive weapons.

Our war on terror is well begun, but it is only begun. This campaign may not be finished on our watch—yet it must be and it will be waged on our watch.

We can't stop short. If we stop now—leaving terror camps intact and terror states unchecked—our sense of security would be false and temporary. History has called America and our allies to action, and it is both our responsibility and our privilege to fight freedom's fight.

Our first priority must always be the security of our nation, and that will be reflected in the budget I send to Congress. My budget supports three great goals for America: We will win this war; we'll protect our homeland; and we will revive our economy.

September the 11th brought out the best in America, and the best in this Congress. And I join the American people in applauding your unity and resolve. Now Americans deserve to have this same spirit directed toward addressing problems here at home. I'm a proud member of my party—yet as we act to win the war, protect our people, and create jobs in America, we must act, first and foremost, not as Republicans, not as Democrats, but as Americans.

It costs a lot to fight this war. We have spent more than a billion dollars a month— over $30 million a day—and we must be prepared for future operations. Afghanistan proved that expensive precision weapons defeat the enemy and spare innocent lives, and we need more of them. We need to replace aging aircraft and make our military more agile, to put our troops anywhere in the world quickly and safely. Our men and women in uniform deserve the best weapons, the best equipment, the best training—and they also deserve another pay raise.

My budget includes the largest increase in defense spending in two decades—because while the price of freedom and security is high, it is never too high. Whatever it costs to defend our country, we will pay.

The next priority of my budget is to do everything possible to protect our citizens and strengthen our nation against the ongoing threat of another attack. Time and distance from the events of September the 11th will not make us safer unless we act on its lessons. America is no longer protected by vast oceans. We are protected from attack only by vigorous action abroad, and increased vigilance at home.

My budget nearly doubles funding for a sustained strategy of homeland security, focused on four key areas: bioterrorism, emergency response, airport and border security, and improved intelligence. We will develop vaccines to fight anthrax and other deadly diseases. We'll increase funding to help states and communities train and equip our heroic police and firefighters. We will improve intelligence collection and sharing, expand patrols at our borders, strengthen the security of air travel, and use technology to track the arrivals and departures of visitors to the United States.

Homeland security will make America not only stronger, but, in many ways, better. Knowledge gained from bioterrorism research will improve public health. Stronger police and fire departments will mean safer neighborhoods. Stricter border enforcement will help combat illegal drugs. And as government works to better secure our homeland, America will continue to depend on the eyes and ears of alert citizens.

A few days before Christmas, an airline flight attendant spotted a passenger lighting a match. The crew and passengers quickly subdued the man, who had been trained by al Qaeda and was armed with explosives. The people on that plane were alert and, as a result, likely saved nearly 200 lives. And tonight we welcome and thank flight attendants Hermis Moutardier and Christina Jones.

Once we have funded our national security and our homeland security, the final great priority of my budget is economic security for the American people. To achieve these great national objectives—to win the war, protect the homeland, and revitalize our economy—our budget will run a deficit that will be small and short-term, so long as Congress restrains spending and acts in a fiscally responsible manner. We have clear priorities and we must act at home with the same purpose and resolve we have shown overseas: We'll prevail in the war, and we will defeat this recession.

Americans who have lost their jobs need our help and I support extending unemployment benefits and direct assistance for health care coverage. Yet, American workers want more than unemployment checks—they want a steady paycheck. When America works, America prospers, so my economic security plan can be summed up in one word: jobs.

Good jobs begin with good schools, and here we've made a fine start. Republicans and Democrats worked together to achieve historic education reform so that no child is left behind. I was proud to work with members of both parties: Chairman John Boehner and Congressman George Miller. Senator Judd Gregg. And I was so proud of our work, I even had nice things to say about my friend, Ted Kennedy. I know the folks at the Crawford coffee shop couldn't believe I'd say such a thing—but our work on this bill shows what is possible if we set aside posturing and focus on results.

There is more to do. We need to prepare our children to read and succeed in school with improved Head Start and early childhood development programs. We must upgrade our teacher colleges and teacher training and launch a major recruiting drive with a great goal for America: a quality teacher in every classroom.

Good jobs also depend on reliable and affordable energy. This Congress must act to encourage conservation, promote technology, build infrastructure, and it must act to increase energy production at home so America is less dependent on foreign oil.

Good jobs depend on expanded trade. Selling into new markets creates new jobs, so I ask Congress to finally approve trade promotion authority. On these two key issues, trade and energy, the House of Representatives has acted to create jobs, and I urge the Senate to pass this legislation.

Good jobs depend on sound tax policy. Last year, some in this hall thought my tax relief plan was too small; some thought it was too big. But when the checks arrived in the mail, most Americans thought tax relief was just about right. Congress listened to the people and responded by reducing tax rates, doubling the child credit, and ending the death tax. For the sake of long-term growth and to help Americans plan for the future, let's make these tax cuts permanent.

The way out of this recession, the way to create jobs, is to grow the economy by encouraging investment in factories and equipment, and by speeding up tax relief so people have more money to spend. For the sake of American workers, let's pass a stimulus package.

Good jobs must be the aim of welfare reform. As we reauthorize these important reforms, we must always remember the goal is to reduce dependency on government and offer every American the dignity of a job.

Americans know economic security can vanish in an instant without health security. I ask Congress to join me this year to enact a patients' bill of rights—to give uninsured workers credits to help buy health coverage—to approve an historic increase in the spending for veterans' health—and to give seniors a sound and modern Medicare system that includes coverage for prescription drugs.

A good job should lead to security in retirement. I ask Congress to enact new safeguards for 401K and pension plans. Employees who have worked hard and saved all their lives should not have to risk losing everything if their company fails. Through stricter accounting standards and tougher disclosure requirements, corporate America must be made more accountable to employees and shareholders and held to the highest standards of conduct.

Retirement security also depends upon keeping the commitments of Social Security, and we will. We must make Social Security financially stable and allow personal retirement accounts for younger workers who choose them.

Members, you and I will work together in the months ahead on other issues: productive farm policy—a cleaner environment—broader home ownership, especially among minorities—and ways to encourage the good work of charities and faith-based groups. I ask you to join me on these important domestic issues in the same spirit of cooperation we've applied to our war against terrorism.

During these last few months, I've been humbled and privileged to see the true character of this country in a time of testing. Our enemies believed America was weak and materialistic, that we would splinter in fear and selfishness. They were as wrong as they are evil.

The American people have responded magnificently, with courage and compassion, strength and resolve. As I have met the heroes, hugged the families, and looked into the tired faces of rescuers, I have stood in awe of the American people.

And I hope you will join me—I hope you will join me in expressing thanks to one American for the strength and calm and comfort she brings to our nation in crisis, our First Lady, Laura Bush.

None of us would ever wish the evil that was done on September the 11th. Yet after America was attacked, it was as if our entire country looked into a mirror and saw our better selves. We were reminded that we are citizens, with obligations to each other, to our country, and to history. We began to think less of the goods we can accumulate, and more about the good we can do.

For too long our culture has said, "If it feels good, do it." Now America is embracing a new ethic and a new creed: "Let's roll." In the sacrifice of soldiers, the fierce brotherhood of firefighters, and the bravery and generosity of ordinary citizens, we have glimpsed what a new culture of responsibility could look like. We want to be a nation that serves goals larger than self. We've been offered a unique opportunity, and we must not let this moment pass.

My call tonight is for every American to commit at least two years—4,000 hours over the rest of your lifetime—to the service of your neighbors and your nation. Many are already serving, and I thank you. If you aren't sure how to help, I've got a good place to start. To sustain and extend the best that has emerged in America, I invite you to join the new USA Freedom Corps. The Freedom Corps will focus on three areas of need: responding in case of crisis at home; rebuilding our communities; and extending American compassion throughout the world.

One purpose of the USA Freedom Corps will be homeland security. America needs retired doctors and nurses who can be mobilized in major emergencies; volunteers to help police and fire departments; transportation and utility workers well-trained in spotting danger.

Our country also needs citizens working to rebuild our communities. We need mentors to love children, especially children whose parents are in prison. And we need more talented teachers in troubled schools. USA Freedom Corps will expand and improve the good efforts of AmeriCorps and Senior Corps to recruit more than 200,000 new volunteers.

And America needs citizens to extend the compassion of our country to every part of the world. So we will renew the promise of the Peace Corps, double its volunteers over the next five years—and ask it to join a new effort to encourage development and education and opportunity in the Islamic world.

This time of adversity offers a unique moment of opportunity—a moment we must seize to change our culture. Through the gathering momentum of millions of acts of service and decency and kindness, I know we can overcome evil with greater good. And we have a great opportunity during this time of war to lead the world toward the values that will bring lasting peace.

All fathers and mothers, in all societies, want their children to be educated, and live free from poverty and violence. No people on Earth yearn to be oppressed, or aspire to servitude, or eagerly await the midnight knock of the secret police.

If anyone doubts this, let them look to Afghanistan, where the Islamic "street" greeted the fall of tyranny with song and celebration. Let the skeptics look to Islam's own rich history, with its centuries of learning, and tolerance and progress. America will lead by defending liberty and justice because they are right and true and unchanging for all people everywhere.

No nation owns these aspirations, and no nation is exempt from them. We have no intention of imposing our culture. But America will always stand firm for the non-negotiable demands of human dignity: the rule of law; limits on the power of the state; respect for women; private property; free speech; equal justice; and religious tolerance.

America will take the side of brave men and women who advocate these values around the world, including the Islamic world, because we have a greater objective than eliminating threats and containing resentment. We seek a just and peaceful world beyond the war on terror.

In this moment of opportunity, a common danger is erasing old rivalries. America is working with Russia and China and India, in ways we have never before, to achieve peace and prosperity. In every region, free markets and free trade and free societies are proving their power to lift lives. Together with friends and allies from Europe to Asia, and Africa to Latin America, we will demonstrate that the forces of terror cannot stop the momentum of freedom.

The last time I spoke here, I expressed the hope that life would return to normal. In some ways, it has. In others, it never will. Those of us who have lived through these challenging times have been changed by them. We've come to know truths that we will never question: evil is real, and it must be opposed. Beyond all differences of race or creed, we are one country, mourning together and facing danger together. Deep in the American character, there is honor, and it is stronger than cynicism. And many have discovered again that even in tragedy—especially in tragedy—God is near.

In a single instant, we realized that this will be a decisive decade in the history of liberty, that we've been called to a unique role in human events. Rarely has the world faced a choice more clear or consequential.

Our enemies send other people's children on missions of suicide and murder. They embrace tyranny and death as a cause and a creed. We stand for a different choice, made long ago, on the day of our founding. We affirm it again today. We choose freedom and the dignity of every life.

Steadfast in our purpose, we now press on. We have known freedom's price. We have shown freedom's power. And in this great conflict, my fellow Americans, we will see freedom's victory.

Thank you all. May God bless.

PRESIDENT BUSH'S COMMENCEMENT SPEECH AT WEST POINT

West Point, New York, June 1, 2002

THE PRESIDENT: Thank you very much, General Lennox. Mr. Secretary, Governor Pataki, members of the United States Congress, Academy staff and faculty, distinguished guests, proud family members, and graduates: I want to thank you for your welcome. Laura and I are especially honored to visit this great institution in your bicentennial year.

In every corner of America, the words "West Point" command immediate respect. This place where the Hudson River bends is more than a fine institution of learning. The United States Military Academy is the guardian of values that have shaped the soldiers who have shaped the history of the world.

A few of you have followed in the path of the perfect West Point graduate, Robert E. Lee, who never received a single demerit in four years. Some of you followed in the path of the imperfect graduate, Ulysses S. Grant, who had his fair share of demerits, and said the happiest day of his life was "the day I left West Point." During my college years I guess you could say I was—During my college years I guess you could say I was a Grant man.

You walk in the tradition of Eisenhower and MacArthur, Patton and Bradley—the commanders who saved a civilization. And you walk in the tradition of second lieutenants who did the same, by fighting and dying on distant battlefields.

Graduates of this academy have brought creativity and courage to every field of endeavor. West Point produced the chief engineer of the Panama Canal, the mind behind the Manhattan Project, the first American to walk in space. This fine institution gave us the man they say invented baseball, and other young men over the years who perfected the game of football.

You know this, but many in America don't—George C. Marshall, a VMI graduate, is said to have given this order: "I want an officer for a secret and dangerous mission. I want a West Point football player."

As you leave here today, I know there's one thing you'll never miss about this place: Being a plebe. But even a plebe at West Point is made to feel he or she has some standing in the world. I'm told that plebes, when asked whom they outrank, are required to answer this: "Sir, the Superintendent's dog—the Commandant's cat, and all the admirals in the whole damn Navy." I probably won't be sharing that with the Secretary of the Navy.

West Point is guided by tradition, and in honor of the "Golden Children of the Corps," will observe one of the traditions you cherish most. As the Commander-in-Chief, I hereby grant amnesty to all cadets who are on restriction for minor conduct offenses. Those of you in the end zone might have cheered a little early. Because, you see, I'm going to let General Lennox define exactly what "minor" means.

Every West Point class is commissioned to the Armed Forces. Some West Point classes are also commissioned by history, to take part in a great new calling for their country. Speaking here to the class of 1942—six months after Pearl Harbor—General Marshall said, "We're determined that before the sun sets on this terrible struggle, our flag will be recognized throughout the world as a symbol of freedom on the one hand, and of overwhelming power on the other."

Officers graduating that year helped fulfill that mission, defeating Japan and Germany, and then reconstructing those nations as allies. West Point graduates of the 1940s saw the rise of a deadly new challenge—the challenge of imperial communism—and opposed it from Korea to Berlin, to Vietnam, and in the Cold War, from beginning to end. And as the sun set on their struggle, many of those West Point officers lived to see a world transformed.

History has also issued its call to your generation. In your last year, America was attacked by a ruthless and resourceful enemy. You graduate from this Academy in a time of war, taking your place in an American military that is powerful and is honorable. Our war on terror is only begun, but in Afghanistan it was begun well.

I am proud of the men and women who have fought on my orders. America is profoundly grateful for all who serve the cause of freedom, and for all who have given their lives in its defense. This nation respects and trusts our military, and we are confident in your victories to come.

This war will take many turns we cannot predict. Yet I am certain of this: Wherever we carry it, the American flag will stand not only for our power, but for freedom. Our nation's cause has always been larger than our nation's defense. We fight, as we always fight, for a just peace—a peace that favors human liberty. We will defend the peace against threats from terrorists and tyrants. We will preserve the peace by building good relations among the great powers. And we will extend the peace by encouraging free and open societies on every continent.

Building this just peace is America's opportunity, and America's duty. From this day forward, it is your challenge, as well, and we will meet this challenge together. You will wear the uniform of a great and unique country. America has no empire to extend or utopia to establish. We wish for others only what we wish for ourselves—safety from violence, the rewards of liberty, and the hope for a better life.

In defending the peace, we face a threat with no precedent. Enemies in the past needed great armies and great industrial capabilities to endanger the American people and our nation. The attacks of September the 11th required a few hundred thousand dollars in the hands of a few dozen evil and deluded men. All of the chaos and suffering they caused came at much less than the cost of a single tank. The dangers have not passed. This government and the American people are on watch, we are ready, because we know the terrorists have more money and more men and more plans.

The gravest danger to freedom lies at the perilous crossroads of radicalism and technology. When the spread of chemical and biological and nuclear weapons, along with ballistic missile technology—when that occurs, even weak states and small groups could attain a catastrophic power to strike great nations. Our enemies have declared this very intention, and have been caught seeking these terrible weapons. They want the capability to blackmail us, or to harm us, or to harm our friends—and we will oppose them with all our power.

For much of the last century, America's defense relied on the Cold War doctrines of deterrence and containment. In some cases, those strategies still apply. But new threats also require new thinking. Deterrence—the promise of massive retaliation against nations—means nothing against shadowy terrorist networks with no nation or citizens to defend. Containment is not possible when unbalanced dictators with weapons of mass destruction can deliver those weapons on missiles or secretly provide them to terrorist allies.

We cannot defend America and our friends by hoping for the best. We cannot put our faith in the word of tyrants, who solemnly sign non-proliferation treaties, and then systemically break them. If we wait for threats to fully materialize, we will have waited too long.

Homeland defense and missile defense are part of stronger security, and they're essential priorities for America. Yet the war on terror will not be won on the defensive. We must take the battle to the enemy, disrupt his plans, and confront the worst threats before they emerge. In the world we have entered, the only path to safety is the path of action. And this nation will act.

Our security will require the best intelligence, to reveal threats hidden in caves and growing in laboratories. Our security will require modernizing domestic agencies such as the FBI, so they're prepared to act, and act quickly, against danger. Our security will require transforming the military you will lead—a military that must be ready to strike at a moment's notice in any dark corner of the world. And our security will require all Americans to be forward-looking and resolute, to be ready for preemptive action when necessary to defend our liberty and to defend our lives.

The work ahead is difficult. The choices we will face are complex. We must uncover terror cells in 60 or more countries, using every tool of finance, intelligence and law enforcement. Along with our friends and allies, we must oppose proliferation and confront regimes that sponsor terror, as each case requires. Some nations need military training to fight terror, and we'll provide it. Other nations oppose terror, but tolerate the hatred that leads to terror—and that must change. We will send diplomats where they are needed, and we will send you, our soldiers, where you're needed.

All nations that decide for aggression and terror will pay a price. We will not leave the safety of America and the peace of the planet at the mercy of a few mad terrorists and tyrants. We will lift this dark threat from our country and from the world.

Because the war on terror will require resolve and patience, it will also require firm moral purpose. In this way our struggle is similar to the Cold War. Now, as then, our enemies are totalitarians, holding a creed of power with no place for human dignity. Now, as then, they seek to impose a joyless conformity, to control every life and all of life.

America confronted imperial communism in many different ways—diplomatic, economic, and military. Yet moral clarity was essential to our victory in the Cold War. When leaders like John F. Kennedy and Ronald Reagan refused to gloss over the brutality of tyrants, they gave hope to prisoners and dissidents and exiles, and rallied free nations to a great cause.

Some worry that it is somehow undiplomatic or impolite to speak the language of right and wrong. I disagree. Different circumstances require different methods, but not different moralities. Moral truth is the same in every culture, in every time, and in every place. Targeting innocent civilians for murder is always and everywhere wrong. Brutality against women is always and everywhere wrong. There can be no neutrality between justice and cruelty, between the innocent and the guilty. We are in a conflict between good and evil, and America will call evil by its name. By confronting evil and lawless regimes, we do not create a problem, we reveal a problem. And we will lead the world in opposing it.

As we defend the peace, we also have an historic opportunity to preserve the peace. We have our best chance since the rise of the nation state in the 17th century to build a world where the great powers compete in peace instead of prepare for war. The history of the last century, in particular, was dominated by a series of destructive national rivalries that left battlefields and graveyards across the Earth. Germany fought France, the Axis fought the Allies, and then the East fought the West, in proxy wars and tense standoffs, against a backdrop of nuclear Armageddon.

Competition between great nations is inevitable, but armed conflict in our world is not. More and more, civilized nations find ourselves on the same side—united by common dangers of terrorist violence and chaos. America has, and intends to keep, military strengths beyond challenge—thereby, making the destabilizing arms races of other eras pointless, and limiting rivalries to trade and other pursuits of peace.

Today the great powers are also increasingly united by common values, instead of divided by conflicting ideologies. The United States, Japan and our Pacific friends, and now all of Europe, share a deep commitment to human freedom, embodied in strong alliances such as NATO. And the tide of liberty is rising in many other nations.

Generations of West Point officers planned and practiced for battles with Soviet Russia. I've just returned from a new Russia, now a country reaching toward democracy, and our partner in the war against terror. Even in China, leaders are discovering that economic freedom is the only lasting source of national wealth. In time, they will find that social and political freedom is the only true source of national greatness.

When the great powers share common values, we are better able to confront serious regional conflicts together, better able to cooperate in preventing the spread of violence or economic chaos. In the past, great power rivals took sides in difficult regional problems, making divisions deeper and more complicated. Today, from the Middle East to South Asia, we are gathering broad international coalitions to increase the pressure for peace. We must build strong and great power relations when times are good; to help manage crisis when times are bad. America needs partners to preserve the peace, and we will work with every nation that shares this noble goal.

And finally, America stands for more than the absence of war. We have a great opportunity to extend a just peace, by replacing poverty, repression, and resentment around the world with hope of a better day. Through most of history, poverty was persistent, inescapable, and almost universal. In the last few decades, we've seen nations from Chile to South Korea build modern economies and freer societies, lifting millions of people out of despair and want. And there's no mystery to this achievement.

The 20th century ended with a single surviving model of human progress, based on non-negotiable demands of human dignity, the rule of law, limits on the power of the state, respect for women and private property and free speech and equal justice and religious tolerance. America cannot impose this vision—yet we can support and reward governments that make the right choices for their own people. In our development aid, in our diplomatic efforts, in our international broadcasting, and in our educational assistance, the United States will promote moderation and tolerance and human rights. And we will defend the peace that makes all progress possible.

When it comes to the common rights and needs of men and women, there is no clash of civilizations. The requirements of freedom apply fully to Africa and Latin America and the entire Islamic world. The peoples of the Islamic nations want and deserve the same freedoms and opportunities as people in every nation. And their governments should listen to their hopes.

A truly strong nation will permit legal avenues of dissent for all groups that pursue their aspirations without violence. An advancing nation will pursue economic reform, to unleash the great entrepreneurial energy of its people. A thriving nation will respect the rights of women, because no society can prosper while denying opportunity to half its citizens. Mothers and fathers and children across the Islamic world, and all the world, share the same fears and aspirations. In poverty, they struggle. In tyranny, they suffer. And as we saw in Afghanistan, in liberation they celebrate.

America has a greater objective than controlling threats and containing resentment. We will work for a just and peaceful world beyond the war on terror.

The bicentennial class of West Point now enters this drama. With all in the United States Army, you will stand between your fellow citizens and grave danger. You will help establish a peace that allows millions around the world to live in liberty and to grow in prosperity. You will face times of calm, and times of crisis. And every test will find you prepared—because you're the men and women of West Point. You leave here marked by the character of this Academy, carrying with you the highest ideals of our nation.

Toward the end of his life, Dwight Eisenhower recalled the first day he stood on the plain at West Point. "The feeling came over me," he said, "that the expression 'the United States of America' would now and henceforth mean something different than it had ever before. From here on, it would be the nation I would be serving, not myself."

Today, your last day at West Point, you begin a life of service in a career unlike any other. You've answered a calling to hardship and purpose, to risk and honor. At the end of every day you will know that you have faithfully done your duty. May you always bring to that duty the high standards of this great American institution. May you always be worthy of the long gray line that stretches two centuries behind you.

On behalf of the nation, I congratulate each one of you for the commission you've earned and for the credit you bring to the United States of America. May God bless you all.

PRESIDENT BUSH'S REMARKS TO UNITED NATIONS GENERAL ASSEMBLY

New York, New York, September 12, 2002

THE PRESIDENT: Mr. Secretary General, Mr. President, distinguished delegates, and ladies and gentlemen: We meet one year and one day after a terrorist attack brought grief to my country, and brought grief to many citizens of our world. Yesterday, we remembered the innocent lives taken that terrible morning. Today, we turn to the urgent duty of protecting other lives, without illusion and without fear.

We've accomplished much in the last year—in Afghanistan and beyond. We have much yet to do—in Afghanistan and beyond. Many nations represented here have joined in the fight against global terror, and the people of the United States are grateful.

The United Nations was born in the hope that survived a world war—the hope of a world moving toward justice, escaping old patterns of conflict and fear. The founding members resolved that the peace of the world must never again be destroyed by the will and wickedness of any man. We created the United Nations Security Council, so that, unlike the League of Nations, our deliberations would be more than talk, our resolutions would be more than wishes. After generations of deceitful dictators and broken treaties and squandered lives, we dedicated ourselves to standards of human dignity shared by all, and to a system of security defended by all.

Today, these standards, and this security, are challenged. Our commitment to human dignity is challenged by persistent poverty and raging disease. The suffering is great, and our responsibilities are clear. The United States is joining with the world to supply aid where it reaches people and lifts up lives, to extend trade and the prosperity it brings, and to bring medical care where it is desperately needed.

As a symbol of our commitment to human dignity, the United States will return to UNESCO. This organization has been reformed and America will participate fully in its mission to advance human rights and tolerance and learning.

Our common security is challenged by regional conflicts—ethnic and religious strife that is ancient, but not inevitable. In the Middle East, there can be no peace for either side without freedom for both sides. America stands committed to an independent and democratic Palestine, living side by side with Israel in peace and security. Like all other people, Palestinians deserve a government that serves their interests and listens to their voices. My nation will continue to encourage all parties to step up to their responsibilities as we seek a just and comprehensive settlement to the conflict.

Above all, our principles and our security are challenged today by outlaw groups and regimes that accept no law of morality and have no limit to their violent ambitions. In the attacks on America a year ago, we saw the destructive intentions of our enemies. This threat hides within many nations, including my own. In cells and camps, terrorists are plotting further destruction, and building new bases for their war against civilization. And our greatest fear is that terrorists will find a shortcut to their mad ambitions when an outlaw regime supplies them with the technologies to kill on a massive scale.

In one place—in one regime—we find all these dangers, in their most lethal and aggressive forms, exactly the kind of aggressive threat the United Nations was born to confront.

Twelve years ago, Iraq invaded Kuwait without provocation. And the regime's forces were poised to continue their march to seize other countries and their resources. Had Saddam Hussein been appeased instead of stopped, he would have endangered the peace and stability of the world. Yet this aggression was stopped—by the might of coalition forces and the will of the United Nations.

To suspend hostilities, to spare himself, Iraq's dictator accepted a series of commitments. The terms were clear, to him and to all. And he agreed to prove he is complying with every one of those obligations.

He has proven instead only his contempt for the United Nations, and for all his pledges. By breaking every pledge—by his deceptions, and by his cruelties—Saddam Hussein has made the case against himself.

In 1991, Security Council Resolution 688 demanded that the Iraqi regime cease at once the repression of its own people, including the systematic repression of minorities—which the Council said, threatened international peace and security in the region. This demand goes ignored.

Last year, the U.N. Commission on Human Rights found that Iraq continues to commit extremely grave violations of human rights, and that the regime's repression is all pervasive. Tens of thousands of political opponents and ordinary citizens have been subjected to arbitrary arrest and imprisonment, summary execution, and torture by beating and burning, electric shock, starvation, mutilation, and rape. Wives are tortured in front of their husbands, children in the presence of their parents—and all of these horrors concealed from the world by the apparatus of a totalitarian state.

In 1991, the U.N. Security Council, through Resolutions 686 and 687, demanded that Iraq return all prisoners from Kuwait and other lands. Iraq's regime agreed. It broke its promise. Last year the Secretary General's high-level coordinator for this issue reported that Kuwait, Saudi, Indian, Syrian, Lebanese, Iranian, Egyptian, Bahraini, and Omani nationals remain unaccounted for—more than 600 people. One American pilot is among them.

In 1991, the U.N. Security Council, through Resolution 687, demanded that Iraq renounce all involvement with terrorism, and permit no terrorist organizations to operate in Iraq. Iraq's regime agreed. It broke this promise. In violation of Security Council Resolution 1373, Iraq continues to shelter and support terrorist organizations that direct violence against Iran, Israel, and Western governments. Iraqi dissidents abroad are targeted for murder. In 1993, Iraq attempted to assassinate the Emir of Kuwait and a former American President. Iraq's government openly praised the attacks of September the 11th. And al Qaeda terrorists escaped from Afghanistan and are known to be in Iraq.

In 1991, the Iraqi regime agreed to destroy and stop developing all weapons of mass destruction and long-range missiles, and to prove to the world it has done so by complying with rigorous inspections. Iraq has broken every aspect of this fundamental pledge.

From 1991 to 1995, the Iraqi regime said it had no biological weapons. After a senior official in its weapons program defected and exposed this lie, the regime admitted to producing tens of thousands of liters of anthrax and other deadly biological agents for use with Scud warheads, aerial bombs, and aircraft spray tanks. U.N. inspectors believe Iraq has produced two to four times the amount of biological agents it declared, and has failed to account for more than three metric tons of material that could be used to produce biological weapons. Right now, Iraq is expanding and improving facilities that were used for the production of biological weapons.

United Nations' inspections also revealed that Iraq likely maintains stockpiles of VX, mustard and other chemical agents, and that the regime is rebuilding and expanding facilities capable of producing chemical weapons.

And in 1995, after four years of deception, Iraq finally admitted it had a crash nuclear weapons program prior to the Gulf War. We know now, were it not for that war, the regime in Iraq would likely have possessed a nuclear weapon no later than 1993.

Today, Iraq continues to withhold important information about its nuclear program—weapons design, procurement logs, experiment data, an accounting of nuclear materials and documentation of foreign assistance. Iraq employs capable nuclear scientists and technicians. It retains physical infrastructure needed to build a nuclear weapon. Iraq has made several attempts to buy high-strength aluminum tubes used to enrich uranium for a nuclear weapon. Should Iraq acquire fissile material, it would be able to build a nuclear weapon within a year. And Iraq's state-controlled media has reported numerous meetings between Saddam Hussein and his nuclear scientists, leaving little doubt about his continued appetite for these weapons.

Iraq also possesses a force of Scud-type missiles with ranges beyond the 150 kilometers permitted by the U.N. Work at testing and production facilities shows that Iraq is building more long-range missiles that it can inflict mass death throughout the region.

In 1990, after Iraq's invasion of Kuwait, the world imposed economic sanctions on Iraq. Those sanctions were maintained after the war to compel the regime's compliance with Security Council resolutions. In time, Iraq was allowed to use oil revenues to buy food. Saddam Hussein has subverted this program, working around the sanctions to buy missile technology and military materials. He blames the suffering of Iraq's people on the United Nations, even as he uses his oil wealth to build lavish palaces for himself, and to buy arms for his country. By refusing to comply with his own agreements, he bears full guilt for the hunger and misery of innocent Iraqi citizens.

In 1991, Iraq promised U.N. inspectors immediate and unrestricted access to verify Iraq's commitment to rid itself of weapons of mass destruction and long-range missiles. Iraq broke this promise, spending seven years deceiving, evading, and harassing U.N. inspectors before ceasing cooperation entirely. Just months after the 1991 cease-fire, the Security Council twice renewed its demand that the Iraqi regime cooperate fully with inspectors, condemning Iraq's serious violations of its obligations. The Security Council again renewed that demand in 1994, and twice more in 1996, deploring Iraq's clear violations of its obligations. The Security Council renewed its demand three more times in 1997, citing flagrant violations; and three more times in 1998, calling Iraq's behavior totally unacceptable. And in 1999, the demand was renewed yet again.

As we meet today, it's been almost four years since the last U.N. inspectors set foot in Iraq, four years for the Iraqi regime to plan, and to build, and to test behind the cloak of secrecy.

We know that Saddam Hussein pursued weapons of mass murder even when inspectors were in his country. Are we to assume that he stopped when they left? The history, the logic, and the facts lead to one conclusion: Saddam Hussein's regime is a grave and gathering danger. To suggest otherwise is to hope against the evidence. To assume this regime's good faith is to bet the lives of millions and the peace of the world in a reckless gamble. And this is a risk we must not take.

Delegates to the General Assembly, we have been more than patient. We've tried sanctions. We've tried the carrot of oil for food, and the stick of coalition military strikes. But Saddam Hussein has defied all these efforts and continues to develop weapons of mass destruction. The first time we may be completely certain he has a—nuclear weapons is when, God forbids, he uses one. We owe it to all our citizens to do everything in our power to prevent that day from coming.

The conduct of the Iraqi regime is a threat to the authority of the United Nations, and a threat to peace. Iraq has answered a decade of U.N. demands with a decade of defiance. All the world now faces a test, and the United Nations a difficult and defining moment. Are Security Council resolutions to be honored and enforced, or cast aside without consequence? Will the United Nations serve the purpose of its founding, or will it be irrelevant?

The United States helped found the United Nations. We want the United Nations to be effective, and respectful, and successful. We want the resolutions of the world's most important multilateral body to be enforced. And right now those resolutions are being unilaterally subverted by the Iraqi regime. Our partnership of nations can meet the test before us, by making clear what we now expect of the Iraqi regime.

If the Iraqi regime wishes peace, it will immediately and unconditionally forswear, disclose, and remove or destroy all weapons of mass destruction, long-range missiles, and all related material.

If the Iraqi regime wishes peace, it will immediately end all support for terrorism and act to suppress it, as all states are required to do by U.N. Security Council resolutions.

If the Iraqi regime wishes peace, it will cease persecution of its civilian population, including Shi'a, Sunnis, Kurds, Turkomans, and others, again as required by Security Council resolutions.

If the Iraqi regime wishes peace, it will release or account for all Gulf War personnel whose fate is still unknown. It will return the remains of any who are deceased, return stolen property, accept liability for losses resulting from the invasion of Kuwait, and fully cooperate with international efforts to resolve these issues, as required by Security Council resolutions.

If the Iraqi regime wishes peace, it will immediately end all illicit trade outside the oil-for-food program. It will accept U.N. administration of funds from that program, to ensure that the money is used fairly and promptly for the benefit of the Iraqi people.

If all these steps are taken, it will signal a new openness and accountability in Iraq. And it could open the prospect of the United Nations helping to build a government that represents all Iraqis—a government based on respect for human rights, economic liberty, and internationally supervised elections.

The United States has no quarrel with the Iraqi people; they've suffered too long in silent captivity. Liberty for the Iraqi people is a great moral cause, and a great strategic goal.

The people of Iraq deserve it; the security of all nations requires it. Free societies do not intimidate through cruelty and conquest, and open societies do not threaten the world with mass murder. The United States supports political and economic liberty in a unified Iraq.

We can harbor no illusions—and that's important today to remember. Saddam Hussein attacked Iran in 1980 and Kuwait in 1990. He's fired ballistic missiles at Iran and Saudi Arabia, Bahrain, and Israel. His regime once ordered the killing of every person between the ages of 15 and 70 in certain Kurdish villages in northern Iraq. He has gassed many Iranians, and 40 Iraqi villages.

My nation will work with the U.N. Security Council to meet our common challenge. If Iraq's regime defies us again, the world must move deliberately, decisively to hold Iraq to account. We will work with the U.N. Security Council for the necessary resolutions. But the purposes of the United States should not be doubted. The Security Council resolutions will be enforced—the just demands of peace and security will be met—or action will be unavoidable. And a regime that has lost its legitimacy will also lose its power.

Events can turn in one of two ways: If we fail to act in the face of danger, the people of Iraq will continue to live in brutal submission. The regime will have new power to bully and dominate and conquer its neighbors, condemning the Middle East to more years of bloodshed and fear. The regime will remain unstable—the region will remain unstable, with little hope of freedom, and isolated from the progress of our times. With every step the Iraqi regime takes toward gaining and deploying the most terrible weapons, our own options to confront that regime will narrow. And if an emboldened regime were to supply these weapons to terrorist allies, then the attacks of September the 11th would be a prelude to far greater horrors.

If we meet our responsibilities, if we overcome this danger, we can arrive at a very different future. The people of Iraq can shake off their captivity. They can one day join a democratic Afghanistan and a democratic Palestine, inspiring reforms throughout the Muslim world. These nations can show by their example that honest government, and respect for women, and the great Islamic tradition of learning can triumph in the Middle East and beyond. And we will show that the promise of the United Nations can be fulfilled in our time.

Neither of these outcomes is certain. Both have been set before us. We must choose between a world of fear and a world of progress. We cannot stand by and do nothing while dangers gather. We must stand up for our security, and for the permanent rights and the hopes of mankind. By heritage and by choice, the United States of America will make that stand. And, delegates to the United Nations, you have the power to make that stand, as well.

Thank you very much.

APPENDIX F

THE CRUCIAL CAMPAIGNS
OF 2004 ON THE WEB

Presidential Race:
www.georgewbush.com

Selected GOP nominees in crucial 2004 U.S. Senate races:

Alaska: Senator Lisa Murkowski (www.lisamurkowski.com)
Arkansas: [to be determined]
California: Bill Jones (www.jonesforcalifornia.com)
Colorado: [to be determined]
Florida: Mel Martinez (www.melforsenate.com)
Georgia: Herman Cain (www.cainforussenate.org)
Illinois: Jack Ryan (www.jackryan2004.com)
Louisiana: Congressman David Vitter (www.vitterforsenate.com)
Nevada: [to be determined]
North Carolina: Congressman Richard Burr (www.richardburrcommittee.com)
North Dakota: [to be determined]
Oklahoma: Kirk Humphreys (www.humphreysforsenate.com)
South Carolina: Congressman Jim DeMint (www.jimdemint.com)
South Dakota: Congressman John Thune (www.johnthune.com)
Washington State: Congressman George Nethercutt (www.nethercuttforsenate.com)

All United States Senate Races:
The National Senate Republican Committee: www.nrsc.org.

All United States House of Representatives Races:
The National Republican Congressional Committee: www.nrcc.org.

252

POLITICAL NEWS FROM THE WEB

These sites carry news from a variety of sources, and can contain crude and obscene language. While RealClearPolitics.com is perhaps the most comprehensive Web site for political news, the thousands of members of FreeRepublic.com and DemocraticUnderground.com continually post breaking news throughout the day and are the best source of late-breaking news while also providing excellent news-nets that sweep tens of thousands of news sources for crucial stories and commentary. Once you have learned how to filter out the nuts from each site and to overlook the unhinged nature of many posters, especially at www.democraticunderground.com, these are the best three sources for national political news throughout the cycle:

www.realclearpolitics.com
www.freerepublic.com
www.democraticunderground.com

California makes the weather in politics quite often, so here are two sites that collect the best in Golden State political news and analysis:

www.californiarepublic.org
www.sacbee.com/static/weblogs/insider

A BEGINNER'S GUIDE
TO THE BLOGS

Blog is short for "Web log"—defined as an online journal with dated postings.

There are millions of blogs run by individuals interested in publishing their thoughts on a variety of subjects. All blog lovers develop their own tastes, but the newcomer is best advised to try these lists for the reliable blogs of 2004. The positions reflected on the various sites are not even close to Republican Party orthodoxy, except at the campaign site of Bush-Cheney 2004, so don't make the mistake of believing everything you read, even on these generally center-right sites.

I link to dozens of blogs at HughHewitt.com, but the starter's kit of the most powerful blogs worth a visit every day includes the following:

The Bleat, www.lileks.com, is owned and operated by center-right comic genius James Lileks.

Powerline, www.powerlineblog.com, is run by a trio of center-right lawyers with superior research skills.

Kausfiles, www.kausfiles.com, is run by center Left Democrat Mickey Kaus.

Andrew Sullivan, www.andrewsullivan.com, is center-right on all issues except gay issues, on which he is an activist from the left.

Instapundit, www.instapundit.com, run by University of Tennessee Law School Professor Glenn Reynolds, is the most visited blog of all.

Joshua Micah Marshall's www.talkingpointsmemo.com is the center of the liberal blog universe.

And Joe Carter's Evangelical Outpost, www.evangelicaloutpost.com, and Mark D. Roberts, www.markdroberts.com, provide portals into the evangelical world, while www.mudvillegazette.com provides an easy jumping-off point to great blogs run by men and women with military experience.

The two most annoying blogs in the world are Fraters Libertas, www.fraterslibertas.com, and Infinite Monkeys, http://blog.infinitemonkeysblog.com (no "www"). Read them only with extreme caution.

THE TEN KEY
TALKING POINTS FOR 2004

1. Our enemies hate and fear George W. Bush because they believe, correctly, that George W. Bush is trying to kill them.

2. George W. Bush will not wait upon the French, the Germans, or the Russians to act to defend the United States. If necessary, he will act alone, though he has not had to in Afghanistan and Iraq.

3. John Kerry voted against the first Gulf War, which stopped Saddam from getting nuclear weapons, and he opposed the second war with Iraq, which made sure Saddam and his crazy sons would never get nuclear weapons.

4. George Bush inherited a lot from Bill Clinton: a recession, a collapsing stock market, a dismal climate for corporate ethics, dozens of terrorist training camps in Afghanistan, and courts packed with judges who think the Pledge of Allegiance is unconstitutional. The recession is over, the markets are up, the terrorist camps are destroyed, and the president hasn't stopped saying the Pledge.

5. The Americans for Democratic Action is the oldest and most beloved of the left-liberal interest groups. It rates legislators on their lifetime record of voting for liberal ideas. At the end of 2002, Ted Kennedy got an 88 out of a possible 100 percent. John Kerry got a 93 percent. John Kerry is not only to the left of Bill Clinton and Al Gore. He's to the left of Joe Lieberman, Howard Dean, John Edwards, and even Teddy Kennedy.

6. If the problem is too much government spending, the answer can't be electing Democrats. That's like saying the answer to a poor harvest is a drought.

7. The war against terror will go on for decades, until every radical Islamist is dead or convinced of the futility of attacking America.

8. John Kerry has opposed researching, developing, and deploying the missile defense system that will protect us against the missiles that North Korea researched, developed,

and deployed under the terms of the agreement that Bill Clinton negotiated with it in 1994. Kerry also opposed other critical weapon systems, including the B-1 and B-2 stealth bombers, the MX missile, the Patriot missile, the M1 Abrams tank, and the Aegis cruiser.

9. The Democrats are patriots, but so are third graders. And you don't trust the national security of the United States to third graders, for third graders are easily confused and fooled.

10. If we are attacked again, who would you rather be in charge: George W. Bush and his team, or John F. Kerry and Bill Clinton's team?

ACKNOWLEDGMENTS

Many hands made for light work.

Amy Schroeder has once again contributed her enormous research and writing talents to this project. Amy's professionalism conquered her political instincts and is greatly appreciated.

Lieutenant Dan Wright and Lieutenant Alex Dorvas, U.S. Marines first and law students second, also helped with research, and I thank them.

Lynne Chapman, my assistant now for fifteen years, has once again shepherded the manuscript from start to finish, even as she kept all the other plates spinning!

Sealy and Curtis Yates again provided the guidance and encouragement that experienced and trusted agents do. Brian Hampton and Kyle Olund of Thomas Nelson contributed great editing and encouragement. Three Hewitts—Diana, Will, and Jamie—kept eyes on the manuscript, and Snow Philip reprised her copyediting tasks, making her and my wife, Betsy, the consistent presence through all five of my books.

The book is a product of the radio show, and the radio show is also the product of many hands.

The day-to-day producing and engineering of Duane Patterson and Adam Ramsey are extraordinary. Jennie O'Hagan continues to bring news affiliates and new listeners. The assistance of Michael Nolf, Alex Caudana, Austen Swaim, Ramin Ahadi, Evan Simon, and Anthony Ochoa are also appreciated.

Russ Hauth, Russell Shubin, Ted Atsinger, and David Spady help keep Salem's message clear, and Greg Anderson and Joe Davis and a legion of station executives have built platforms from which that message can be sent. Ed Atsinger and Stuart Epperson had the vision and skill to bring all these people and hundreds more into the project of building a profitable communications company with a purpose worth pursuing.

Chapman University and its Law School remain places of great inno-vation and talent. Many thanks to Jim Doti and Parham Williams specifically, and to many faculty colleagues generally, for creating one of the rare islands in academia where conservatives can flourish.

Some of these chapters began as columns for WorldNetDaily.com and the WeeklyStandard.com. Tom Ambrose and Jonathan Last are fine edi-tors, whose encouragement has been crucial. JVL, especially, has welcomed the unexpected and the unusual.

Richard Botkin, Tim Cook, Terry Eastland, Bill Lobdell, and Mark Roberts have all debated the ideas in this book with me, each helping me to refine my arguments, even when they disagreed, sometimes forcefully.

And Betsy, as always, has kept smiling and kept her eye on the most important things, even when the writing, the blogging, the teaching, and the talking made the days crowded. For twenty-two years, she has been my editor in chief, and I hope and pray that our partnership never does any-thing but grow longer and better with the years.

ABOUT THE AUTHOR

Hugh Hewitt is the host of a nationally syndicated radio talk show heard in more than sixty cities nationwide, and a professor of law at Chapman University Law School, where he teaches Constitutional Law. He is a graduate of Harvard College and the University of Michigan Law School, and is the author of four previous books, including his most recent work *In, But Not Of: A Guide to Christian Ambition and the Desire to Influence the World*. Hewitt received three Emmys during his decade of work as cohost of the PBS Los Angeles affiliate KCET's nightly news and public affairs show *Life & Times*. He is a weekly columnist for *The Daily Standard*, the online edition of *The Weekly Standard*, and a weekly columnist for WorldNetDaily.com. He can be reached at hugh@hughhewitt.com.